LF

Protest and Reform

The British Social Narrative by Women

1827–1867

Joseph Kestner

Protest and Reform

The British Social Narrative by Women

1827–1867

The University of Wisconsin Press

Published 1985 in the United States of America by

The University of Wisconsin Press
114 North Murray Street
Madison, Wisconsin 53715

Published in Great Britain by
Methuen & Co. Ltd
11 New Fetter Lane
London EC4P 4EE

First printing

Printed in the United States of America

Library of Congress Cataloging in Publication Data
Kestner, Joseph A.
    Protest and reform.
    Bibliography: pp. 217–231.
    Includes index.
    1. English fiction — 19th century — History and
criticism. 2. English fiction — Women authors — History and
criticism. 3. Social problems in literature. I. Title.
PR868.S62K4 1985   823′.8′099287   84-40498
ISBN 0-299-10060-X

For Anna

Contents

Acknowledgments

The author would like to express his gratitude to the following institutions for their assistance in the preparation of this book: in the United States the libraries of Columbia University, Harvard University, Indiana University, Princeton University, the University of Texas at Austin, the University of Tulsa, and Yale University; in Great Britain the collections of the Birmingham Public Library, the Bodleian Library of Oxford University, the British Library, the British Public Records Office at Kew, the Liverpool Library, the Manchester Central Library, the Norwich Public Library, and the John Rylands Library of the University of Manchester.

At the McFarlin Library of the University of Tulsa the author wishes especially to thank Alberta Frost, Mary Grant, and Jeanne Rehberg.

The author wishes to express his gratitude to the University of Tulsa for a Faculty Fellowship which enabled him to pursue this study. A grant from the Cities Service Corporation, administered by the College of Business Administration at the University, supported the initial phase of this research.

The author is particularly grateful to the following for their assistance at various stages of the development of this book: David Farmer, Monica Fryckstedt, David Gilson, Thomas Horne, Coral Lansbury, Joseph Nichols, Winston Weathers, Joseph Wiesenfarth, and Carl Woodring.

The author is grateful to the following for their insightful suggestions: Bernard Duyfhuizen, Darcy O'Brien, Thomas Staley, and Gordon Taylor.

ix

To the editors of the following journals the author expresses his gratitude for permission to incorporate material which appeared in another form in their publications: *Tulsa Studies in Women's Literature* 2 (Fall 1983); *Papers on Language and Literature* 19 (Winter 1983); and the *Bulletin of the John Rylands University Library* 67 (Autumn 1984).

The tables included in this book are reproduced with the permission of the Edinburgh University Press and Fontana Collins Ltd. The author is grateful to Miss Helen Valentine and the Royal Academy for permission to reproduce Hubert von Herkomer's *On Strike* as the jacket illustration.

For their incisive advice during the production of this book, the author wishes to thank Allen Fitchen, Peter Givler, and Elizabeth Steinberg of the University of Wisconsin Press.

Joseph Kestner
The University of Tulsa

Protest and Reform

The British Social Narrative by Women

1827–1867

1   The Social Narrative

Social protest fiction in the nineteenth century has been recognized as a substratum of the development of the novel during the last century. Reviewers of the time observed the importance of contemporaneous subject matter and commented upon the use of research materials by such authors as Charlotte Brontë and Elizabeth Gaskell. Louis Cazamian inaugurated the careful study of this subgenre in the early twentieth century. During the last decade several studies have analyzed elements of this type of prose, such as the portrayal of the captain of industry, the use of poetry and fiction for reformist purposes, and the presentation of the poor in such literature.

Considerations of the social novel during the nineteenth century rely on a small canon of writers: Elizabeth Gaskell, Benjamin Disraeli, Charles Kingsley, perhaps Charlotte Brontë or Charles Dickens. The tradition has been conceived as being predominantly male. A recent critic has declared: "Few women novelists of this period are active reformers (at least in their fiction), and their books are generally not the forerunners of social change" (Gorsky, "Doubters" 29). This presupposition by critics has created a distortion of the facts concerning the social narrative during the nineteenth century. Far from being the province of male writers, the reverse assertion, that it was a literary form much practiced by women, constitutes the truth. Not only were many women part of this tradition; they also entered it far earlier than their male counterparts. Women identified with the disenfranchised working classes and sought to influence legislative reform through social protest narratives that depicted conditions requiring improvement. In these nar-

3

ratives they were responding to the transitional nature of their historical situation.

The history of the novel during the nineteenth century, particularly as it concerns women authors, remains an established canon of greatness, consisting of Jane Austen, the Brontës, and George Eliot, with Elizabeth Gaskell frequently considered in their company. If one advantage of studying social narratives by women is an appraisal of their historical value, another result is the redefinition of the canon of female authors during the Victorian period. Writers like Maria Edgeworth and Harriet Martineau occupy a much more important place in the history of the social narrative, while other writers exhibit strengths that argue for a revision of the exclusive canon. Charlotte Elizabeth Tonna and Fanny Mayne were both novelists and journal editors, while Julia Kavanagh and Elizabeth Stone pioneered in the sober, unadorned depiction of the working and managerial classes. Serial authors, such as Eliza Meteyard, described conditions in millinery and factory labor, often explicitly depicting women as independent agents in a period of severe economic transition.

Many of these women did extensive research, familiarizing themselves with data and social documentation. All challenged the idea that novel reading was a superficial activity. Instead, demanding that their readers confront social realities, they elevated the seriousness of the novel as a literary form. This book is therefore concerned with two central issues: the role of women protest writers in a period of economic transition; and the revision of the canon of female authorship during the nineteenth century. Elaine Showalter has noted that "the ongoing history of women's writing has been suppressed, leaving large and mysterious gaps in accounts of the development of genre" ("Feminist" 33). Studying one segment of this development of a genre during the nineteenth century—the social narrative by women—makes it evident that a redefinition and revaluation of fictional prose is necessary. Women form an interlocking chain of contributions in creating the genre of the social narrative, integrating and perfecting its use of statistical and governmental evidence in conjunction with personal experience to advance reform during the nineteenth century in Britain.

While the origin of social fiction antedates Thomas Carlyle's essay *Chartism* (1839), the basic function of this fiction accords with Carlyle's behest in the opening chapter of his monograph, "Condition-of-England Question": "A feeling very generally exists that the condition and disposition of the Working Classes is a rather ominous matter at present; that something ought to be said, something ought to be done, in regard to it. And surely, at an epoch of history when the 'National Petition' carts itself in wagons along the streets, and is presented . . . to a Reformed House of Commons; and Chartism numbered by the million and half . . . breaks out into brickbats, cheap pikes, and even into sputterings of conflagrations, such very general feeling cannot be considered unnatural! To us individually this matter appears, and has for many years appeared, to be the most ominous of all practical matters whatever; a matter in regard to which if something be not done, something will *do* itself one day, and in a fashion that will please nobody. The time is verily come for acting in it; how much more for consultation about acting in it, for speech and articulate inquiry about it!" (118). Writing in 1839 Carlyle was asking a new direction for inquiry, one which not only recounted physical and financial circumstance ("condition") but also accounted for individual emotive and attitudinal reaction ("disposition") to the transitional status caused by an industrializing economic system. One element of that inquiry was social fiction, whether in the form of the novel, the novella, or the tale.

The urgency of the request for inquiry arose because, as Humphry House notes, "Carlyle, in *Chartism* and *Past and Present,* is not only an angry but a frightened man" (49). Inquiry had already begun, however, had in fact already produced results by the time Carlyle exhorted his readers to begin. Such works as Hannah More's *The Lancashire Collier Girl,* Maria Edgeworth's *Castle Rackrent* and *The Absentee,* Harriet Martineau's *The Rioters* and *The Turn-out,* and Charlotte Tonna's *The System* and *Combination* had appeared, anticipating Carlyle's plea and prefiguring the development of social literature in the forties and fifties. By the time Carlyle's monograph was printed in December 1839, Frances Trollope's *Michael Armstrong, the Factory Boy* and Charlotte Tonna's *Helen Fleetwood* had begun to appear in serial form. It was to be Trollope and Tonna who would pursue this fiction in the forties before men like Disraeli and Kingsley contributed to the tradition.

In *An Essay on the Principle of Population,* Thomas Malthus had noted "that the histories of mankind which we possess are only of the higher classes. We have but few accounts that can be depended upon of the manners and customs of that part of mankind, where these retrograde and progressive movements chiefly take place" (25).

Social literature is one response to this situation. The value of social fiction to the historian and literary historian is twofold. Its validity as one record of a transitional society is significant for the former. For the literary historian, social fiction represents an important development of the art of the novel during the period. The historical value of fiction in the nineteenth century is attested by scholars, such as Asa Briggs in *The Age of Improvement:* "Literature is much more revealing than economic data for the understanding of the attitudes of contemporaries to the social gulfs of the 1840s" (298). Steven Marcus regards literature itself as an historical datum: "Literature is, among many other things, a historical phenomenon and . . . therefore it plays a part — and a most important part — in the historical development of consciousness" (*Engels* 138–39). If literature is part of the historical development, however, it is still necessary to study it against the background of other factors that contribute to historical understanding. Peter Laslett cautions: "It is true, and very important to the social historian, that the spontaneous assumptions in the literature of any age, the behavior of the minor characters, the conventions against which irony and humour must be understood, reveal with great precision, facts of considerable interest about the structure of society. . . . But it is indeed hazardous to infer an institution or a habit characteristic of a whole society or a whole era from the central character of a literature work and its story. . . . The outcome may be to make people believe that what was the entirely exceptional, was in fact the perfectly normal" (87). An additional danger is "a circular process of response, in effect relating the novels to a pseudo-reality deduced from them" (213). Social writers were themselves aware of this circumstance, which gives their productions a validity that may not apply to more famous or more exceptional literary works. Throughout this study non-fictional nineteenth-century investigations (such as those by James Phillips Kay, Peter Gaskell, E. C. Tufnell, William Cooke Taylor, William Dodd, and John Fielden) have been used to demonstrate that these social narratives did reflect reality as perceived by early social analysts of industrialism.

Those novelists who instituted and pursued the inquiry demanded by Carlyle were compelled to adhere to external factual data, although the degree of allegiance might vary from writer to writer. The assurance that a story was "founded on fact" had to be given some, even if cursory, mention. The importance of authenticity was emphasized by the critic Fitzjames Stephen when he noted, in his essay "The License of Modern Novelists," that "the most influential of all indirect moral teachers" were "contemporary novelists" and "the educational influence of novels," especially since "their influence is enormously increased by the facilities which cheap publication affords to them" (65). William Aydelotte cautions that "the historical interest of these novels lies . . . in what they reveal about the opinions and attitudes of the men who wrote them. A novel helps to show not the facts of the age, but the mind of the novelist, not social conditions, but attitudes toward social conditions. The historical value of fiction . . . is not for the history of facts but for the history of opinions" ("England" 43). Some of these writers were to depict both conditions and attitudes toward them. The reviewer of *Mary Barton* in *Fraser's Magazine* felt that such a novel provided data and a supplement to other social investigations as a means of altering attitudes: "For we must hope—we dare not but hope for the honour of humanity, that in spite of blue-books and commissions, in spite of newspaper horrors and parliamentary speeches, Manchester riots and the 10th of April, the mass of the higher orders cannot yet be aware of what a workman's home is like in the manufacturing districts" (429).

In appraising the role of female writers in the tradition of social fiction, the appropriate context includes two elements, the concept of intervention and the interest women had in the process of intervention. Intervention was the central preoccupation of the early and developing phases of industrialism in Britain, prompted by the recognition that the nineteenth century was distinguished by economic transition. Writing of the industrial era in 1833, Peter Gaskell declared: "One generation even now is but passing away since this epoch, and what mighty alterations has it already wrought in the condition of society—changing in many respects the very framework of the social confederacy, and opening to view a long vista of rapid transitions" (6). For Gaskell the most conspicuous aspect of this state of economic transition was "the rapidity of increase in the manufacturing population" (219). He regards industrialization as inevitable: "To endeavour to arrest its progress would be madness: they cannot turn back the stream of events—the onward current of the age" (325). James Kay, writing in 1832 of *The Moral and Physical Condition of the Working Classes Employed in the Cotton Manufacture in Manchester,* saw transition as not only generally applicable, but specifically so, trade by trade. He emphasized the hand-loom weavers "existing in this state of *transition*" as a result of advances in means of production: "The state of transition in employment consequent on a new invention . . . will always be followed by an embarrassment . . . determined . . . by the extent of the market for manufactures" (44, 84–85). Frederick Harrison commented in retrospect: "The eighty years which passed between the death of the fourth George and the accession of George V (1830–1910) were pre-eminently an age of transition" (Black, *Victorian* 458–59). The transition from an agrarian to an industrial-based economic system, from the "domestic" to the "factory" system of production, was marked by the consolidation of labor within a large area and the breakdown of the production process into small units. Social fiction mirrors this emphasis by its selection of one character or one family from a large anonymous entity.

The conditions generated by rapid transition gradually increased the recognition by society that intervention was necessary to maintain social cohesion. As Kitson Clark notes, if the industrial revolution was "morally neutral," it was nonetheless a "blind force" (*Making* 93, 108). Despite the belief of someone like David Ricardo in 1817 that wages "should never be controlled by the interference of the legislature" (61), state control did become necessary. It was the growth in population, above all, that made intervention, initially desirable, ultimately essential. Roberts contends that the "industrial revolution did not create abuses where none existed before; it concentrated them and brought them into the open" (*Victorian* 101). Social novelists wrote in a context of interventionism and were not immune to the debate between adherents of laissez-faire and partisans of interventionism, as the contrasting beliefs of Harriet Martineau and Charlotte Tonna illustrate. A. V. Dicey's misreading of Bentham, by which he contended that early nineteenth-century Britain was an "age of laissez-faire," is distorted. "Although laissez faire never prevailed in Great Britain or in any other modern state, many men have been led to believe that it did. . . . Neither laissez faire nor state intervention was the engine of change in nineteenth-century Britain. Instead, both were constant accompaniments of the basic force — industrialization" (Brebner 60, 69). Peter Gaskell in 1833 recognized as an important question "how far the interference of Government in questions of this nature is likely to prove beneficial" (12). The social novelists became part of the interventionist reaction to industrialization, whether their political allegiances were toward local or central control, or no control. "State intervention may not have been policy but it was the growing reality" (Finlayson, *Decade* 66).

When William Gladstone in 1844 proposed government involvement in registering joint stock companies with the Board of Trade, John Bright denounced the procedure by warning of "the entering wedge of government interference" (Roberts, *Victorian* 64), but despite objections, the country pursued what Ashley advocated in 1844: "The state has an *interest* and a right to watch over and provide for the moral and physical well being of her people" (Hutchins 93). Interventionism prevailed because "the line between what the State may do and what it must leave alone had been drawn in the wrong place, and . . . there was a whole world of things where the individual simply could not help himself at all" (Young, *Victorian* 52). The question for legislators and writers was to define the nature of this intervention, moral or physical or both, and its extent. The growth of population made this intervention imperative. The population of England and Wales in 1780 was 7.5 million; by 1801, it was 9 million, and fifty years later it was 18 million. In 1831 the population of the British Isles was 24.1 million; in 1841, 26.7 million; in 1851, 27.3 million (B. R. Mitchell, *Abstract* 6–7). These decennial increases demonstrate the basis of transition. Cities were to experience similar growth. The figures for Manchester, for example, indicate the nature and acceleration of this increase: 1801, 75,000; in 1831, 182,000; 1841, 235,000; 1851, 303,000 (B. R. Mitchell, *Abstract* 24). By 1851, 54 percent of the population was urban. As Briggs notes, "population change was one of the most important determinants of the structure and prosperity of any society" (*Age* 15). Writers and politicians had to reckon with the social conditions produced by such growth. This was difficult, as it could not be automatically assumed that such increases were known to everyone. R. A. Slaney, addressing Parliament in 1837 about education, felt compelled to state: "There were . . . many new members who might be unacquainted with the immense increase which had taken place in the manufacturing population" (4).

The fiction that responded to Carlyle's inquiry and to the social pressures created by population growth and economic transition was social fiction, the "novel with a purpose." In the nineteenth century critics like the author of "Novels with a Purpose" in *The Westminster Review* noted that "the current of public feeling at present sets in favour of prose fiction." He then wondered, "Is it given to the novelist to accomplish any definite social object, to solve, or even help towards the solution of any vexed social question? . . . Is there any real use in producing that class of books which our readers can easily and distinctly identify if we call them, for lack of a better generic title, Novels with a Purpose?" He explained the impulse behind such works: "The author seems to have written, not because he or she felt inspired to tell a story, but because certain meditations, or convictions, or doubts, on some subject connected with human society, seemed to find convenient and emphatic expression through the medium of a work of fiction. In each of these books the philosophical critic of humanity, the social reformer, or the social accuser, stands behind the story-teller and inspires and guides his utterance. . . . In all alike the story is not the end, but only the means." The critic added the caveat: "A novelist is free to write a book with a purpose if he likes, but having done so, he must submit to be judged according to the nature of his purpose and the clearness with which he has developed it" (28–32). Kettle contends there is a distinction between the social novel like Gaskell's *Ruth* and a novel like *Mary Barton,* but this distorts Carlyle's intention in calling for inquiry. No complete inquiry would be possible if industrial literature were not perceived as part of the tradition of social problem literature. The standard in determining whether a particular book might be called a social narrative should be the urgency of its subject, the presentation of the necessity for remediation, its use of sources, and the use of story as a function of its protest. The most convincing social fiction observes the cautious parameters laid down by Aydelotte and Laslett. While such fiction might include a political thesis, social fiction may exist apart from a specific political program or ideology, although it may promote a political tendency.

Ellen Moers notes "the predominant female presence in the early history of industrial literature" (39). There are several explanations of this phenomenon. Amid the changes produced by the transition from a cottage to a factory system of production, social changes important to women emerged in the twenties and thirties to alter the roles women had played in a preindustrial era. Disraeli's definition of the Two Nations in *Sybil* in 1845, in a conversation between Stephen Morley and Lord Egremont, is given point because the two men discuss the Queen who reigns over the two groups: "She reigns over . . . Two nations; between whom there is no intercourse and no sympathy; who are as ignorant of each other's habits, thoughts, and feelings, as if they were dwellers in different zones, or inhabitants of different planets; who are formed by a different breeding, are fed by a different food, are ordered by different manners, and are not governed by the same laws . . . THE RICH AND THE POOR" (65–66). This classification was not original with Disraeli. In 1805 Charles Hall had noted that for purposes of studying the people of a nation, "they need only be divided into two classes, viz. the rich and the poor" (Briggs, *Age* 65). These two nations may be interpreted as rich/poor, employer/ employee, or industrial/agricultural, but, as Hamilton notes, "the division is psychological" (103). For women writers there was the further division of male and female, not isolated from these other divisions but included within them.

In 1864 *The Westminster Review* noted of social novels that: "They have their purpose written clearly on them like a motto, and they hold to it perseveringly. The greatest social difficulty in the England of today is not that which is created by the relations between wealth and poverty. . . . A much more complicated difficulty is found in the relations between men and women. . . . The social life of England today shows scarcely any improvement in this direction" ("Novels Purpose" 40). Concern with women's issues was a result of an identification of women with workers: "The profound sense of injustice that the feminine novelists had represented as class struggle in their novels of factory life becomes an all-out war of the sexes in the novels of the feminists" (29); Showalter defines the feminine phase of authorship from 1840 to 1880, the feminist from 1880 to 1920. This labeling of phases compartmentalizes areas of concern that are not so separable. As the case of Charlotte Tonna was to demonstrate, a "feminine" concern with work conditions in the thirties was not separable from a "feminist" concern with domestic legislation in the sixties. As Asa Briggs has noted, change "is a process and not an event" (*Age* 4). If women writers could identify with workers for reasons such as economic discrimination, there were other powerful reasons for their attraction to this substratum of fiction.

In *A Room of One's Own* Virginia Woolf observed that "toward the end of the eighteenth century a change came about which, if I were rewriting history, I should describe more fully and think of greater importance than the Crusades or the Wars of the Roses. The middle-class woman began to write. . . . When the middle-class woman took to writing, she naturally wrote novels. . . . The novel alone was young enough to be soft in her hands" (66, 68, 77). There were cultural factors that contributed to this new disposition. Patricia Branca isolates "the declining influence of religion" in middle-class women's lives as one factor contributing to their new identities, as well as "a declining sense of fatalism" that increased during the century with improvement in health care (146, 62). Both these factors permitted women to be more direct in expressing themselves. In 1869 John Stuart Mill noted in *The Subjection of Women* that "Literary women are becoming more freespoken, and more willing to express their real sentiments," although he believed that "If women's literature is destined to have a different collective character from that of men . . . much longer time is necessary than has yet elapsed" (153, 207).

The social literature examined in this book spans the late 1790s to the mid-1860s. This entry by middle-class woman was facilitated by "a revolutionary social concept; that of the democracy of print. . . . Under the conditions of industrial life the ability to read was acquiring an importance it had never had before" (Altick 1, 4). Industrialism directly caused a new demand for literacy and literature. There were obstacles in general toward the advance of literature in the early nineteenth century. R. K. Webb notes that "most of the middle classes and aristocracy were abominably educated," and this situation was even more damaging for women. Furthermore, fiction did not represent a large percentage of the material published in Britain during the first half of the nineteenth century. "Of the roughly 45,000 books published in England between 1816 and 1851, well over 10,000 were religious works, far outdistancing the next largest category — history and geography, with 4,900, and fiction with 3,500" ("Victorian" 207, 206). "The great Victorian reading public and the mass market that went with it were formed in the early 1850s" (Sutherland 62). Women writers of social fiction had to confront many situations to achieve recognition. Perhaps most distressing, as Sutherland observes, was the fact that "no firm of name regarded fiction as its most respectable line of goods" (2).

The fact that government reports were accessible to these women supplemented or in fact substituted for their lack of direct contact through traveling and social intercourse with the other classes, although some writers, such as Charlotte Tonna, Fanny Mayne, and Elizabeth Gaskell, had wide and immediate association with the working-class poor. There is validity in Moers' argument that "denial of access to the Real made it fascinating to women. Simple curiosity . . . drove literary women to overachievement in their quest for fact." The availability of data through Blue Books, first sold to the public in 1836, allowed women access to information that contained revealing miniatures, encapsulated case histories of individuals. "It was by reading . . . that women writers acquired the remarkable quantity and quality of information about workaday realities that they brought to literature" (125–27).

Writing social fiction allowed women, although not enfranchised, to participate in the legislative process. Charlotte Tonna wrote *The Perils of the Nation* in 1843 at the behest of Lord Ashley. Women writers followed Tonna's argument that women, by becoming familiar with social conditions, could influence their voting husbands, fathers, and brothers to meliorate conditions. The difficulty of enforcing legislation meant that there was much to be done after as well as before the passage of a law. The culture was such that "the machinery of life designed to control an aristocratic, agricultural, and mercantile society could not control the society that industrial capitalism had imposed upon the older scheme" (H. House 182). Spacks claims that women writers "have characteristically concerned themselves with matters more or less peripheral to male concerns, or at least slightly skewed from them" (7) but women's social fiction, while having special emphases, was not divorced from the preoccupations of male contemporaries.

Fiction "founded on fact" provided middle-class women not only with "something to do," for which Florence Nightingale pleaded in *Cassandra,* but with something important to do. Women writers' appeals to fact constituted "integrity" as Woolf later defined it, "the conviction that [the novelist] gives one that this is the truth." Although Woolf cautioned against too great "deference to external authority," female social novelists gave received authority (from Parliamentary commissions, for example) expanded authority (*Room* 72, 74). Writers such as Tonna and Stone were concerned with maintaining an influence over legislation, whether enfranchised or not. Women writers realized that in the working classes there was a curious equality of men and women in so far as both were potential victims of unemployment, social ostracism, lack of sanitation, and undervaluation. Their awareness of separate issues concerning women, which were not confined to the working classes, made their arguments about child care or female alcoholism relevant to women in general, whether or not the specific story concerned a lower-class woman. It is erroneous to believe that middle-class women knew nothing of poverty, since much of it existed in the lower strata of their own class. In certain specialized kinds of fiction, such as Elizabeth Stone's *The Young Milliner,* the middle-class or upper-class woman was shown to be the oppressor of her lower-class sister. The middle-class writer recognized that her own class was both victim and oppressor. Women sought to intervene in social conditions through literature for a range of reasons, some, like Charlotte Tonna, driven by Evangelical fervor, while Elizabeth Stone became involved in writing through family occupations. Marital circumstances encouraged Elizabeth Gaskell's writings, while the unmarried status of Julia Kavanagh provided her particular angle of vision. In all these instances, female writers sought to influence social action. Reviewing *Mary Barton* in 1849, the *Westminster Review* emphasized its protesting rather than its reforming intention: "It is an appropriate and valuable contribution to the literature of the age. It embodies the dominant feeling of our times — a feeling that the ignorance, destitution and vice which pervade and corrupt society, must be got rid of. The ability to point out how they are to be got rid of, is not the characteristic of this age. That will be the characteristic of the age which is coming" (26). Female writers, however, regarded protest not only as a stage toward reform but as a function of reform.

The appearance of women in literature during the century did not go unrecognized, partially because, as W. R. Greg declared in 1859, "it is not easy to overestimate the importance of novels. . . . This literature is effective by reason of its very lightness. . . . There are many reasons why we should look upon novels in this serious point of view. They are the sole or the chief reading of numbers. . . . They are the reading of most men in their idler and more impressionable hours. . . . They form, too, an unfortunately large proportion of the habitual reading of the young. . . . Finally, novels constitute a principal part of the reading of women, who are always impressionable" ("False" 144–45). Lewes used his review of *Shirley* in 1850 to discuss the degree of intellectual equality of men and women. In 1852, he declared: "The appearance of Woman in the field of literature is a significant fact. It is the correlate of her position in society. . . . It is certain that the philosophic eye sees in this fact of literature cultivated by women, a significance not lightly to be passed over. It touches both society and literature." "What does the literature of women mean? It means this . . . the advent of female literature promises woman's view of life, woman's experience: in other words, a new element. . . . The literature of women has fallen short of its function, owing to a very natural and very explicable weakness — it has been too much a literature of imitation. To write as men write is the aim and besetting sin of women; to write as women, is the real office they have to perform. . . . To imitate is to abdicate. We are in no need of more male writers; we are in need of genuine female experience" ("Lady," 129–32).

Greg was less enthusiastic about the advent of women writers on the literary scene, declaring that "there are vast numbers of lady novelists, for much the same reason that there are vast numbers of sempstresses. Thousands of women have nothing to do, and yet are under the necessity of doing something." Writing in 1859, Greg felt that novels by women would be "inherently defective" because of women's lack of intelligence and experience (147–48). He condemned a novel like *Ruth* for its "faulty religion" and "false morality" (167). Lewes was more speculative in his review of *Ruth* and *Villette:* "Should a work of Art have a moral? . . . A narrative can prove nothing" (474). The opinions of Greg and Lewes define the milieu in which female novelists wrote, one questioning their purposes, capabilities, artistry, and uniqueness.

There are additional reasons for studying this group of female writers beyond their involvement in social issues. While their individual observations of the social conditions of nineteenth-century England are interesting in themselves, a further benefit derived from studying these writers is an enlargement of literary history from two perspectives. First, the contributions of several of these women, such as Tonna, Stone, Kavanagh, Toulmin, Jewsbury, Mayne, even Martineau, have been ignored, not only in appraisals of the development of the novel in the nineteenth century in general but also in appraisals of women writers in the century. This is probably a result of the implicit canon of "great predecessors" contained in Virginia Woolf's monograph: "Lady Winchelsea, Charlotte Brontë, Emily Brontë, Jane Austen, and George Eliot" (91). This is not to say that Woolf ignored other writers, as her essay on Jane Carlyle and Geraldine Jewsbury illustrates. Largely ignored in *A Room of One's Own* is Woolf's recognition of another body of writers outside the canon of the great but essential to it: "But there was a fence beyond that and a fence beyond that. Whether she had the staying power I was doubtful. . . . But she did her best. . . . Give her another hundred years, I concluded . . . and she will write a better book one of these days" (93). Woolf recognizes that the achievement of women like the Brontës or Eliot derives from a larger group of less exceptional but not less significant women. "Thanks to the toils of those obscure women in the past, of whom I wish we knew more," conditions are improving (106). There is a tradition involving women, important to the development of both literary and social history, that is part of the tradition of nineteenth-century female authorship without being its most distinguished part. This is not a reason, however, for it to remain indistinguishable.

In the canon of female social fiction, the names of More, Martineau, Tonna, Trollope, Stone, Jewsbury, Meteyard, Toulmin, Kavanagh, Mayne, and Craik must be included along with the more habitually recognized Edgeworth, Charlotte Brontë, Elizabeth Gaskell, and George Eliot. Lewes discussed as a representative selection Austen, Sand, Gore, Jewsbury, Lynn, Brontë, Trollope, and Gaskell. The achievement of these women as social novelists can only be understood by association with the work of their contemporaries or important predecessors who dealt with similar concerns. Even if one takes the received designations of the various decades of the nineteenth century during the flourishing of the social novel (the collectivist twenties, the radical thirties, the hungry forties, the becalmed fifties, and the equilibrated sixties), women writers confronted varied conditions with responses that not only reinforce but also undermine conventional designations. All these women were disenfranchised from the political process but were neither uninvolved nor uninfluential. "I want to be doing something with the pen since no other means of action in politics are in a woman's power," wrote Harriet Martineau (Moers 30). A tradition of women writing social fiction existed well before Lewes' statement in 1852, having been established in the twenties, thirties, and forties. It is the intention of this study to examine this tradition.

If assimilation was one of the problems of industrialism, women were as concerned as their male associates with their position in this transition. For middle-class women, Branca notes, "the dominant problem was assimilation to a very new life-style" (2). Although female social fiction must be considered against the broad spectrum of intervention and assimilation, there were a number of specific issues that concerned women writers. Harriet Taylor Mill noted that "the manufacturing districts of the North" were "that part of England where every serious movement in the direction of political progress has its commencement" (120–21). Dealing with this material revealed new fictional subjects to women. Although some of these considerations were shared by male counterparts, such as Benjamin Disraeli and Charles Kingsley, women dominated the social fiction narrative and their interests reflected this preoccupation. Spacks notes that "the differences between traditional female preoccupations and roles and male ones make a difference in female writing" (7). Topics suggested by social conditions allowed women to explore areas of behavior that enlarged their process of self-identification. In this fiction the woman was often not the Angel in the House, not married, not a mother. Often there was no house. They opposed the cult of the "wife-guide" (Basch 59) and the stereotype set forth in Ruskin's *Of Queens' Gardens.* Florence Nightingale noted in *Cassandra:* "There is perhaps no century where the woman shows so meanly as in this" (50).

While the writers under consideration in this study were middle-class women, their range of education and their political allegiances and religious background varied considerably. Martineau was anti-interventionist as strenuously as Tonna was the opposite. George Eliot was agnostic, Tonna was strongly Low Church Evangelical, Gaskell was Unitarian. Yet these differences did not divide them in their concern for social issues. The issue of emigration, used by Kingsley in *Alton Locke,* was previously a part of works like *Michael Armstrong, Mary Barton,* or *Lucy Dean,* especially as women such as governesses and milliners were often not successful in emigration settlement. The issue of family size concerned Trollope in *Jessie Phillips* and Tonna in *Helen Fleetwood,* while preferential hiring (of women over men) was criticized by Tonna in *Helen Fleetwood* and *The Wrongs of Woman* for decreasing women's domesticity. Stone in *William Langshawe, the Cotton Lord* and Jewsbury in *Marian Withers* were concerned with education. The plight of the protagonist in Stone's *The Young Milliner* arises because she has no useful skills when she is orphaned. The motherless working girl is conspicuous in *Mary Barton* and *Jane Rutherford,* while a novel like *Rachel Gray* discusses the corresponding situation in the shabby genteel world. The futile existence of middle-class women is a broad concern in *Marian Withers, John Halifax, Gentleman, North and South, Felix Holt, the Radical,* and *Shirley.* These show the difficulty for the middle-class woman of finding an occupation or a means of economic survival during the transition.

Some writers concentrated as well on the plight of women unable to survive in the new environment, such as the seduced working-class women of *Mary Barton, The Young Milliner, Lizzie Leigh, William Langshawe, Helen Fleetwood,* and *The Wrongs of Woman.* Male writers like Kingsley and Disraeli avoided such a subject, but female novelists concentrated on these situations to mark a specific social group destroyed during the transition, each woman discussing the issue in her individual manner. Middle-class female authors also focused on the relationship of the middle-class woman to her lower-class sister, as in *The Young Milliner* or *William Langshawe*. Altick notes that "working class" during the century was "the lower middle and lower classes together . . . at least three-quarters of the total population" (82). Depictions of the daughters of industrialists in novels like *Marian Withers* and *William Langshawe* brought to prominence second-generation upward mobility. The transition opened a new field for female novelists, and also a new role: writing, more than "something to do," became a genuine involvement in the transition itself.

If these women brought to their observations a class bias, it was nevertheless true, as Louis Cazamian notes, that in politics the middle and working classes had some similar interests despite their economic separation. The situation of women during the economic change was a subject that could be dealt with by middle-class women despite the difference in monetary status, since many middle-and working-class women in their social situation differed more in degree than in kind. As Branca has commented, such issues as family size, the difficulty of raising children, and precarious economic circumstances bound women during the nineteenth century. The emphasis on "facts" with these writers had, as one advantage, the goal of recording accurately without class bias. While selectivity of fact could result in distortions, more often than not a novelist avoided the harshest details more from fear of censorship by a publisher than from presumed female modesty. Female social novelists were more aggressive than male novelists like Disraeli or Kingsley in their specificity. Particularly in showing interactions among women of different classes these novelists surpassed their male counterparts. If in some social fiction by women—*Michael Armstrong, Helen Fleetwood,* or *The Rioters,* for example—women were not successful in depicting male characters, *A Manchester Strike, North and South, Rachel Gray, Felix Holt, Sylvia's Lovers,* and *Lizzie Leigh* showed that women could deal with men in domestic and occupational circumstances with conviction. In the prefaces to *Marian Withers, William Langshawe,* and *Mary Barton,* the writers demonstrated that their motivation was purposeful, their intentions reformist, their concerns universal.

During the period of this study, social fiction, primarily used for advancing theses, became social literature with varying degrees of artistry. This study uses the term "social fiction" or "social narrative," rather than "social novel," because it embraces texts of variable artistic quality. Kathleen Tillotson notes that in social fictions "the novelist's 'purpose' may too firmly predestine the individual fates of his characters, destroying both suspense and spontaneity." She establishes "gradations," with *Mary Barton* being more satisfactory than *Sybil* or *Yeast,* which are in turn more artistic than *Helen Fleetwood.* From another perspective, however, the challenges were so great that these writers may be considered successful artists: "The formal ordering of ideas into narratives, the presentation of 'views' through persons, the creating of a world which bore a strangely close relation to the actual contemporary world . . . — all these were problems which exercised the novelist's art to the utmost" (118–19). Martineau grows in formal awareness between *The Rioters* and *The Turn-out* (themselves contrasting narrative experiments) and between *The Hill and the Valley* and *A Manchester Strike.* The same is true of Elizabeth Stone between *William Langshawe* and *The Young Milliner,* separated by less than a year, or Elizabeth Gaskell between *Mary Barton* and *Ruth, North and South,* and *Sylvia's Lovers.* Charlotte Tonna subdivides her concerns in *The Wrongs of Woman* and thereby avoids the presentation of one family as in *Helen Fleetwood.*

The variety of formats used by women writers is evidence of their dealing with the publishing world in diverse circumstances. While triple-deckers like *Marian Withers* and *Ruth* were typical of one kind of publishing, other formats were tried successfully: the tract (*The Lancashire Collier Girl*), the tale (*A Manchester Strike*), the single volume (*Rachel Gray, The Young Milliner*), the double volume (*Mary Barton, William Langshawe*), the serial, monthly or weekly (*Jane Rutherford, Lucy Dean, Michael Armstrong, Helen Fleetwood, Jessie Phillips*), and part-publication (*The Wrongs of Woman*). Such diversity of published formats reveals an inclination toward rapid audience accessibility. This diversity of narrative form was paralled by specific narrative strategy, exemplified by the contrast between Martineau's *The Rioters* and *The Turn-out.* The novelists relied on varying degrees of striking incident, with Trollope and Tonna representing one pole of this tendency, and Kavanagh, Stone, and Gaskell the other, which subdued or abolished such tendencies. Writing in "The Lady Novelists" about *Jane Eyre* and *Mary Barton,* Lewes said "Whatever of weakness may be pointed out in their works, will . . . be mostly in those parts where experience is deserted, and the supposed requirements of fiction have been listened to" (138). Social fiction has been discounted as art, however important as documentation, but the artistry was considerable, and, considering the intentions, even exceptional. The bleakness of London has rarely been so sharply seen as in a few brief paragraphs of Stone's *The Young Milliner* nor has its blankness been better chronicled than by Kavanagh in *Rachel Gray*.

While these women do not constitute a school, the extent to which they knew of one another can be ascertained with some exactitude. Lewes relates writers as diverse as Jewsbury, Eliot, and Charlotte Brontë. Gaskell feared for a while to compete with George Eliot and knew of Stone's and Kavanagh's writings. Martineau and Trollope were names familiar to their successors, while Charlotte Tonna may have been known to writers of the fifties. Jewsbury reviewed Craik and strongly endorsed George Eliot's *Adam Bede*. Eliot reviewed Kavanagh's *Rachel Gray,* while Fanny Mayne indicates an awareness of novels like Gaskell's *Ruth*. George Eliot disliked being compared to Dinah Mulock Craik, and Harriet Martineau did not acknowledge, although she knew of, Maria Edgeworth's contributions to social fiction. Lewes praised Martineau's *History of the Peace,* while Eliot declared in 1859 about Martineau, "I respect her so much as an authoress" (Haight, *Letters* 3:201). Several days earlier she had written Elizabeth Gaskell that "my feelings towards Life and Art had some affinity with the feeling which had inspired . . . the earlier chapters of 'Mary Barton'" (3:198).

Because these narratives concentrate on issues rooted in the decades in which they appear, the development of the female social narrative is treated in this book by decade. Such a method reveals the continuity of this tradition and the alteration of subject matter. The depiction of working-class conditions in the twenties and thirties expands in the forties to include the middle class, which becomes the subject matter of the fifties. The period from the later eighteenth century until the thirties is dominated by More, Edgeworth, Tonna, and the early Martineau. The latter two inaugurate the thirties and are joined in that decade by Trollope. In the forties, several new women emerge as important writers, particularly Elizabeth Stone, Camilla Toulmin, Elizabeth Gaskell, and Geraldine Jewsbury, while the fifties show Gaskell and Jewsbury in the company of Dinah Mulock Craik, Julia Kavanagh, and Fanny Mayne. This study concludes with Gaskell and George Eliot, who represent the culmination of the tradition before it enters a hiatus in the seventies and eighties.

The reasons for the interruption of the social narrative tradition in the later decades of the nineteenth century are various. Cazamian notes that the Crimean War refocused attention on foreign affairs, while Smith observes that the poor were receding from fiction at this time. Clark regards the fifties and sixties as a respite from the reforms of the previous decades, a stage Burn regards as maintaining equilibrium. When social fiction reappeared in the eighties and nineties, its focus was the East End, not Manchester: the industrial novel was transformed into the urban novel. The history of the English novel in the nineteenth century and the canon of female authorship during the period are examined as part of this study of the evolution of the female social novel. The evaluation of these works in literary and social contexts is the purpose of this study, not in their separateness so much as in their interaction. Geoffrey Best in *Mid-Victorian Britain* has noted that "the questions which they were trying to answer with the aid of this sort of evidence, are the very questions we still most dearly want to get answered" (57). A study of female social fiction is a reappraisal of the role of women writers in nineteenth-century Britain with their diversity of subjects and narrative practices, their protest, and their influence. Such an appraisal results in a redefinition of the role of women writers during a period of historical change and a revision of the canon of literary achievement during the nineteenth century.

2 The Early Decades

In his review of Harriet Martineau's *Illustrations of Political Economy* in 1833, the political economist George Poulett Scrope compared her work to that of an important predecessor, Maria Edgeworth, a significant notice, since it associates Maria Edgeworth with the tradition of the social novel. After commenting adversely on several tales in the *Illustrations,* Scrope observes that Harriet Martineau would do well to "study the works of a lady who, with immeasurably greater abilities in every way, was her predecessor in the line she considers so wholly original — the illustrating by fiction the natural laws of social welfare. Political economy is far more ingeniously as well as justly illustrated in *The Absentee* and *Castle Rackrent* than in *Ireland*. . . . The moral of Miss Edgeworth's tales is naturally suggested to the reader by the course of events of which he peruses the narrative; that of Miss Martineau is embodied in elaborate dialogues or most unnatural incidents, with which her stories are interlarded and interrupted, to the utter destruction of the interest of all but detached bits of them" (151–52). Scrope's review, unflattering though it may be, is interesting in its suggestion that even as early as the thirties contemporary critics were able to recognize the social novel as belonging to a tradition and to identify significant predecessors in the tradition. Kettle concurs, noting that "the novel with a specific moral, social, or even overtly political purpose did not begin with the publication of *Coningsby* (1844) or *Sybil* (1845). On the contrary, the social-problem novelists of the forties were not more earnest in their aims nor half so abstract in their methods as their predecessors of half a century before" (171–72).

In the latter part of the eighteenth century, and during the first three decades of the nineteenth century, several practitioners of the social novel were active. Among those one must include Hannah More and Maria Edgeworth, as well as Charlotte Elizabeth Tonna and Harriet Martineau. It was Hannah More "who initiated this important literary trend" of using "fiction for propagandist purposes" (Kovacevic, *Fact* 147). Hannah More (1745–1833) was an "Evangelical best-seller of the period" (Jay 98), "condemned for her innocent attempts to instruct the poor" (Altick 73). Two of her stories, *Village Politics* and *The Lancashire Collier Girl,* deserve notice as early forms of social fiction or fiction with a purpose. Both stories illustrate qualities of later social fiction in the use of dialogue concerning economics and the focus on a single protagonist whose story is a success fable about the lower classes. As Vineta Colby observes, More wrote to "refute the radical political tracts of the Jacobins" (156). *Village Politics* and *The Lancashire Collier Girl* are presented with a conservative bias against some of the political ideas existing in her time. Thomas Day, for instance, a friend of Maria Edgeworth's father, was a disciple of Rousseau who "could not endure . . . any pretensions of birth, fortune or fashion" (Butler 105). More writes to support the idea of proper stations for the rich and poor, the artistocracy and the working classes. She opposes rioting and radicalism, illustrating the essential virtue of the existing social order.

Village Politics is a dialogue between Jack Anvil, a blacksmith, and Tom Hod, a mason, the former being a spokesman for More's Tory conservatism. Published in 1793, this pamphlet indicts both the legacy of the French Revolution and the tendencies of Tom Paine's *The Rights of Man* (1791, 1793). For More "every new reader in the lower ranks of society meant another potential victim of radical contagion" (Altick 76). While the mason desires liberty, equality, and the "rights of man," and condemns taxation, Jack Anvil espouses a contrary position. He condemns the French as atheists, points out their lack of a poor rate, and reveals that freedom of conscience does not exist in the Revolution. His beliefs are clear, particularly "the more we riot, the more we will have to pay" (161). Anticipating the argument of Harriet Martineau in *The Rioters* (1827), this statement suggests much of the ideology of thirties social fiction. Anvil believes that "the poor have as much share in the government as they well know how to manage" (161). More noted of the style of *Village Politics:* "It is as vulgar as heart can wish; but it is only designed for the most vulgar class of readers. I heartily hope I shall not be discovered; as it is a sort of writing repugnant to my nature" (Jay 152). More's artistry is not that negligible. While the dialogue form is derivative from drama and philosophy, More also uses analogies, comparing England to a castle or the body to a political organism, that establish domestic, civil, physical, and political equivalencies. At the end of the dialogue, Hod summarizes the evidence, a device later used in Martineau's *Illustrations*. Now converted to Jack's thinking, Hod follows his prescript that there be "no drinking, no riot, no bonfires" (168). The names Hod and Anvil, with the latter being the ideologically correct position, mark the ascendancy of the industrial over the agricultural. Hannah More believes: "Beautiful is the order of Society when each, according to his place — pays willing honour to his superiors . . . when high, low, rich and poor — when landlord and tenant, master and workman, minister and people, . . . sit down each satisfied with his own place" (Altick 105).

The Lancashire Collier Girl is subtitled *A True Story*. Published in 1795, the tale indicates another direction of social fiction: the success fable, concentrating in the space of a tract a myth of the value of Christian endurance. It is based on a story of the same name that appeared in *The Gentleman's Magazine* of the same year written by "A Rambler." It is not surprising that More wrote a similar story, since in the original the author asserts: "Could our collier-girl have had the advantages of a Sterne, or a Hannah More, who takes the poor under her protection, she would justly appear in the first line of characters" (198). More's tale recounts the rise to respectability of a young girl, Mary, who at age nine works in the mines hauling corves for her father. When he is killed in an accident, she willingly agrees to work a double shift, as in the Rambler's original. More notes that even before the accident, Mary was not "ever much over-worked." In the mines Mary's "virtue was safe" (170, 172). However, Mary succumbs to fatigue and overwork; eventually she is taken to be a domestic servant, albeit girls from the mines, as the narrator notes, were unlikely to make this transition. Mary's "good character" allows her to make this shift. The narrator attributes her respectability to the miners' conduct: "This rule of decency and propriety towards young women, established by a set of coarse miners, is here recorded for the benefit of some of those persons, who are pleased to call themselves their betters" (174). More admits that Mary's tribulations could prompt one to lose faith in God, but naturally Mary does not. However, she notes that "the calamities of Mary were not risen to such a height, that those who are accustomed to view things in this religious and most comforting light, might be ready to imagine that the Almighty had forsaken her, and that there is little use in serving him" (173). Subsequent social writers had also to confront the discrepancy between the sufferings of workers and providential divinity. Many did not succeed any better than More when she concluded that sufferings exist to increase trust in God. The Rambler, obviously a reader of More, noted that she made "considerable alterations" from the original (*Letter* 993). More's stories establish some of the elements of succeeding social fiction: the emphasis on dialogues of conflicting ideologies, the focus on lower-class characters, the promulgation of the gospel of work, and the assumption that the ideology has been illustrated by evidence or is itself sufficiently evidentiary. "Tom Paine and Hannah More between them had opened the book to the common English reader" (Altick 77).

Several of these traits are represented in fiction by men during the corresponding period. William Paley's *Equality, as consistent with the British Constitution,* written in 1793, employs the dialogue format, this time between a workman and his master. The title of Paley's (1743–1805) 1781 publication, *Reasons for Contentment,* indicates his belief. The Workman, on his way to a liberty club, encounters his Master, and the dialogue ensues. This device recalls the meeting that initiates Plato's *Symposium.* The Master, who seldom reads anything "except my Bible and Ledger" (139), tells the Workman, "I was the son of a small farmer, whose condition was little better than that of a common labourer. I had learned to read and write at a charity-school. I was first porter, then clerk, and afterwards partner in the house I entered into" (141). He believes his sons, who are in the military and the law, have an opportunity to rise even higher than himself, an early illustration of self-help ideology. The Workman accepts the lesson, believing that "if I go on as you do, and mind my business, I may in time be as rich and as happy as you" (145). Ivan Melada argues that the ideology of the story is that inequality is natural and that one should accept one's situation (50). On the contrary, the position espoused is that an individual need not accept his lot at all if he is willing to apply self-help. Kingsley later cited Paley's *Evidences of Christianity* in *Alton Locke,* showing the strength of his influence even into the mid-nineteenth century. Paley's opposition to absentee landlordism in *The Principles of Moral and Political Philosophy*

(1785) anticipates the arguments of Maria Edgeworth in *Castle Rackrent* and *The Absentee* in the early nineteenth century.

Albeit those are three examples, there are contrasts between the male and female social fictions. More is concerned with domestic situations and couches her dialogue strictly among lower-class participants. Paley's workman believes in a doctrine of self-help, while More's Mary can only suffer until a lady alerts her to the position of servant. The woman is regarded as lacking in resources to improve her lot. The man is obliged to do so by his gender. Despite the fact that both More and Paley argue from Church premises, neither addresses the conflict between a providential divinity and the lot of the wretched.

The social fiction of Maria Edgeworth (1767–1849) illustrates advances over that of Hannah More. Concerned with the aesthetic values of her texts, Edgeworth is able to write detailed treatments of the social questions to which she addresses herself. The two most important novels are those cited by Scrope, *Castle Rackrent* (1800) and *The Absentee* (1812). As her titles indicate, Edgeworth is concerned with two specific, but interrelated, abuses: the charging of exorbitant rent by a landlord and the absenteeism of the landlord. In the tradition of the social novel, it is not merely the focus on a servant such as Thady Quirk in *Castle Rackrent* that makes the tales of value. Their narrative strategies illustrate two different modes of approach to the social novel.

Castle Rackrent was composed in three parts. The first, written between 1793 and 1795, concerns Thady Quirk's first three masters, Sir Patrick, Sir Murtagh, and Sir Kit. Around 1798 Edgeworth added the narrative about Sir Condy Rackrent. The third stage of composition was the Glossary of 1800. The depiction of the abuse of tenants by spendthrift, profligate, albeit generous landlords, is astute, but it is the creation of her narrator-servant that marks Edgeworth's distinction in *Castle Rackrent*. After the dialogues of Paley and More, one encounters a virtual monologue by a proletarian character. By this device, the narrative discourse imitates the thought pattern and expression of the narrator. *Castle Rackrent* is located in a tradition of social fiction but also exists in a context of classical theatre, with the Rackrents being the bragging *alazons* of Roman comedy, Thady the clever *eiron* who observes the erratic existence of his masters. The first three masters and their lives are presented in Thady's narrative with a degree of ironic expression which suggests that Edgeworth's ideology is reformist and progressive. The profligate Sir Patrick is so indebted that his corpse is seized. Sir Murtagh and Sir Kit marry a Scottish and a Jewish woman respectively, both of whom suffer at the hands of their husbands. With the tale of Sir Condy, Edgeworth's political attitude veers away from the progressive stance implicit in the first part, evincing sympathy for the ruined but benevolent landlords.

Castle Rackrent is important for the development of the social novel. Its proletarian narrator is presented with force. The doctrine of self-help, to be promulgated later by writers like Craik, is given a bitter depiction in the story of Jason Quirk's ascendancy over the Rackrents by his appropriation of their mismanaged estates. "Every thing at Castle Rackrent was seized by the gripers, and my son Jason, to his shame be it spoken, amongst them. I wondered, for the life of me, how he could harden himself to do it, but then he had been studying the law, and had made himself attorney Quirk" (71-72). Edgeworth, in the guise of the Editor, declares that "he lays it before the English reader as a specimen of manners and characters, which are perhaps unknown in England" (96-97). The story anticipates later social fictions with its declaration that "all the features in the fore-going sketch were taken from the life" (97). In her Preface Edgeworth declares: "We are surely justified in this eager desire to collect the most minute facts relative to the domestic lives, not only of the great and good, but even of the worthless and insignificant" (2). The desire for authenticity explains Thady's dialect: "He had it once in contemplation to translate the language of Thady into plain English; but Thady's idiom is incapable of translation, and besides, the authenticity of his story would have been more exposed to doubt" (4). "The best that can happen will be the introduction of British manufacturers" in the place of these landlords (97). Engels was to note a generation later that in Ireland "rents are twice, three times and even four times greater than in England" (306), so the abuse criticized in *Castle Rackrent* remained. In 1826 the distress of weavers was expressed in a petition as follows: "The occupiers of land are with very few exceptions tenants at rack rents of small farms, the rents of which they raise partly by the sale of milk and butter to the cottagers and partly by the weaving of calicoes" (Aspin 46). So significant is Edgeworth's depiction in her novels that they remained a mark of "the one irreparable disaster of our history" to Young in 1936 (186). The passage of the first General Enclosure Act in 1801 reveals that the profligate mismanagement depicted in *Castle Rackrent* was untenable in a period of agricultural reform. The fact that the first census was taken in that year further validates Edgeworth's strategy emphasizing the individuality of her narrator. Her concentration on the suffering of the Irish anticipates later recognition of this situation, such as Carlyle's chapter "Finest Peasantry in the World" from *Chartism* in 1839. Carlyle's reference to *Castle Rackrent* in *Past and Present* signifies its importance as a text of social protest. Disraeli in *Sybil* was to contrast medieval resident monks with nineteenth-century absentee landlords. Later in the century Flintcomb-Ash in Thomas Hardy's *Tess of the d'Urbervilles* is owned by an absentee proprietor.

The *Absentee* is a more serious indictment of the political situation. Published twelve years after the Act of Union, it is among other novels like *Ormond* and *Ennui* which "are more specifically political, and more liberal in their underlying tendency, than ever *Castle Rackrent* was" (Butler 392). In *The Absentee* Edgeworth incorporates the problem of rack rent into the larger abuse of the profligate habits of absentee landlords who had to exact extreme rent to cover the cost of their extravagant behavior in England. *The Absentee* originated as a drama, but the objective of both the drama and the novel was the same, an indictment of a disastrous system of conduct. The novel is a *Bildungsroman* centered upon Lord Colambre (a predecessor of the enlightened aristocrats of Disraeli) who travels to Ireland and discovers the effect of the abuses resulting from absenteeism. He is an early social investigator. Through his political education, the reader is in turn enlightened.

The range of characters in *The Absentee* supports Edgeworth's presentation of a variety of attitudes toward the social question. "Lord and Lady Killpatrick, who had lived always for the fashionable world, had taken little pains to improve the condition of their tenants . . . every thing let go to ruin for the want of a moment's care, or pulled to pieces for the sake of the most surreptitious profit" (107–8). Count O'Halloran indicts the behavior of "those cruel absentees" who destroy property to subvent their spending (121). Lord and Lady Oranmore represent the conscientious Anglo-Irish landowners who remain to supervise their estates. Two kinds of agents are presented to counterpoint the political situation. On the Colambre estate Mr. Burke is careful in his supervision of tenants. His wife runs a school in which Catholic and Protestant children are "sitting on the same benches, learning from the same books, and speaking to one another with the same cordial familiarity" (132). In contrast, the tenants of the Clonbrony estate are at the mercy of the Garraghty brothers, who rackrent the land in Lord Clonbrony's absence. At the conclusion of *The Absentee,* Lord Colambre declares: "I think more of your tenants — of those left under the tyranny of a bad agent, at the expense of every comfort, every hope they enjoyed" (199). The influence of Edgeworth on Scott suggests that her tendency to use the novel for reformist purposes was to have a considerable legacy in the nineteenth century.

While *The Absentee* is not nearly so experimental in its narratology as *Castle Rackrent,* the work is a broader indictment of social abuses. The significance of Edgeworth's depiction of schooling, for example, is indicated by Henry Brougham's belief in *Practical Observations upon the Education of the People* (1825) that "if in any part of the kingdom more than another the education of the working classes is of importance, that part surely is Ireland" (27). In its interest in the total society, *The Absentee* is indicative of a direction the social novel would take in its development during the century. Edgeworth's novels were impressive enough that some male reviewers liked to believe that they were written by her father. In showing the condition of Ireland, Edgeworth marked the basic situation which would cause its brutal hardships later in the century: the fact that it had no industrial revolution. The landlord/tenant relationship in succeeding decades was cited by social critics of the factory system, like Cooke Taylor: "There exists such identity of interest between a proprietor and the labourers whose industry renders his property valuable, but in countless instances this identity escapes the ken of both, as the relations between landlord and tenant in Ireland too often and too notoriously testify" (120). As an Irishman Cooke Taylor is transferring a social distress recorded by Edgeworth and applying it to Lancashire. *The Absentee* would be given particular point because 1812 saw food riots in Oldham, Manchester, and Bolton, while a power loom was attacked in Middleton. A malnourished, discontented populace was not peculiar to Ireland.

Social fiction by such writers as William Paley, Hannah More, and Maria Edgeworth established norms for the subsequent expansion of the form. The use of a dialogue between master and man formed a strong part of the narratives of Harriet Martineau. The concentration on women's distress in *The Lancashire Collier Girl* reappeared in the work of Charlotte Tonna in the forties. Edgeworth's proletarian Thady Quirk was important for later treatment of working-class characters. The concentration by More and Edgeworth on the domestic consequences of abuses was expanded by such writers as Tonna, Stone, and Toulmin. The social novel of the twenties was to retain traits that had appeared earlier.

The decade of the twenties was difficult and disturbing. "Nineteenth-century Britain, especially early nineteenth-century Britain, was a very harsh place" (Clark, *Making* 12). Between the publication of *The Absentee* in 1812 and the first important social fiction of the twenties, Martineau's *The Rioters* and Tonna's *The System* in 1827, social unrest was frequent in British society. The appearance of *The Absentee* in 1812 records a changing milieu for the industrial narrative. While the riots in Ireland in 1798 prompted Edgeworth to write her narratives, two years before the appearance of *The Absentee* Britain had experienced the Spinners' Strike in Manchester. The Luddite Rebellion, which had prompted machine breaking during 1811 and 1812, was followed by several years of continuing war, first 1812–1814, with the United States, and until 1815, with Napoleon. During the economic depression that followed, 1816–1817, social action, such as the Blanketeers' March in 1817 and the rioting of colliers in Newcastle the same year, evinced dissatisfaction. In 1818 strikes in the cotton industry and in 1819 strikes by weavers focused on specific trades. Growing desperation prompted the founding of groups like the Mendicity Society in 1818. The Peterloo affair in Manchester in 1819 and the enforcement of the Six Acts concluded the second decade with tension between workers and management. While the period saw the passage of some key legislation, such as the Health and Morals of Apprentices Act in 1802, it was becoming evident that the passage of legislation did not guarantee its enforcement. A 16 percent growth rate in the population during the period 1811–1821 produced distress in the forties, particularly when coupled with the Corn Law of 1815, which cut off foreign wheat. The second decade of the nineteenth century was responsible for much later disturbance.

The 1820s saw the rise of such social writers as Harriet Martineau and Charlotte Tonna. The period demonstrated the same tendency toward unrest that had marked the previous decades. The repeal of the Combination Act in 1824 offered workers' associations a brief period of legitimacy, but by 1825 the purposes of combinations were restricted. That same year, Hobhouse's Factory Act attempted further government intervention in industry. The speculations crash of 1825–1826 exposed the uncertainty of financial markets and later furnished substance to novels like *Marian Withers* and *John Halifax*. New forces were revealed in such groups as the 1825 Friendly Union of Mechanics and the 1829 Grand Union of Spinners. By the end of the decade such changes as the repeal of the Test and Corporation Act in 1828 and the Catholic Emancipation Act in 1829 showed reformist impulses emerging in the legislative process. Nevertheless, it was not the positive achievements of legislation that social novelists of this decade isolated for consideration. It was rather the strikes and other social disturbances that caught their attention. Finlayson notes that "the social consequences of this aspect of industrialism — the hours worked in factories and the environment in which they were worked — had attracted attention before the 1830s" (2), an interest indicated in Martineau's two early stories. "Hostility to novels which had been building up for several decades reached its peak in the early nineteenth century." "Reading literature was a form of dilettantism and an especially deplorable one. . . . Literature . . . was judged above all in terms of its didactic power, its moral usefulness" (Altick 123, 135–36). The writer in the twenties had to prove his or her utility. Two early tales by Harriet Martineau (1802–1876), *The Rioters* and *The Turn-out,* and Charlotte Tonna's *The System,* confronted these situations. Industrial literature of the twenties is especially important to study because "by the 1820's Britain was no longer a pre-industrial economy" (Deane 212).

John Stuart Mill noted in *The Subjection of Women* that "Two women, since political economy has been made a science, have known enough of it to write usefully on the subject" (205). One of these was Martineau. Martineau's apprenticeship in the social narrative began with *The Rioters* the year following the speculations crash. She recorded her entrance to the form in 1833: "A country bookseller asked me to compose for him some little work of fiction; I thought that I might join the useful to the agreeable, as I had the choice of the subject, if I could show the folly of the populace of Manchester, who had just been destroying the machinery, to the great detriment of the manufactures, on which their bread depended. I produced a little story, entitled 'The Rioters,' and the following year another, on wages, called the 'Turn-out.' I was far from suspecting while I wrote them that wages and machinery had anything to do with political economy; I do not even know whether I had ever heard the name of the science" ("Autobiographical" 613). Martineau's particular interest in economic questions was not that of an observer. In 1826 her father died, having lost a great deal of money in 1825. She recorded in her *Autobiography* that there was a "desperate struggle" in the family during this period: "My father never speculated; but he was well nigh ruined during that calamitous season by the deterioration in value of his stock" (1:98). The Martineau family was to experience total financial collapse in 1829, but there was sufficient distress by 1826 to make financial conditions a subject of personal interest. Furthermore, accompanying the depression of 1826, Norwich, where she was still residing, had experienced several riots, as had towns in Wiltshire. The immediate impetus for *The Rioters* came from an account in the *Globe:* "My Globe newspaper readings suggested to me the subject of machine-breaking as a good one, — some recent outrages of that sort having taken place: but I had not the remotest idea that I was meditating writing on Political Economy, the very name of which was then either unknown to me, or conveyed no meaning. I wrote the little story called 'The Rioters' and its success was such that some hosiers and lace-makers of Derby and Nottingham sent me a request to write a tale on the subject of Wages, which I did, calling it 'The Turn-out'" (1:103).

In the autumn of 1827, Martineau encountered the principles of political economy in Jane Marcet's *Conversations on Political Economy* (1817), which used the dialogue form and in which Edgeworth was mentioned as a predecessor in discussing social conditions. From Martineau's *Autobiography,* it would seem that both *The Rioters* and *The Turn-out* had been written prior to her exposure to Marcet: "Great was my surprise to find that I had been teaching it [political economy] unawares, by my stories about Machinery and Wages. It struck me at once that the principles of the whole science might be advantageously conveyed in the same way — not by being smothered up in a story, but by being exhibited in their natural working in selected passages of social life" (1:105). Both *The Rioters* and *The Turn-out* reflect conditions prevailing in Britain, and particularly Norwich, in the 1820s. They derive their force from Martineau's own financial situation, becoming social fictions written outside but parallel to the orthodoxy of Ricardo and Smith. A reading of these two tales indicates their importance to the fiction that Martineau was to write in the *Illustrations of Political Economy.* There are some differences between the two stories. *The Rioters* is told in the first person by a traveling company representative, *The Turn-out* in the third person. In the former a religious emphasis exists that has been eliminated in the lat-

ter. Both narratives employ a modified form of the debate format that
More had used in the eighteenth century. Both *The Rioters* and *The
Turn-out* are particularly important because they deal with a period
of industrial development that was later to interest George Eliot.

Harriet Martineau recorded specific aspects of the period covered
by the two stories in her *History of the Peace, 1816–1854,* which Lewes
reviewed in the *British Quarterly Review* in 1850. One section of her
History Martineau devoted to disturbances in 1825–1826, which particularly form the basis of *The Rioters.* She records a sequence of
riots, beginning in August 1825 in Sunderland, then in November in
the Isle of Man. In 1826, as a result of trade depression, riots occurred
in Lancashire during the first week in April, in Manchester during
the first week in May (specifically cited as the incident prompting *The
Rioters*), with additional disturbances that spring in Carlisle and in
her birthplace, Norwich. During the April riots "twenty-one mills were
attacked and more than 1,000 power looms destroyed" (Aspin 48).
"In Norwich, the unemployed weavers, who could not take work at
the wages which the manufacturers could afford, kept watch at the
city gates for goods brought in from the country. . . . [They] kept the
magistracy busy and alarmed for some weeks. About 12,000 weavers
in Norwich were then unemployed, and the whole city in a state of
depression" (2:428). During the Lancashire riots, she records, workers were "leaping from two-story windows to escape the soldiery"
(2:426), an incident transferred to the opening pages of *The Rioters.*
In her *History* Martineau discussed emigration as a solution to the
workers' difficulties. When George Eliot wrote *Felix Holt, the Radical* in the sixties, she was familiar with Martineau's account of the
Reform period, which Eliot claimed was "treated with great vigour"
(Wiesenfarth, *Notebook* 153). Martineau, one of the earliest writers
of protest fiction, is linked through the *History of the Peace* with a
much later practitioner like George Eliot. Although there is no evidence that Eliot had read *The Rioters* and *The Turn-out* by the time
she wrote *Felix Holt,* the personal acquaintance of the two women
would make this possible.

The Rioters (1827) concerns protest against the introduction of
power-looms into the factories of Manchester. By 1832 James Kay
in *The Moral and Physical Condition of the Working Classes Employed in the Cotton Manufacture in Manchester* was to describe machine riots as "the most frightful devastations on the property of . . .
masters" (42). The following year, in *The Manufacturing Population*

of England, Peter Gaskell devoted an entire section to the "influence of machinery on human labour" (326–41), noting that it is unrealistic to expect people will not be thrown out of work by machinery. Martineau takes the longer view, that ultimately such practices will lead to greater employment. The unnamed commercial traveler, the narrator, arrives on a Wednesday evening in the city. After he has helped a distressed woman, Mary Brett, he witnesses an assault on a factory. During the riot her sons George and John are arrested. Cruikshank has shown that machinery is a "threat to the family and to parental authority" (11). It is Martineau's achievement to relate machinery and parental authority early in industrial literature with *The Rioters.* In the course of his stay the narrator visits Mrs. Brett's father, who has taken in his granddaughter Hannah on his small farm outside the city, which allows Martineau to contrast the rural with the urban. After an interval of four months, the narrator returns to Manchester when George and John Brett are tried, the former receiving three years (with clemency) and the latter six months. Interspersed with these events are commentaries and conversations about the introduction of machinery, the nature of rioting, and the position of law enforcement.

The arrangement of events in the text reflects the combined practices of More and Paley. The narrator's interest in the social question begins by his assisting Mary Brett, the mother of the arrested boys: the initial point of contact is domestic. By this technique, Martineau individualizes the effects of the riot. Having an outside narrator-observer further localizes the effects of the story. This immediacy is enhanced by the compression of the first part of the tale (until the four months' hiatus) into a mere four days, the narrator arriving on Wednesday and leaving on the following Saturday evening. This narrative compression increases the tension of the subject itself. The text begins late in March, and it is interesting that the story was published on 13 March 1827. The fictional and publishing times are thus coordinated.

The Rioters is an account of the crisis that affected British industry after the Napoleonic Wars. The boys' father declares that "when the war was over, we were told that we should always be prosperous, because trade is always brisk in time of peace" (27). The distress occasioned by general economic decline, and especially by the collapse of 1826, rouses the mob to destroy power loom machinery. The narrator, however, when first viewing the riot in torchlight, reflects when he sees the Brett boys: "The young men both attempted to escape; and I really could not help wishing they might, so strong was the compassion excited by their famished and miserable appearance" (15). The night before their trial four months later, he notes: "I could not forget their care-worn countenances" (108). The recurrence of the datum recalls the mother and directs the reader's response. This is not to say that Martineau neglects her political arguments in the tale. There are several discussions between the narrator and the Bretts' father, one concerning the destruction of machinery, another on law. In the former the narrator comments that "the poor cut their own throats by destroying their masters' property," arguing that the introduction of machinery is the only possible means of confronting competition (34). In the discussion about law, Martineau is adamant. When Brett notes that his class neither makes nor approves the laws, the narrator replies that a person "should strictly observe the laws, whether he understands them all or not" (93). Later in the social novel, the middle-class Philip Hepburn in *Sylvia's Lovers* (1863) states this same position regarding the poor and law. Although the two debates in *The Rioters* sound like hardline political economy, Martineau complicates the narrator's reactions.

On the first evening of his stay in Manchester, the narrator writes to his wife, admitting that "I had learned a new lesson by what I had already seen; I had learned how to be thankful for daily bread." He attempts to secure peace of mind from "having brought myself to reflect on these awful dispensations as ordained by the Father of mercies. . . . I remembered also that in that hand evil is the instrument of greater good. . . . The best way of tranquilizing the mind is to contemplate our feelings in the relation which they bear to the whole of our existence, and with a reference to their Author" (24–25). Such assurance is not easily obtained: "To witness such violences was afflicting; and it was no less so to reflect how the perpetrators had been driven to them. Where, and how soon a remedy was to be found, was a puzzling question. Time and patience were, no doubt, the best remedies: but how to preach patience to starving people . . . was the difficulty. That these trying events were in better hands than ours, and at the disposal of a wiser Being than ourselves, was the only consolation I could find, the only means of soothing my harassing doubts and fears" (45–46). This is the central passage of *The Rioters,* for a member of the mercantile middle class senses a social tremor. Martineau invokes the Judgement of Death Act of 1823, by which mercy could be recommended, to explain the commutation of George's death sentence. The trial at the conclusion of this story indicates a situation which the Hammonds noted: "The art of politics was not the art of keeping the attachment of the people. . . . It was the art of preserving discipline among a vast population destitute of traditions and restraints" (82). While the story concludes with the narrator ruminating on the dangers of rioting, it is the alternative story of the narrator's perception of his and the state's situation that remains important.

Martineau's attitude toward rioting was taken up by Peter Gaskell in 1833 in his study, when he noted that "the men . . . have chiefly erred" (7), but one can also claim that the workers in *The Rioters* have realized that "the basis of power lay in machine-wrecking, rioting and the destruction of property in general" (Hobsbawm 6). The fact that the narrator is unnamed and that the working class family has a name suggests that the narrator is a bourgeois everyman. Martineau may be recording the dawning awareness by the middle class that the laborers have distinct identities. When *The Rioters* was reprinted in 1842, the *Athenaeum* noted that it was written "with the direct purpose of informing the working classes; and it has, no doubt, been re-issued at this moment, with reference to the late outbreak in the manufacturing districts" (930). The reviewer believes it one of the *Illustrations.* Its reissue during a period of Chartist unrest indicates its contemporary relevance.

The Turn-out was published in 1829, although according to Martineau it was written like *The Rioters* in 1827 before she had read Jane Marcet. It appeared in a year that saw riots in Manchester in May 1829, when conditions "were as bad as those of 1826–27"(Aspin 52). The tale is subtitled *Patience the Best Policy,* indicating that Martineau is telescoping two forms of narrative, the industrial tale and the tract. The difference between this tale and its predecessor is the absence of religion as having any function among the working classes. The patience advised is no longer a Christian virtue. It is a secularized standard. Melada notes that the later *A Manchester Strike* is devoid of religion, but this secularization began with *The Turn-out.* Like its predecessor, the story focuses on one family, the Gilberts. Henry Gilbert incites the millhands to a strike, encouraging his brother James to join. James, engaged to Maria Field, has doubts but postpones his marriage to engage in the strike against Maria's inclination. Robert Wallace, the mill owner, advises against the strike and gives an address terminating the strike at the conclusion of the text.

Henry Gilbert travels to Leicester to seek support for his strikers, encountering his cousin George Gilbert, who has been involved in a strike and has turned to drink after losing his job. To understand Martineau's attitude toward an industrial action like a strike, one must realize that "a workman who broke his contract of employment (which he might do by absenting himself in the course of a suddenly-called strike) was guilty of a criminal offence under the Act of 1823" (Burn 243). Striking was or could be an indictable offense. "The courts repeatedly used interpretations of conspiracy and of the master-servant relationship to wear away statutory legalization of trade-unions" (Brebner 71). Martineau's condemnation, and the later criticism of Charlotte Tonna in *Combination,* concern not merely disruptive but criminal behavior.

Unlike *The Rioters, The Turn-out* is composed in chapters, but it does have a similar compressed time scheme for part of its development. It begins on a Saturday afternoon in August. The first chapter is confined to events of Saturday evening, when Henry Gilbert delivers his first speech and tries to lead his brother to strike. The second chapter occurs on Sunday (with the workers' march) and Monday, when James recounts the events of the meeting to Robert Wallace. On Tuesday morning in chapter three Henry leaves for Derby, Nottingham, and Leicester (in deference to the manufacturers who requested the story). On the coach he meets another factory owner who restates what Wallace had told James in the previous chapter, to emphasize the argument. In the sixth chapter, a climactic meeting including speeches by Henry Gilbert and Robert Wallace, the latter ending the strike, brings events to a close. The strength of this construction resides in the parallelism between chapters two and three and the reiteration of that parallelism in the final chapter. One of Martineau's weaknesses is not showing the initial stages of the strike but only the situation after one month. James and Maria have postponed their marriage, but the formation of this decision is not explored. Martineau keeps her two central ideological characters, Henry and Wallace, separated through the device of the brother as intermediary until the conclusion. *The Turn-out* uses contemporary events and circumstances like Peterloo and the postwar economy to give it the illusion of history. The contrast between the two brothers, Henry and James Gilbert, derives from Cain and Abel but with the secularization that marks *The Turn-out.*

The Turn-out is didactic, with workers encouraged to use savings banks, train their children in different occupations, and postpone marriage. The harshness of this last point Martineau makes unwittingly poignant by the plight of Maria Field and James Gilbert. Martineau's owners anticipate the Preface to *Mary Barton* but not with Elizabeth Gaskell's sympathetic attitude: "Their interests are the same as those of their men"; "Your interest and ours are the same" (56, 127). The nameless gentleman traveler expresses a noninterventionist belief: "They will best mend their condition by conforming to the natural course of things, instead of trying to control events which are beyond the power of any one set of men" (59). Henry's first address pits God against man: "When his sufferings proceed from men, instead of from Providence, it is his duty to struggle against them to the utmost" (16). This comment anticipates Engels' observation in *The Condition of the Working Class in England:* "It may well be asked why the workers go on strike when it is clear that the stoppage cannot prevent a reduction in wages. . . . The answer is, simply, that the workers must protest both against a reduction in wages and also against the circumstances which make that reduction necessary. They must assert that since they are human beings they do not propose to submit to the pressure of inexorable economic forces. . . . If trade unionists failed to register their protest by striking, their silence would be regarded as an admission that they acquiesced in the pre-eminence of economic forces over human welfare" (247). Martineau stated in her *Autobiography,* "I believe that I may so write on subjects of universal concern as to inform some minds and stir up others" (2:166). Brougham declared in 1825 that the "doctrines of political economy . . . ought to be much more extensively circulated for the good of the working classes, as well as of their superiors. . . . I can hardly imagine, for example, a greater service being rendered to the men, than expounding to them the true principles and mutual relations of population and wages; and both they and their masters will assuredly experience the effects of the prevailing ignorance upon such questions, as soon as any interruption shall happen in the commercial prosperity of the country, if indeed the present course of things, daily tending to lower wages as well as profits, and set the two classes in opposition to each other, shall not of itself bring on a crisis" (4–5). *The Rioters* and *The Turn-out* indicate the validity of Brougham's admonition two years later, as Martineau, under these changed conditions, tries to "inform some minds." Narratives like *The Rioters* and *The Turn-out* illustrate that, intentionally or not, Martineau's depictions can be read apart from her politics, supporting the attitudes either of an Engels or a Peter Gaskell or a James Kay. "The vivid sketches of the degradation and demoralization of the poor that emerged in Disraeli, . . . Dickens, Kingsley, Mrs. Trollope, . . . Charlotte Elizabeth, and Mrs. Gaskell are anticipated by Harriet Martineau" (V. Colby 221–22).

"Of all the minor women of the epic age, . . . Mrs. Tonna . . . is the one about whom I most wish to satisfy my curosity" wrote Moers (36). Charlotte Elizabeth Tonna (1790–1846) published *The System* in 1827, "designed as part of the Evangelical campaign against slavery" (Jay 170). Although the slave trade had been abolished in 1807, the end of slavery in the colonies did not occur until 1 August 1834 (the date of the conclusion of *John Halifax*). Like Martineau's *The Rioters,* Tonna's *System* has an outsider serving as a reader-surrogate. In Tonna's novel Sir William Belmont visits his brother George, a planter in the West Indies. He encounters a variety of attitudes about slave ownership. The planter Seldon has two children by negroes, a son Caesar and a daughter Lilias, and a cruel wife. On his plantation there is the vicious overseer Whalley and the kind overseer Thomas Cowper. The insidious planter Green infiltrates the revolt of Caesar, then has his own slaves inform against Caesar at the concluding trial. Green has seduced Lilias and degraded her. The Moravian teacher Kerffmann instructs the slaves in Christian tolerance and the masters in Christian sympathy. The judge and attorney Dallas becomes repentant at the conclusion of the novel.

Tonna presents the condition of the West Indies with the same oppositions that were to mark the protest literature of the thirties: the conflict between rebellion and Christian resignation, the relationship of social revolt to Christianity, and the meaning of equality in a religious society. Although Tonna was a strong Low Church Evangelical, she presents the black slaves as doubting whether a white man's God is solicitous of their fates. "Me did pray, massa; but what good dat?" (130). Advised by Sir William that Christ is their brother, the slaves reason: "He no call me broder — he no give me noting" (149). When the imprisoned Caesar is told he is a "determined impenitent offender against the laws of God," he replies: "I should not have become a beast of prey, had they not hunted me from society and drove me from defensive to aggressive warfare" (209). There is no explanation of God's toleration of slavery; Tonna is compelled to present her opponent's case. To reinforce her beliefs, she uses evidence, appended

verbatim in footnotes to her novel. In the year of the publication of
The System, 1827, the *Bolton Chronicle* noted the poor "are compelled to work more and to endure much greater hardship than negro
slaves" (Aspin 71).

That *The System* anticipates the terms of thirties literature is made
apparent if one examines Richard Oastler's letter to the Leeds *Mercury* on "Yorkshire Slavery," October 1830. He notes: "The pious and
able champions of *negro* liberty and *colonial* rights should . . . have
gone farther than they did; or perhaps, to speak more correctly, before they had travelled so far as the West Indies, should, at least for
a few moments, have sojourned in our own immediate neighbourhood, and have directed the attention of the meeting to scenes of
misery, acts of oppression, and victims of slavery, even on the threshold of our homes." Tonna does not shrink from depicting sexual profligacy and squalor in the community of *The System.* Oastler argues:
"Let truth speak out, appalling as the statement may appear. The fact
is true. Thousands of our fellow-creatures and fellow-subjects, both
male and female, the miserable inhabitants of a *Yorkshire town . . .*
are this very moment existing in a state of slavery, *more horrid* than
are the victims of that hellish system '*colonial slavery*'" (Cole and
Filson 316). "Senex" in his essay on Wage Slavery in the *Pioneer* noted:
"I would banish the word wages from the language, and consign it
with the word slavery, to historians and dictionaries" (275). Engels
was to state that "the worker is both legally and in fact the slave of
the middle-class capitalists" (92). *The System* perceptively anticipates
the worker = slave equation of labor agitation. Peter Gaskell in 1833
observed: "The moral evils of the truck and cottage systems . . . de-
grade [the laborer] to a condition of mere slavery, compared to which
the West Indian slave may indeed congratulate himself on his good
fortune" (358). The same equation appears in Parliamentary documents of the sixties. Mill in *The Subjection of Women* was to declare
that "no slave is a slave to the same lengths, and in so full a sense
of the word, as a wife is" (159), while the Chartists were to refer to
their "slavery" in the National Petition in the late thirties (Cole and
Filson 354). Tonna's novel thus isolates a system that symbolically
if not literally referred to many conditions on the British mainland.
The anti-slavery campaign in *The System* suggests the process of "information, agitation, the parent society" that "Evangelicals and hu-
manitarians used and that became part of reformist processes in succeeding decades" (Young, *Victorian* 81).

By the end of the twenties the social narrative had assumed distinguishing characteristics: the use of partisan dialogues, the contrasting opinions of various spokesmen, the presentation of individualized lower-class characters, and the use of narrative to express didactic beliefs. *The Absentee* and *Castle Rackrent,* with *The Rioters, The Turn-out,* and *The System,* prepared for the emergence of a strong form of protest fiction in the next decade. If the achievements of the next decade, and of the forties and fifties, are better known, it is because the early work of writers like Tonna and Martineau has been neglected. The works of Edgeworth have not traditionally been included in the canon of this literature, but she was significant in the evolution of the social novel. Altick mentions that social investigators such as Kay and Chadwick "never showed the slightest curiosity . . . about the inner lives of the workers" (94), but the social novel prior to the thirties had initiated this area of investigation. Edgeworth, Tonna, and Martineau were writing at a time when Greg could note, in 1831: "It is wonderful how little curiosity has been excited respecting the moral and physical condition of so large a portion of our fellow countrymen, and how lamentable and pernicious an ignorance prevails on these subjects in almost every part of the kingdom. The effects of manufactures on the health and morals of those engaged in them, are scarcely known" (2). These women pioneered in a new form, directing the moral direction of the early century. During the first three decades of the nineteenth century, "no English artist could consider the moral stance of art as a neutral, abstract, aesthetic question. And this outlook left its mark on the novel more than any other genre" (Cazamian 37). These writers developed a new direction of this morality in social protest. The optimism Carlyle expressed at the conclusion of *Signs of the Times* in 1829 was not universally believed.

Steven Marcus has observed that "on any account, the 1830s are a decade of critical importance" (*Engels* 15). The decade is prominent in the industrial era for being the period of three far-reaching if not entirely satisfactory pieces of legislation: the Reform Bill of 1832, the Factory Act of 1833, and the Poor Law Amendment Act of 1834. "The reforms of the thirties started a process which has never wholly stopped, and which, in some respects, is still in progress" (Finlayson, *Decade* 3). The decade divides itself naturally between 1836 and 1837, when economic depression (which would last at least until 1842) began and a typhus epidemic caused distress, as had the cholera of 1831–1832. Prior to 1837, the country experienced a number of upheavals that drew the attention of the industrial writers. Eighteen-thirty saw incendiarism and the riot of field laborers near London, as well as the Swing Riots. Riots broke out in Bristol in 1831 when the Lords rejected the Reform Bill. In the winter of 1830–1831 agricultural laborers rioted. By 1833, the incidents involving the Tolpuddle Martyrs in Dorset and the Cold Bath Fields Riots had demonstrated the timeliness of Martineau's tales, whatever one's political sentiments. In the middle of the decade it was apparent that legislation, such as the prohibition of the truck system in 1830 and the Factory Act, was not proving enforceable or effective as a deterrent to social unrest.

The rise of workers' organizations, such as the Northern Typographical Union in 1830, the Grand National Consolidated Trades Union in 1834, and the London Working Men's Association in 1836, made the idea of combination an obvious subject to social writers. Three important documents dealing with this early stage of the thirties reflect the transition from the twenties. Writing of strikes and combinations made this literature typical of the period. In 1832 two stories concerning labor actions, Martineau's *A Manchester Strike* and Tonna's *Combination,* focused on the middle-class fear of unions. *The Hill and the Valley,* published in the same year, is a fable of the destruction of an industrial Eden. This writing in the early decades responds to Carlyle's request in his essay on Diderot: "What were far better, sweep their Novel-fabric into the dust-cart, and betake them with such faculty as they have to understand and record what is *true*" (178). Kathleen Tillotson wonders why "the rapid emergence and multiplication of such [protest] novels should belong to the forties and not to the thirties" (123), but the thirties saw many examples of protest fiction.

When Charlotte Tonna published *Combination* in 1832, she appended the subtitle *A Tale, Founded on Facts,* and the story, although crude in its artistry, is important for several reasons. *Combination* concerns two brothers, William and Thomas Riley. The Cain/Abel analogy is significant, since in the course of the tale the young brother Thomas actually participates in the killing of another laborer. The story reflects its times in that the parents of the two brothers died of fever, probably reflecting the visitation of cholera in England during 1831–1832. The story opens in Ireland, but after Thomas is implicated in the murder of Collyer, the brothers and their sister Judy go to Manchester to stay with their aunt, Mrs. Harris. This study of early Irish emigration to England indicates an awareness of the social consequences of this phenomenon as noticed by Engels, Kay, and others later in the decade and in the forties. Having lived in Ireland from 1819 to 1824, Tonna was acquainted with Irish customs and is one of the first writers to note this emigration.

The subject of *Combination* is strike action, and therefore the characters are predominantly male. The two brothers lose their father, who was of "a good moral character, and a sensible man. . . . As he wished to be respectable and prosperous, he avoided all immoral practices." William, the older brother, has "a mild amiable character," but he is influenced by the younger Thomas, whose pride was "immoderate" (3–5). Their employer Mr. Hall is "very benevolent," a man who continues to pay one wage despite reductions by other manufacturers because of economic distress. Tonna contrasts the union agitator Smith and the beneficent gentleman Mr. Bolton, who is temporarily employing the brothers' sister. Smith presents a strong case for striking, despite Tonna's antiunion position, while Bolton, who "knew to what dreadful crimes combination was daily leading the working classes," argues against the influence of the agitator Smith (16). Bolton's argument is presented without the narrator's own antiunion bias. He regards oath-taking as inconsistent with being a Christian. Combination to the narrator is rebellion, "the first crime committed," she notes (75), after Thomas Riley becomes involved in the murder of Collyer.

As an Evangelical, Tonna imposes a biblical allegory on industrial conditions. She marks Thomas as a Prodigal Son, a common practice of "trying to equate contemporary events with biblical symbols" (Jay 97). When in Manchester, he becomes initiated into a drunken group of free thinkers, which Tonna calls a "synagogue of Satan" (112). A new character is introduced, the Riley's cousin Michael Burke, a soldier quartered in Manchester to prevent dissension. Burke has led a dissolute life but, having been saved by Christ, has become "a true soldier of the Cross" (163), a prefigurement of Kingsley's Muscular Christian. Tonna's indictment of the factory system and particularly of unions is strident. The narrator interprets a fever infecting the workers' district as a visitation from God: "Such was a part of the miseries that followed from the wicked principle of combining to raise wages; and thus did the displeasure of the Lord help on the affliction which they had wantonly brought on themselves and others" (178). Combination is associated with rebellion and therefore with "a sinful way" (27). At the conclusion the narrator notes: "There are a thousand ways to hell, but only one way to heaven; and the man who breaks the laws of his country is already breaking the law of God, and is therefore in one of those thousand ways" (208). As does Martineau in *The Rioters,* Tonna seems to refer to the 1823 Master and Servant Act, viewing it almost as a divine ordinance, associating civil with religious rebellion.

Two aspects of *Combination* are particularly significant. Both Thomas and William Riley, who contract fever, die outside the influence of religion, Thomas blaspheming and William indifferent to religion. George Eliot was to ask in 1856: "Why, then, cannot our Evangelical lady novelists show us the operation of their religious views among people . . . who keep no carriage?" (Pinney 318–19). In *Combination* Tonna was already doing something more striking, showing the failure of her own religion among workers. Its sustaining value she saved for *Helen Fleetwood.* The National Petition of 1837 was to include a statement that "Heaven has dealt graciously by the people; but the foolishness of our rulers has made the goodness of God of none effect" (Cole and Filson 354). The undercurrent of skepticism or sheer disbelief is evident in this comment, and in *Combination* Tonna has distinguished this consciousness in her workmen. Houghton notes that "the decline of faith among members of the working class doubled the fear of revolution. . . . Atheism [was] more common in this class than in any other single group" (59). With these two brothers Tonna creates early portraits of agnostic or atheistical workingmen, which would have successors in works like Kingsley's *Alton Locke.* Tonna's *Combination* is typical of a transition by the novelist, "when he began to explain, judge, evaluate man in terms of *man,* not of God" (J. Mitchell 249).

Tonna can present the grim urban landscape with some perception as a background to the industrial world as a religious battlefield: "It was bitterly cold, and yet did he half grudge himself of the comfort of his warm surtout coat, while beholding the shivering objects that wandered about the streets even at that hour, in utter despair, driven from their homes by the hungry cries which they had no means of stilling: some reeling like drunkards from the effects of starvation, and others really intoxicated, having spent the pence that they had begged during the day, in liquor that would make them insensible, as they madly wished to be, to the horrors of their hopeless condition" (185). This description, paralleling the record of the narrator of *The Rioters,* indicates the nature of the urban world in the early thirties and the interest in it as a background for industrial unrest. Like her fellow Evangelical Hannah More, Tonna isolates the two domestic situations, the parentless home in Ireland, the Christian but ineffectual residence of Mrs. Harris in Manchester, to show the domestic consequences of industrial dislocation. The only Irishman in the story who is assimilated to England is Michael Burke, who joins the military.

Humphry House notes that combinations "were revolutionary in the sense that they did not accept the doctrine of the natural indentity of interests between Capital and Labour" (209). Tonna's *Combination* is an accurate reflection of middle-class fear and suspicion during the decade. The following statement from Cooke Taylor indicates the extent of this fear even into the forties: "Rome fell, not because its finances were exhausted or its armies routed, but because the lower ranks of its population were systematically corrupted" (129). Tonna's rhetoric in *Combination* is excusable if one considers she is writing a decade earlier than Cooke Taylor. *Combination* was published two years before E. C. Tufnell's *Character, Object, and Effects of Trades' Unions* (1834), which chronicles the bases for anxiety about unions, including a series of strikes that would have been known to Tonna: spinners of Manchester in 1810, spinners in Hyde in 1824, shipwrights in Liverpool in 1816, an 1829 action against machinery in Manchester, London hatters in 1820, spinners in Ashton both in 1825 and in December 1830. Like Tonna, Tufnell was to note the practices of union intimidation and tyranny, the decline in the work ethic from idleness during strikes, and the fact that many workers, if returned to work, had to accept even lower wages than before striking. The murder of Collyer in *Combination* was prophetic of the December, 1832 murder of "a man who had refused to join in a turn-out" in Leeds (73).

Harriet Martineau's *A Manchester Strike,* also published in 1832, is among the better-known of her *Illustrations of Political Economy.* Based on an 1829 strike, Martineau's book advances a pro-Malthusian, anti-interventionist, laissez-faire position. Her arguments are couched in a doctrine of Necessarianism, which she stated in her *Autobiography:* "All human action proceeds on the assumption that all the workings of the universe are governed by laws which cannot be broken by human will" (1:185). This philosophy "required the utmost exertion on the part of the individual to bring himself into line with the natural laws of society" (Webb, *Martineau* 110). In her *Autobiography* Martineau states that in constructing the *Illustrations* she intended "to embody each leading principle in a character . . . and the mutual operation of these embodied principles supplied the action of the story" (1:147). Some of these are "lively novels in miniature, but complete in cast of characters, setting, dialogue, and plot" (Moers 29).

Martineau used reports and statistics for her series and never revised. Her forthrightness about her processes of composition and a later statement about her "own inability to make a plot" have prejudiced readers against her art (*Autobiography* 1:180). In *A Manchester Strike,* Martineau's emphasis on factuality and the possibility that William Allen is modeled after John Tester (the leader of the Bedford Strike of 1825–1826) have, along with her own statements about her artistry, obscured appreciation of her strengths. John Doherty remarked that "Every incident of the tale is drawn from real life" (Webb, *Martineau* 122). The 1829 strike and Francis Place supplied her with information for the story. Although it seems *A Manchester Strike* "describes in stereotype the operation of the law of wages and its meaning for strikes" (Brantlinger, "Case" 46) the elements of individuation Martineau introduces into her story elevate it to a higher plane.

A Manchester Strike concerns a rebellion against masters to force equalization of wages. The central character William Allen is a spokesman for the striking workers. A new element in this tale is a recognizable family life for the protagonist. Allen's wife Mary is opposed to striking, his little daughter Martha is a piecer with painful knees. The union organizer Clack instigates the workers to strike, and the workers must deal with three employers, Rowe/Mortimer, Elliott, and Wentworth. Allen begins by thinking striking is the worst possible alternative, but the intransigence of the three firms in refusing to equalize wages compels him to join the strike action. He believes that "where both parties are so necessary to each other, it is a pity they should fall out" (230). The ideological pivot of *A Manchester Strike* is the opposition of two addresses, one by Allen early in the strike, the other at the climax. As in *The Turn-out* an address by the master marks the end of the strike. In chapter four Allen presents in detail the value of combination for the workers: "Combination on our part is necessary from power being lodged unequally in the hands of individuals, and it is necessary for labourers to husband their strength by union" (252). Wentworth's address in chapter nine propounds the basic tenets of political economy: "The masters' capital does not return enough to pay you all at the rate you desire" (280).

A Manchester Strike shows advances over Martineau's previous stories in the rhythm of the narrative. The ideological dialogue has receded to a more realistic milieu, with events intervening between the various dialogues: Martha's health declines from inhaling cotton dust; the relationship between Clack and Allen deteriorates; Clack's fiancée Ann Howlett is imprisoned under the 1823 Act for breach of contract. While Martineau might have felt she was using her characters as spokesmen, *A Manchester Strike,* with its multifarious events, gives doctrine a more satisfactory context. Martineau strengthens her depiction in this story by several details. The urban landscape is grim: "There were heaps of rubbish, pools of muddy water, stones and brickbats lying about, and cabbage-leaves on which the unwary might slip, and bones over which pigs were grunting and curs snarling and fighting" (226). This depiction is made convincing because it is seen through the eyes of Allen's daughter Martha as she "tried to avoid all these obstacles." The domestic emphasis of the tale is another reason for its credibility. Allen arrives home to find his wife in a bitter dispute with Sally Field, a neighbor. Little Martha plays with Hannah Bray, daughter of a former worker turned itinerant musician; fathers abuse their children as the strike continues. In these ways Martineau creates a fuller milieu for her characters than she had in *The Rioters* and *The Turn-out.* Bray is a forerunner of the Jupes in *Hard Times,* providing a sharp contrast by his occupation to the drabness of the factory workers' existences. Martineau presents arguments against imprudent marriages (on which Wentworth bases his claim that labor controls wages), government interference, and the necessity of teaching children alternative employment. Her choice of details is astute. Children laid off from work spend their time "playing at being cotton-spinners"; and little Martha tells time by watching the sunbeams: "The sunbeams rested now on the ceiling, and Martha knew that they must travel down to the floor and be turned full on her frame and some way past it, before she could be released" from her night shift (287, 262). Martineau's tale is more successful than Tonna's in creating a domestic milieu for the workers and for being free of stridency. In *Combination* Tonna has not mastered the gradual unfolding of a narrative that is part of the artistry of *A Manchester Strike.* The novel is a significant predecessor of works like *North and South, Hard Times,* and *Sybil.*

Before her depiction of a strike in 1832, Martineau wrote *The Hill and the Valley* to show the process of the rise of an iron works in

Wales, the importation of machinery, a riot, and the collapse of the industry. *The Hill and the Valley* "enlarges upon the question of labor-saving machinery that was the subordinate theme of *The Rioters*" (Melada 53). The central characters, Wallace, a partner in the iron works, and John Armstrong, an opponent of the factory system living reclusively on the hill overlooking the industrial valley, are created convincingly, especially the latter. Armstrong is a portrait of an aging individualist, methodical in his habits. The scenes between him and his housekeeper, Margaret Blake, are tinged with warm affection. Armstrong had been in trade, but "had lost money through the knavery of his partner. He immediately took a disgust to business" (5). He hoards his savings rather than investing them to produce capital. When trade declines from French and American competition, Wallace installs machinery, which the workers destroy in a fire-burning riot after James Fry, a local boy, is killed through carelessness in an accident at the factory. Martineau captures "the inexplicable economic crashes which burst in on capitalist and worker alike with a diabolical regularity" (J. Mitchell 264).

Martineau expands her portraits of subsidiary characters in *The Hill and the Valley,* especially of women. Wallace's shy wife learns to live with the working people. His partner Bernard has a son Francis who comes to the valley with Mrs. Sydney, teacher of his sisters. This woman is at ease with the operatives. She is especially interested during a tour of the iron works, in a manner later used by Elizabeth Stone in *William Langshawe* or by Geraldine Jewsbury in *Marian Withers.* The first view one is given of the iron works is effective, coming through the eyes of Mr. Bernard's children: "In a moment the carriage turned the corner, and the children started up, forgetting cold and hunger and fear, to gaze at the extraordinary scene before them. Strange sounds rose when the gust fell—a roaring like that of a mighty wind, which their father told them was caused by the blast of the furnaces. . . . There were black figures of men, brandishing long rakes, sometimes half-hidden by red smoke, and sometimes distinctly marked against a mass of flame" (55).

Although Martineau uses the riot as a device, she does so with credibility. The overwrought mob, after James Fry's funeral, proceeds to burn the buildings of the works. Eventually soldiers arrive. Many are arrested and taken away as prisoners, with the women refusing to see them off: "Some took a shorter leave still; for there were wives and sisters — though not one mother — who would not own a relation in disgrace" (125). *In The Hill and the Valley* Martineau shows women suffering particularly. Some try to see their imprisoned men: "Many an entreaty was addressed to the soldiers just to be permitted to step up to the window between the horses, and see whether John, or Will, or George wanted anything or had anything to say. This could not of course be allowed; but it was long after dark before the last lingerer had shut herself into her cheerless home to watch for the morning" (124). Wallace delivers a programmatic defense of the closing of the ruined works, but the gradualness of the narrative disguises its dogmatism.

The final meeting between Armstrong and Wallace shows the older man an altered individual who has accepted the principle of change. When Wallace asks if Armstrong regrets the departure of the factory, he responds: "I might not say so perhaps . . . if yonder valley could be made what it once was. But that can never be; and there is no comparison between a settlement where art and industry thrive, and a greater number of human beings share its prosperity every year, and a scene like that, where there is everything to put one in mind of men but man himself" (138). Cooke Taylor writes of an instance of machine-breaking during the Luddite period that "ended in the destruction of the mill by incendiary violence." The consequence was that the mill "took its flight from persecution . . . and has been allowed to remain in quietude" in another locale (171, 172). Martineau's critique embraces not only a contemporary situation but one two decades earlier. When Armstrong gathers the departing Mrs. Wallace a bouquet of flowers as the novel ends, Martineau has learned to humanize her doctrine. The accuracy of the circumstance recounted in *The Hill and the Valley* is indicated in Peter Gaskell's study the following year: "So far have these [combinations] gone sometimes, as to threaten the ruin of an entire and flourishing town or district, and have involved in it not only the interests of the two conflicting parties, but the race of shopkeepers and others dependent upon them for their support" (299).

Martineau's artistry has advanced from her earlier tales of the twenties. *A Manchester Strike* and *The Hill and the Valley* show advances in use of settings, the domestic emphasis, the growth in the number of characters, the evocation of milieu, and the transformation of dogmatic dialogues into conversations. From *The Rioters* to *The Hill and the Valley,* Martineau develops from a writer of industrial fiction to a writer of industrial literature. Her success can be measured by the fact that Edward Bulwer-Lytton found her comparable to, if not quite the equal of, Maria Edgeworth.

The period after the writing of *The Hill and the Valley* and *A Manchester Strike* saw dramatic alterations in British society that were to influence social fiction by the end of the decade. The creation of the Statistical Department of the Board of Trade in 1832, of the Manchester Statistical Society in 1833, and of the Statistical Society of London in 1834, confirmed the emerging power of documentation about social conditions. The publication of the *Journal of the Statistical Society* in 1838 represents a revolution. J. R. McCulloch's *A Statistical Account of the British Empire* appeared in 1837. As Young notes, "It was the business of the thirties to transfer the treatment of affairs from a polemical to a statistical basis" (*Victorian* 32). Carlyle remained a skeptic in *Chartism:* "Tables are like cobwebs . . . beautifully reticulated, orderly to look upon, but which will hold no conclusion. . . . Statistical Inquiry, with its limited means, with its short vision and headlong extensive dogmatism, as yet too often throws not light, but error worse than darkness" (124, 126). Statistics "present averages and . . . the average is the life led by no man" (112). Still, quantification was a revolution, for it compelled the social fiction writer to seek new sources of data and information. Newspaper accounts, such as those used by Martineau in *The Rioters,* were no longer sufficient. When Blue Books began to be sold to the public in 1836, access to material was not merely facilitated—it became compulsory. The rise of statistical analysis implied the existence of government intervention on a new scale. While Parliamentary commissions had explored social conditions of laborers, for example in 1816, the new dissemination of this material and its transformation into social policy was significant for the thirties. By the end of the decade, events were to make recourse to data more significant than it had been in the twenties.

Several events after mid-decade sharpened writers' observation. The financial recession of 1836–1837 marked the beginning of a depression that lasted until 1842 or later. Bad harvests, 1839–1842, exacerbated the effects of the Corn Laws on the poor, while a smallpox epidemic 1837–1841 aroused interest in sanitation and housing. The Anti-Corn Law Association in Manchester in 1838, and the Anti-Corn Law League of 1839, were further evidence of dissatisfaction with the Reform Bill. By the end of the decade discontent with social legislation, such as the Reform Bill, the Factory Act, and the New

Poor Law, was pronounced. The formation of the National Char-
ter in 1838, the defeat of the first Chartist petition in 1839, with the
uprisings in Newport, Birmingham and Wales, emphasized the anger. Novelists began to respond to this distress, among them Frances
Trollope.

The Ten Hours Movement, begun in 1831, assumed prominence
for many writers, such as Frances Trollope (1780–1863), whose *Michael
Armstrong* reflects this dismay. The review of its first numbers in the
Athenaeum of August 1839 indicted the novel for being too late: "But
we pray Mrs. Trollope to reflect that this contingency has passed away.
A cry, a fanatical cry has been raised on the subject; the evil is in
the hands of the legislature, and fully before the public; for all purpose of practical good the Factory Boy has come too late" (590). This
is to miss the point of Trollope's novel. She is writing in defense of
the Ten Hours Movement, albeit using the conditions of the 1820s
and 1830s as her ostensible subject. There is an overt and a covert
subject of the novel: it describes conditions of the previous decade
and the early thirties, while it is actually about the insufficiency of
the legislation then existing. Further evidence of the contemporaneity
of *Michael Armstrong* is found in John Fielden's *The Curse of the
Factory System* (1836). Fielden criticizes a plan "to persuade the gentry and farmers to send the 'redundant supply' of rustic infants down
into the manufacturing districts, and the parents to comply in this
species of what is called 'home colonization'! A proposition at which
I shudder. . . . I am decidedly opposed to sending the little children
of the south into the northern manufactories" (36, 69). Therefore,
although shipping apprentice children was not an issue in 1839, there
was still serious discussion about transporting young children from
agricultural areas to work in factories. Trollope is thus not dealing
with abuses that have vanished. She is dealing with a contemporary
subject in slightly distanced form.

Published in twelve-shilling parts beginning in February 1839, *Michael Armstrong, the Factory Boy* was influential. Samuel Kydd in
1857 noted that "Mrs. Trollope's novel *Michael Armstrong* has been
much abused; it has, however, been useful, and so, also, has *Helen
Fleetwood* by Charlotte Elizabeth." Mrs. Trollope herself said, "I don't
think any one cares much for *Michael Armstrong*—except the Chartists. A new kind of patrons for me!" Cazamian concluded that "*Michael Armstrong* was without question one of the least effective social novels, as it was one of the worst" (Cazamian 237). While no

claims of artistic perfection are tenable, *Michael Armstrong* is not so devoid of craft as its reputation has suggested. The process by which the novel was constructed and Trollope's use of sources reveal one technique of research by social novelists. On 20 February 1839, she traveled from London to Manchester to view conditions for herself. She was praised for this excursion by the *Northern Star* in March 1839: "The lady is taking the right way to write the truth about 'The factory boy'" it declared (Chaloner 160). The contemporary relevance of Trollope's novel is clear if compared to the assertions James Kay made in *The Training of Pauper Children* the same year that saw the novel published: "The payment of premiums for apprenticeship has been shown to be a system having many most pernicious tendencies," he argued, adding that "the training of a child should not be procured by coercion and restraint" (9, 14). Rather than being dated *Michael Armstrong* is rooted in the year of its appearance.

Trollope's sources for *Michael Armstrong* included information from Lord Ashley, the leader of the Ten Hours Movement in the House of Commons, Parliamentary Blue Books, including the material of the Sadler Committee *Report* of 1832 on children's employment, and John Brown's *Memoir of Robert Blincoe,* first serialized and then issued in a pamphlet in 1828, reprinted in Manchester in 1832. Lord Ashley recommended Kay's 1832 monograph, later used by Engels in *The Condition of the Working Class.* Behind *Michael Armstrong* is dissatisfaction with the Factory Acts of 1802, 1819, and 1833. The emphasis on factuality is strong. The narrator informs the reader in footnotes accompanying her description of the hellish Deep Valley Mill: "The real name of this valley (which most assuredly is no creation of romance) is not given, lest an action for libel should be the consequence. The scenes which have passed there, and which the few following pages will describe, have been stated to the author on authority not to be impeached" (180). "Let none dare to say this picture is exaggerated, till he has taken the trouble to ascertain by his own personal investigation, that it is so. . . . But woe to those who supinely sit in contented ignorance of the facts" (186). The source of this material, as Chaloner comments, was the *Memoir of Robert Blincoe.* One can identify Deep Valley Mill with Litton Mill in Derbyshire, owned by Ellice Needham, who became the Elgood Sharpton of *Michael Armstrong.* Brown described Litton Mill thus: "Its situation at the bottom of a sequestered glen, and surrounded by rugged rocks, remote from any human habitation, marked a place fitted to the foul crimes of frequent occurrence which hurried so many of the friendless victims of insatiate avarice, to an untimely grave" (45). Trollope observed: "It is hardly possible to conceive a spot more effectually hidden from the eyes of all men, than this singular valley. Hundreds may pass their lives within a few miles of it, without having the least idea that such a spot exists" (180). Cruikshank notes that "in the remote areas labour was scarce and many employers imported child apprentices, parish orphans from workhouses far and near" (13).

A comparison of Blincoe and Trollope illustrates Trollope's practice with sources. Trollope's description of events in Deep Valley Mill parallels experiences Blincoe had at his first mill, Lowdham Cotton Mill near Nottingham. The arrivals of Blincoe and Armstrong are described in parallel terms. At his first meal in the mill, Michael is dismayed: "To Michael, the spectacle was appalling; and young as he was, he seemed to feel that the filthy, half-starved wretches before him, were so many ghostly representations of what he was himself to be. A sickness like that of death came over him, and he would have given a limb, only for the freedom to stretch himself down upon the floor and see no more. But the master of the ceremonies at this feast of misery bore a huge horsewhip in his hand. . . . The food placed before him consisted of a small bowl of what was denominated stir-pudding, a sort of miserable water-porridge, and a lump of oaten cake" (182–83). At first the new apprentices in Blincoe are alone: "The supper set before them consisted of milk-porridge, of a very blue complexion! The bread was partly made of rye, very black, and so soft, they could scarcely swallow it, as it stuck like bird-lime to their teeth. . . . This caught the eye of the governor . . . who had served in the army, and had been a drill serjeant; unexpectedly he produced a large horse-whip. . . . In a moment [all] were reduced to solemn silence and abject submission. Yet the master of the house had not uttered a single threat; nor indeed had he occasion; his carbuncled nose, his stern and forbidding aspect and his terrible horsewhip inspired quite as much terror as was requisite" (24). From Blincoe's second location, the Litton Mill, Trollope extracted the detail of the soap allowance: "No soap was allowed — a small quantity of meal was given as a substitute; and this from the effects of keen hunger, was generally eaten" (46). Trollope wrote: "The persons of the children [were] permitted to be filthy to excess, from having no soap allowed to assist their ablutions — though from the greasy nature of their employment it was peculiarly required, while the coarse meal occasionally given out to supply its place was invariably swallowed, being all too precious in the eyes of the hungry children to be applied to the purpose for which it was designed" (212). Trollope likewise derives the appearance of fever from Blincoe's account of Litton Mill.

Trollope's celebrated borrowing is the account in Blincoe of eating from the pig trough. "The fatting pigs fared luxuriously, compared with the apprentices! Blincoe . . . as soon as he saw the swineherd withdraw . . . used to slip down stairs, and steal slyly toward the trough, plunge his hand in at the loop holes, and steal as many dumplings as he could grasp! The food thus obtained from a pig's trough . . . [was] devoured with a much keener appetite than it would have been by the pigs" (62). The same episode occurs on Michael's first day at Deep Valley Mill: "Seven or eight boys had already made their way to the sort of rude farm-yard upon which this door opened, one and all of them were intent upon purloining from a filthy trough just replenished for the morning meal of two stout hogs . . . leaving Michael gazing with disgust and horror at the contest between the fierce snouts of the angry pigs and the active fingers of the wretched crew who contested with them for the offal thus cast forth" (184). From Blincoe Trollope derived the comparison of apprentices to slaves. Brown demanded the legislators "rescue their nation from a worse stain, than even the African Slave Trade, horrible as was that odious traffic" (42). "It would be difficult, if not impossible, from the record of sufferings inflicted upon Negro slaves, to quote instances of greater atrocity . . . incomparably worse than that of the field-slave in the West Indian plantations" (52). Trollope declared, following the analogy of Blincoe and Tonna: "It is a very fearful crime in a country where public opinion has proved (as in the African Slave Trade) to be omnipotent" (186).

The inadequacies of the Factory Act of 1802, limiting the hours of apprentices, are emphasized by both Brown/Blincoe and Trollope. Brown was amazed to learn that Blincoe knew nothing of the 1802 act for years; Brown calls it a "dead-letter" (44). The vicious Sir Matthew Dowling refers to the nuisance the government interference has made in making it more difficult to secure apprentices. Even Trollope's beneficent heiress Mary Brotherton is not untouched by the act, since her father "had been a manufacturer of the old apprentice-system school, and his fortune made long before the humane bill of Sir Robert Peel" (84). Middle-class wealth and respectability are erected on a foundation of slave apprentice labor.

The Parliamentary evidence available to Trollope was consider-able. Francis Horner had noted in the Commons in 1815 that children were considered as property, and the *Report on Children Employed in Manufactories* of 1816 contained numerous accounts of abuses, despite the provisions of the 1802 Act, with records of overlookers such as John Moss molesting female operatives. William Evans ad-mitted that the "Act was not of any efficient service" and thus refused to read it, although he was Manchester magistrate (Pike, *Industrial,* 96). Sadler condemned "infantile slavery" to parents who "purchase idleness by the toil of their infants . . . [and] count upon their chil-dren as upon their cattle" in a speech in March 1832 (117–18). In the Parliamentary papers 1831–1832, numerous accounts of beatings and strappings occur. The reports of 1833 tell of children dragged from beds and weighted with iron as punishment. A Manchester spinner, Grant, said, "Much was said of black slaves and their chains; no doubt they were entitled to freedom, but were there no slaves except those of sable hue?" (145).

Peter Gaskell admitted in 1833 that the apprentices "suffered very severely" (176). Some of the more gruesome episodes recounted in Blincoe's memoir are omitted in Trollope. Mr. Bell, the clergymen in *Michael Armstrong,* makes a plea for the Ten Hours Bill, stating: "All that we ask for . . . all that the poor creatures ask for themselves, is that by Act of Parliament it should be rendered illegal for men, women, and children to be kept . . . for more than ten hours out of every day" (206). Trollope enlists the data of the second and third decades of the century to advance her crusade in the fourth. In her advocacy of the Ten Hours Bill, she was far from being late: Cooke Taylor in 1842 could describe it as "a remedy . . . which assuredly has no parallel in the annals of quackery" (131).

It is the overdrawn characters in *Michael Armstrong,* rather than the situations, that undermine the novel. In its earliest chapters, this tendency is clear in the treatment of Sir Matthew Dowling, the fac-tory owner, when he adopts Michael Armstrong to gain favor in the area: "The idea of being thus entrapped, and forced to adopt *'a bag of rags out of his own factory'* (for it was thus he inwardly designated little Michael), galled him for a moment so severely, that he was within an ace of exclaiming 'Confound you, and the beggar's brat together, you old fool!'"(17). Sir Matthew is described by his gardener Mac-nab as "raising his arm like one of his own steam-engines" (26). Other oppressors include the evil factory superintendent Joseph Parsons, who "had a Napoleon-like promptitude of action" and the insensitive physician Dr. Crockley, who encourages Dowling in his greed and his dislike of government intervention, health commissions, and child labor regulations (37). These three men decide that Michael "is to be made a gentleman of" (44), although he is a natural gentleman. These expressions are close to several of those used later in *Great Expectations.*

If the lower classes are kept in subjection by these men, women of the middle class are kept in ignorance, as is Mary Brotherton: "No one speaks of the factory in the house of the manufacturer." Trollope dislikes the "extraordinary degree of ignorance in which the ladies of the great manufacturing families are brought up" (93). Mary Brotherton, orphan heiress, begins to wonder about this control: "What is the cause of this strange degradation of one peculiar class of human beings? It surely cannot arise from the nature of their employment; for if it did, of course the clergy of the neighbourhood would interfere to stop it" (107). When she attempts to get Mr. Thomas, a medical practitioner in the town of Ashleigh, to visit a dying woman, he thinks of "the very *unnatural conduct* of the rich young lady" (135). Before Mary Brotherton goes to investigate the conditions of the Sharpton mill, she is counseled by the Reverend George Bell, a reforming minister regarded as "wrong-headed" by his neighbors for saying that factory work "is bad for the children's health" (197).

From Bell, Mary Brotherton hears Trollope's most severe condemnation of the factory system. "Nothing except personal investigation can enable the inquirer to arrive at the whole truth respecting it" (202). Like the author, Mary Brotherton undertakes the investigation, which indicates that she is an alter ego of Trollope herself. Although Bell argues strenuously for government intervention, he tells Mary: "I cannot in conscience tell you that it is in your power effectually to assist them. That you may save your own excellent heart from the palsy of hopeless and helpless pity, by the indulgence of your benevolence in individual cases of distress, I need not point out to you; but that any of the ordinary modes of being useful on a larger scale, such as organising schools, founding benefit societies, or the like, could be of any use to beings so crushed, so toil-worn, and so degraded, it would be idle to hope" (208-9). When he suggests Mary cannot travel to Derbyshire without attendants, she tells him:

"Do not set me down in your judgments as a hot-headed girl, indifferent to the opinions of society, and anxious only to follow the whim of the moment. . . . The only way I know of, by which I can make this desolate sort of freedom endurable, is by fearlessly, and without respect to any prejudices or opinions whatever, employing my preposterous wealth in assisting the miserable race from whose labours it has been extracted. If you can aid me in doing this, you will do me good; but you will do me none, Mr. Bell, by pointing out to me the etiquettes by which the movements of other young ladies are regulated. I cannot think that I have any right place among them; and I therefore feel that to check any possible usefulness by a constant reference to the usages of persons with whom I have little or nothing in common, would be putting on very heavy harness, neither effective for use, nor for ornament." (232)

This passage is an important assessment of the middle-class woman's position in society. Probably without knowing it, Trollope gave her heroine the same surname as that of Joseph Brotherton, Radical M.P. for Salford, himself a former "factory boy." For the first time in this literature, a female becomes the repository of the social conscience, not a male as in *The System* or *The Rioters*. Moers' belief that *Michael Armstrong* is "a crude but occasionally effective transposition of the *Oliver Twist* formula to the industrial setting" is unjust (35). Trollope repudiates the female role expectation established even by benevolent male authority figures like Bell.

At the conclusion of the novel, Mary Brotherton adopts a female apprentice, Fanny Fletcher, and Michael's brother Edward. All four go to live in Germany, an instance not of working-class but of middle-class emigration. For Mary "circumstances . . . had rendered her own country less dear to her than it is to most others" (386). Fanny and Michael are reunited after he escapes from Sharpton's mill, works as a shepherd, and attends the Yorkshire meeting for the Ten Hours Bill on Easter Monday, 24 April 1832. Symbolically indicating the interdependence of the social classes, Mary Brotherton marries Edward Armstrong, a man of working-class origin, finding no man of her own class satisfactory, an unusual example of male hypergamy. This device of interclass marriage will be important to later social fiction. In Mary, Trollope shows a woman unwilling to conform to predetermined standards of behavior. Her name *Brotherton* is ironic, as it is now a woman who can be brother.

Peter Gaskell's study indicates that child laborers, even if not apprentices, suffered severely in the thirties. As Sadler's *Report* illustrates, the Acts of 1802 and 1819 were ineffectual. Trollope had the advantage of knowing that the Act of 1833 was full of difficulties for enforcement. The book sold well for this reason. Neff calls Trollope's story "unreliable" (44), but the use of sources, from Blincoe's *Memoir,* Sadler, the Parliamentary papers of 1816, and her own excursion constitutes an earnest probing of conditions. While the *Athenaeum* correctly criticizes Trollope's *a priori* assumption that mill owners are crude barbarians (588), there is much of value in the novel. With its emphasis on documentation, its new role for women, and the new authority it gives to the female social novelist, Trollope's campaign for government intervention (contrary to the beliefs of Harriet Martineau) advances the female social novel to a different plane by its care for sources and its involvement of a middle-class woman in working-class affairs. Like *Helen Fleetwood, Michael Armstrong* is a novel of the late thirties: "Evils which had once seemed to be part of the unalterable structure of the world, the inescapable fate of man, now appeared to be removeable and therefore intolerable" (Burn 64). For this reason the language and characterization of *Michael Armstrong,* excessive from a later perspective, are appropriate to Trollope's own time.

Like Frances Trollope, Charlotte Elizabeth Tonna was influenced by the Sadler Committee when she supported the Ten Hours Movement in *Helen Fleetwood,* serialized in Tonna's *The Christian Lady's Magazine* from September 1839 to March 1841. Tonna marks a change in political literature, "the shift in standpoint of the novelists from the 'philosophical' to the 'social/evangelical' and even practical political" (Kettle 173). Although advocating the same cause as Trollope, and equally a proponent of government intervention, Tonna is also a critic of intervention, finding it inadequate to deal with existing conditions. Between *Combination* in 1832 and the beginning of *Helen Fleetwood* in 1839, Tonna had done considerable writing about industry. In 1837 she initiated a series in *The Christian Lady's Magazine* on St. Giles, which continued until 1838. She also in 1838 wrote a series of essays on the factory system. When *Helen Fleetwood* concluded in March 1841, she published several more criticisms of the system in 1842.

In the introduction to the first issue of *The Christian Lady's Magazine* in January 1834, Tonna stated her purpose: "Is then our little periodical to be numbered among works exclusively theological? We mean not so: we have sketched a wider range for our kind contributors to occupy. . . . Against love-tales we enter our solemn protest: the youthful mind needs no incitement to lead it into that perilous tract—doubly perilous to those for whom we principally expect to write. . . . It is our ambition, not merely to supply our friends with a periodical that may amuse them for a fleeting hour, but to furnish their shelves with an occasional volume of useful reference on topics of permanent importance" (1:4–6). In the second issue Tonna published an essay, "Politics," a conversation between an uncle and his niece.

The immediate occasion of the essay was probably the publication of the minutes presented before the Sadler Committee, the *Report from the Select Committee on the Bill to Regulate the Labour of Children in Mills and Factories* of August 1832. Tonna calls Sadler "a humane M.P." (1:155). The uncle criticizes the final bill passed, which did not include a ten hours provision for those under eighteen, as had originally been proposed: "This was considered unreasonable by the majority, and the indulgence is restricted to those who are under thirteen. Thus, however weak, delicate, or backward in growth a girl may be, no sooner is her thirteenth year completed, than she is liable to be fixed at her destructive employment, for sixteen or eighteen hours out of every twenty-four" (1:155). Topics like ventilation, work hours, powers of overseers, and fencing of machinery are discussed. Two practices of this 1834 essay characterize Tonna's approach: the inclusion of documentation and the exhortation to the female audience to become reformist. The uncle quotes from newspapers actual cases of child abuse and of death by machinery.

Tonna asks her reader to become involved in legislative reform: "Female influence is very powerful; it was exerted with persevering energy, and most happy effect, throughout the thirty years' struggle on behalf of oppressed negroes. The work to which you are now called, is comparatively easy: the scenes described are within a short journey of any person who desires to investigate the matter. . . . The sources of information are so numerous, so near at hand, that it is enough to point it out to our readers;—interest when awakened will lead to inquiry; and, under the divine blessing, we shall see it followed by results that will bring health and comfort to thousands, who now pine under the wasting domination of sin and suffering" (1:159–60). Tonna emphasizes the fact that women must inform themselves about factory conditions by traveling or reading and then influence their male associates for legislative change. She supplies them with material for "inquiry" before Carlyle's *Chartism.* In December 1835 she published an essay concerning "Remuneration for Needle-work," asking her readers to pay a just return for millinery since "there is something . . . in the very occupation — so quiet, so harmless, so domestic, so exclusively *womanish* — it seems to have a peculiar interest to a woman's feeling" (4:536). In July 1838, she published "English Slavery," which picks up the ideas of Oastler's letter to the Leeds *Mercury:* "About *three thousand* petitions, bearing above a *million* of signatures, have been offered to parliament in behalf of the negro apprentices. And yet we have in our own land a system of far more fearful character. . . . We allude to the myriads of little English victims who are now suffering the horrors of a lingering, torturing death, in . . . our cotton-mills and factories" (10:47). From Tonna's perspective, *Michael Armstrong* would be relevant in the years of its appearance. To reinforce her contentions, she cites authorities like Fielden in his *The Curse of the Factory System.* In 1836 she quotes letters from Hannah More to reinforce her objectives, recognizing an affiliation with her predecessor in the social novel.

Between the initial installment of *Michael Armstrong* and the initial installment of *Helen Fleetwood,* the Chartist petition had been rejected in July by a vote of 235 to 46. In an important footnote to the first installment of *Helen Fleetwood,* Tonna noted: "Some of our readers may be ready to imagine, when they discover the nature and drift of this story, that the idea has been borrowed from some of the works on the same subject which are now being extensively advertised. The writer, therefore, wishes to say in explanation, that she has never seen a single page of any of those works, and that the plan of the present narrative was fixed upon before either of them were so much as announced. Although subsequently laid aside, from illness and other obstacles, all that is here printed, and several chapters more, were written upwards of eight or nine months since" (12:193). One of the works referred to is probably *Michael Armstrong.* Unlike Frances Trollope, Tonna selects a female protagonist.

In December 1839, Tonna informed her readers that *Helen Fleetwood* was not a fiction: "Let no one suppose we are going to write fiction, or to conjure up phantoms of a heated imagination, to aid the cause which we avowedly embrace. Names may be altered, characters may be grouped, with some latitude of license; but not an incident shall be coined to serve the purpose, however good, so far as relates to the main subject — that is, to the factories of this, our free and happy England. Vivid indeed, and fertile in devices must the fancy be that could invent a horror beyond the bare, every-day reality of the thing! Nay, we will set forth nothing but what has been stated on oath, corroborated on oath, and on oath confirmed beyond the possibility of an evasive question. Neither will we lift the veil that piety and modesty would draw over the hidden atrocities of this diabolical child-market. Blasphemy and indecency may, they do abound, turning every mill into a pandemonium; but it is not needful to sully our pages with either" (519). Tonna later inquires: "Does slavery, such as our law repudiates, and to which the very act of inhaling British air is supposed to be fatal, dwell and reign over thousands in our most public, most populous cities? This question must be answered by an appeal to facts: and should the charge that so it is be substantiated by the evidence adduced, the next inquiry is, Shall this state of things be allowed to continue?" (545).

Tonna's anger and contempt are if anything more exacerbated than Trollope's. Because she has selected a contemporaneous period for her narrative, rather than distancing it to the 1820s as Trollope had done, Tonna can naturally include the futility not only of the 1809 and 1819 laws but also of Althorp's Factory Act of 1833. The 1802 Health and Morals of Apprentices Act had signaled the beginning of awareness by government of factory conditions. It concerned not only factors of production but also questions of health relative to factory workers. No apprentice was supposed to work more than twelve hours per day and there was to be no night work. Legislation involved housing as well. This "early example of State intervention in private enterprise" did not arouse controversy since its provisions were so narrow (Thomas 11). The 1819 Act for Regulation of Cotton Mills and Factories did arouse controversy. Lord Stanley during the debate contended that the "Bill was an interference with free labour" (23). The Act did establish "the fundamental principle of State interference with free labour, as the laissez-faire school realized only too well" (26). The Act "broke down the barriers. The State had intervened between employer and employed" (27). However, it dealt with "free" children, not pauper apprentices. Reiterating Brown on the 1802 Act, Tonna realized that the 1819 Act was, as the Hammonds later contended, a "dead letter" (148). The Amendment of 1820 did not alter this circumstance. Tonna quotes a Manchester observer about this act in *The*

Wrongs of Woman in 1844: "The velocity of the machinery has been increased fourfold since 1819, and the child who had then to walk eight miles a day has now to travel thirty-two!" (471).

John Fielden in *The Curse of the Factory System* recorded the "greater attention and activity required by the greatly-increased speed which is given to the machinery" (32). By 1825 only two convictions for violation of the 1819 Act had been undertaken. In *Helen Fleetwood,* when Mrs. Green applies to the manufacturer Mr. M for work, Tonna alludes to the 1833 Act, which provided that none under nine could be employed in mills and factories (524). Tonna states about the acts that in looking for work there were two classes of persons with whom to deal, "those who knew little or nothing of the legalized regulations, and those who were well disposed to evade them" (523). She sees, as had Frances Trollope and John Brown, the inadequacy of the 1802 and 1819 provisions, but in *Helen Fleetwood* she is also critical of the 1833 Act. The reform-minded Hudson suggests that Blue Books have helped: "The facts are brought before Parliament, by having witnesses up to be examined on oath before the committee; these reports, as they are called, are printed, and sold too" (611). He praises Lord Ashley's assistance in reforms. To reinforce the contemporaneity of her book, Tonna quotes Leonard Horner's testimony of 11 March 1840. The surname of her titular character is identical to that of Hesketh Fleetwood, a Member from Preston who tried to improve the conditions of handloom weavers. Tonna also derived the name from Fleetwood, a working class resort, a practice that may have induced Dickens to do the same with Blackpool in *Hard Times.*

Tonna's strength as a writer, as Kovacevic notes, is that she was "the only novelist to describe actual conditions in the factories of the time, more especially the miseries of the child and female operatives" ("Bluebook" 157). She includes in her novel actual definitions and depictions of activities like piecing and scavenging, emphasizing disease-causing hazards like cotton fluff in the lungs or the use of opiates among the working class. Frequently she compares the sufferings of the workers to white slavery. The deluded widow Green thinks: "It is not possible that in this English town there should be some thousands of slaves — white slaves — free-born slaves — and my own children among them" (561–62). When Tonna presents the reader with a tour of the factories, the operative is called "a human piece of mechanism" (616). The narrator thinks that to a person from the country the factory looks like the torments of Sisyphus. Children are still regarded, despite the Act of 1833, "as bare matter of merchandize between two parties" (619). Tonna introduces her middle-class female readership to new conditions by this tour and by detailing the nature of the occupations signified by new terms like "scavenger" or "piecer." This description of processes marked several contemporary studies of the system, like Andrew Ure's *The Philosophy of Manufactures* (1835). Ure describes the relationship between a slubber and his "piecener," admitting that the children are "subject to the caprice of individual operatives" (180).

Helen Fleetwood concerns a single family, the Greens, headed by the grandmother and consisting of her grandchildren, Richard, Mary, James, and Willy, and the orphan Helen Fleetwood, adopted by Mrs. Green. The family is dispossessed after a lease on their farm is not renewed by the new landlord. Deluded by recruiters from the cities (already censured in "English Slavery"), the Greens migrate to Manchester, where Mrs. Green's daughter Sally Wright lives with her four children, Sarah, John, Phoebe, and Charles. William Dodd in *The Factory System Illustrated* (1842) confirmed Tonna's point about the practice of luring agricultural families to the industrial centers, citing the prevalence of the practice during 1835 and 1836, when "vast numbers . . . were induced to migrate from the Agricultural to the Manufacturing counties" (245). The actual distress of the Green family is provoked by unfeeling Poor Law administrators. In the second chapter these men meet "to administer the funds of the parish, whose representatives we are; and our object must be, to secure the greatest possible saving in all branches of our expenditure" (508). With the exception of the clergyman Barlow, the remainder of these men were "sacrificing on the shrine of supposed public duty, not only all the finer feelings of humanity, all the brotherly observances that man owes to man, but also the obedience due from every professing follower of Christ" (509). The factory agents work in collusion with the Poor Law board to entice the dispossessed off the parish rolls: "The poor-law and factory system had merely played into each other's hands" (568). Eventually, Mrs. Green manages to place Helen at the works of the callous Mr. Z. Because she is religious, she is attacked by the juvenile workers and harassed by adults, an example, noted by Gaskell in 1833, of "the facilities for lascivious indulgence afforded [overlookers] by the number of females brought under their immediate control" (58). Tonna does not use this material melodramatically, however. She describes the factory as a "scene of trial," allegorizing it as a Christian's testing ground (551).

Tonna's critique is emphasized through her character Tom South, a discontented father who has already lost several children to the factory system. Through him Tonna locates her arguments in a working-class consciousness, unlike the device of using the middle-class Mary Brotherton in *Michael Armstrong*. South's name is an implicit criticism of the industrial north, as is the pastoral name Green. South finds the education mandated by the factory acts mere verbiage: "What school? This act mocks us with an order that every child should go to school twelve hours in the week, and have a ticket for it; but when it comes to pass, how do they manage?" (530). While the poor had great hopes that inspection might lead to improvements, he observes that one inspector must deal with six counties: "The number of mills that he has to superintend is about eighteen hundred. Now there are little more than three hundred days to a year . . . the inspector's district lies spread over many hundred miles of country; the mills are greatly scattered" (565). South is the spokesman for Tonna's criticism of the legislative process: "Yes, but the laws don't make themselves, you know; and we send up members to Parliament on purpose to make good laws for us, or to alter what are bad. . . . There never was a body of men brought together that thought so little of their pledges, or cared so little for the poor, or trifled so with the liberties that they had always in their mouths, as this reformed House of Commons" (597). Tonna's ire was to make *Helen Fleetwood* "more influential in its day than Mrs. Gaskell's *Mary Barton*" (V. Colby 175).

Tonna contrasts the factory system with the tradition of the squirearchy when she recounts a harvest home in the country, where the grandson Richard Green remains: "The owner of the field was the principal landed proprietor in this place; and the spot was chosen among many, just because it had, from time immemorial, been the scene of the annual celebration. . . . The 'Squire was pleased with the diligence with which they had availed themselves of the favourable season; the men were gratified by his praises. . . . Each, both old and young, enjoyed that peculiar feeling, the value of which the poor are seldom aware until they experience its absence, 'My employer knows me; I am not in his sight a mere piece of machinery, regarded only while it works in his service. There's a tie between us that he, though a rich man, would not disown'" (578). Lamenting the passing of this association, Tonna notes the emergence of two nations, anticipating Disraeli's *Sybil*: "An unnatural state of things, wholly foreign to the old English character, is transforming 'a bold peasantry, their country's pride,' into a degraded, discontented, restless, reckless, turbulent mob. Two classes, hitherto bound together by mutual interest and mutual respect, are daily becoming more opposed the one to the other" (627). Tonna fears that the neglect by government "will yet recoil . . . in some terrible outbreak, aided by those who are made desperate by oppression," which she later identifies as likely to be inspired by either socialism or Chartism: "The Beast of Socialism fails not indeed to stalk over our fields. . . . There the Chartist is taught secretly to whet his pike" (610, 630). The language is Carlylean.

At the conclusion of *Helen Fleetwood,* most of the characters become casualties of the system. Helen dies after a seizure at the mill; James Green and Sarah Wright die in religious ecstasy; Mrs. Green goes to the workhouse; Phoebe Wright becomes a prostitute; and Mary Green is apprenticed to a business. Only Richard Green, working in the country, has any decent existence. He has rescued his brother Willy with the aid of Barlow. Tonna does not avoid subjects like Sally Wright's loss of religion or Phoebe's prostitution. Unlike Trollope in *Michael Armstrong,* Tonna can depict no amorous life for her operatives. She creates characters like Tom South, who in his skepticism anticipates the workmen of *Yeast* and *Alton Locke.* Neff observes that "Mrs. Tonna, by giving the Government investigations a fictional framework, brought to the lay reader a rudimentary knowledge of the factory. *Helen Fleetwood* is the most effective single literary agency in getting technical information before the general public. Only a writer who had a greater regard for truth than for art, who sacrificed the interest of her tale for what it taught, could be so wilfully dull and, at the same time, so important" (87). Tillotson does not find *Helen Fleetwood* dull; it is rather a "vivid and authentic tale of factory life" (127). The thirties show the development of both a "working-class consciousness which had been forming since the 1790s . . . and . . . a developing middle class consciousness" (Finlayson 97). Both *Michael Armstrong* and *Helen Fleetwood* testify to that development. Each marks a change from "the post-war crudities of the 'twenties [to] the passionate but less selfish hopes of the 'thirties" (Burn 73). In this respect *Michael Armstrong* and *Helen Fleetwood* are strong protests of their decade at conditions that the next period would strive to improve. Narratives of the 1830s, such as *Combination, A Man-*

chester Strike, Michael Armstrong, and *Helen Fleetwood,* indicate that prose fiction during this decade, usually bypassed in appraisals of nineteenth-century fiction, must be reintegrated into the canon of literary history. This is so because such narratives elucidate Carlyle's premise in *Characteristics* in 1832: "To understand man . . . we must look beyond the individual man and his actions or interests, and view him in combination with his fellows. It is in Society that man first feels what he is" (10). The nature of this new "Society" is distinguished by one quality: "Change, or the inevitable approach of Change, is manifest everywhere" (21). These narratives of the thirties confronted the transformation made inevitable by the industrialization of Britain.

3   The Eighteen Forties

The transition from the thirties to the early forties is marked by changes in the social literature by women made to confront the conditions revealed by Parliamentary committees during the early part of the decade. One in eleven of the population was a pauper in 1842. Even authors who wrote without documents knew from newspaper accounts something of the issues concerning the economy and the condition of workers. The decade is important for purposes of this study because it exhibits a new interest in the condition of women and particularly in the nature and consequences of their employment. In 1841, forty percent of women were unmarried, with many compelled to seek a livelihood (J. Harrison 26). The economic depression that had begun in 1837 continued into the period, until at least 1842, as did the bad harvests and the smallpox epidemic which had originated in the later years of the thirties. The appearance of Carlyle's *Past and Present* in 1843 renewed in polemical language the awareness of the discrepancy between the professed and the actual situation of Britain. Labor actions were frequent during the decade. The second Chartist petition was defeated in 1842, weakening the movement, but events like the Miners' Strike in 1844 in Northumberland, which lasted five months, proved working class dissatisfaction. Agricultural distress, which was to be recorded by Kingsley in *Yeast,* was apparent from incidents of rick burning during the winter of 1843–1844 and was a subject of some note in Cooke Taylor.

During 1847 and 1848 unemployment in textiles was high, with riots in London, Glasgow, and Liverpool. Sanitary conditions received new attention with Edwin Chadwick's *Report on the Sanitary Condition of the Labouring Population of Great Britain* and with the establishment of Lord Ashley's Mine Commission in the same year. The *First Report of the Children's Employment Commission* of 1842, and the *Second Report* of 1843, were to affect novelists as the period advanced. Brantlinger notes that the forties emphasized exposé rather than the didacticism favored by the thirties (*Spirit* 24), although Trollope and Tonna, important in both decades, had initiated the shift. On the local level efforts for improved sanitation had been a significant movement. For example, Liverpool passed a Sanitary Act in 1846, the same year which saw the exposure of the abusive conditions in Andover Workhouse. By the end of the decade, from 1846 to 1849, Britain experienced another visitation of cholera, coincident with the 1848 Public Health Act which established the Board of Health. Mayhew's articles in the *Morning Chronicle* revealed personal testimonies of hardship when they appeared in 1849. The potato failure in Ireland in 1845 initiated the massive migration to the cities that strained employment and housing conditions in industrial centers. That England experienced a poor harvest the same year only made the distress worse.

Social legislation during the period fought to curb the abuses that the "Hungry Forties" witnessed. The Coal Mines Act of 1842 mandated inspectors and prohibited women or children under ten from working underground, while the Factory Act of 1844 required a maximum working day of six and a half hours for children and twelve for women, the first time that women were included in employment legislation. Sanitation was encouraged locally by such practices as the prohibition of back-to-back housing in Manchester in 1844. The repeal of the Corn Laws in 1846, long advocated by others but staunchly resisted by landed interests, demonstrated the first political alliance between the middle and lower classes as a result of the Reform Act. The most important labor legislation of the period was the passage in 1847 of the Act to Limit the Hours of Labour of Young Persons and Females in Factories, the Ten Hours Bill. The daily hours of work for young people under eighteen and females was restricted to ten hours or fifty-eight hours per week. As Young notes, "In the sixties one social observer laid his finger not on the repeal of the Corn Laws in 1846 but on the Factory Act of 1847, as the turning-point of the age and, with longer perspective, we can hardly doubt that he was right" (*Victorian* 47).

The establishment of the Governess's Benevolent Association in 1843, the appearance of Marian Reid's *A Plea for Women* the same year, and the issuing of the first women's suffrage pamphlet in 1847 revealed new analysis of the status of women. The founding of the Society for Prevention of Cruelty to Children in 1844 was a result of the 1840 law against chimney-sweeping and the revelations of the 1842 and 1843 Parliamentary reports. While the decade saw improvements in many sectors of the society, the work of the social novelists, and particularly of female social novelists, was not finished. By the conclusion of the decade they were monitors of the success of legislation passed during the earlier years of the period. The decade saw the emergence of new social writers such as Elizabeth Stone, Charles Kingsley, and Elizabeth Gaskell, as well as the continuing careers of Tonna, Trollope, and Dickens from the previous decade. The novel in the 1840s "was in process of becoming the dominant form" (Tillotson 13).

In early years of the decade Elizabeth Wheeler Stone (1803–1856?), with her two novels *William Langshawe, the Cotton Lord* (1842) and *The Young Milliner* (1843), represented these vigilant tendencies. Readers familiar with *William Langshawe* believed that *Mary Barton,* published anonymously in 1848, was written by Elizabeth Stone. Elizabeth Gaskell, confusing Stone's married and maiden names, recorded her reactions to this attribution: "Marianne Darbishire told me it was ascertained to be the production of a Mrs Wheeler, a clergyman's wife, who once upon a time was a Miss Stone, and wrote a book called 'The Cotton-Lord'. Marianne gave many proofs which I don't think worth repeating, but I think they were quite convincing." To her publisher Edward Chapman she added: "I find everyone here has most convinving [sic] proofs that the authorship of Mary Barton should be attributed to a Mrs Wheeler, née Miss Stone, and authoress of some book called the 'Cotton Lord'" (Chapple 62–63). Despite some resemblances between *William Langshawe* and *Mary Barton,* it appears Gaskell had not read Stone's novel. In the tradition of industrial fiction, *William Langshawe* and *The Young Milliner* are transitional between the earlier writing of Trollope, Martineau, and Tonna and the later achievements of Gaskell and Kingsley.

Elizabeth Wheeler Stone was fortunate to have several factors favor her development as an industrial writer. Born into a prominent Manchester family in 1803, she was influenced by the journalistic and literary activities of her father and her brothers. Her grandfather Charles Wheeler had founded the *Manchester Chronicle* in 1781 and in 1783 had published a monograph, *A Description of Manchester, by a native of the town.* Wheeler's son John, Elizabeth's father, assumed the management of the *Manchester Chronicle* in 1827 on his father's death. Her brother Charles Henry published in *Blackwood's.* Another brother, James, wrote *Manchester: Its Political, Social and Commercial History* in 1836 and in 1838 edited *Manchester Poetry,* an anthology of poems by, among others, Samuel Bamford, Harrison Ainsworth, and the Reverend William Gaskell, husband of Elizabeth Gaskell. In his *History* Wheeler declares: "The Author . . . is content that in his statistical details he has opened valuable productive mines hitherto unexplored" (vi). In the introductory essay to *Manchester Poetry* in 1838, Wheeler gave his sister a programmatic statement that became important to her as a novelist. He stresses "the peculiar properties which characterize a 'Manchester Man'" and the process of assimilation by which "the learned professions are crowded with the aspiring scions of commerce" (ix, vii). (The volume included poems by a Mrs. Fletcher, née Jewsbury, probably a relative of the Geraldine Jewsbury who was to write of Manchester in *Marian Withers,* 1851.) In *William Langshawe* Stone adopts the tone of her brother's introductory essay in *Manchester Poetry.* They are both presenting Mancunian ways to a curious but skeptical audience of English men and women to whom Manchester is a foreign country. Stone elects to discuss the effect of industrialism on the managerial classes in *William Langshawe* and on the working classes in *The Young Milliner.*

As Monica Fryckstedt observes, *William Langshawe* is important because its author "was the first Manchester resident to write a novel about the manufacturing districts" ("Early" 17). Published in two volumes, as *Mary Barton* was to be later, *William Langshawe* exhibits several distinct qualities. One of these is the difficulty of distinguishing its author from its narrator. With footnotes appended as authentications and with its chapters editorializing about Mancunian habits, *William Langshawe* virtually ignores such separation. As the daughter of a middle-class family, but one not involved in manufacturing, Elizabeth Stone is both observer and commentator in her narrative, emphatic for example about women's education and the lack of domestic training among female operatives. She is a careful observer of social change in *William Langshawe,* including details about the transitional status of handloom weavers, the divergent characters of sons of industrialists, union agitation, trade depression, factory conditions, and assimilation. While a reviewer in the *Athenaeum* criticized *William Langshawe* as "an attack on the social circles of Manchester" (846), this represents a misreading of Stone's intentions. She clarifies her objectives in her introduction to the novel.

Stone appears as both guide and provider of documentation in the introduction to *William Langshawe*. The introduction merits attention since she is aware that she is an innovator in her fictional account. In its opening paragraphs she establishes a scene deliberately conforming to the reader's expectations: "The scene of our tale lies in the manufacturing districts. . . . Cotton bags, cotton mills, spinning-jennies, power-looms, and steam-engines; smoking chimneys, odious factories, vulgar proprietors, and their still more vulgar wives, and their superlatively-vulgar pretensions; dense population, filthy streets, drunken men, reckless women, immoral girls, and squalid children; dirt, filth, misery, and crime; — such are the interesting images which rise . . . at the bare mention of the 'manufacturing districts:' vulgarity and vice walking side by side; ostentatious extravagance on the one hand, battening on the miseries of degraded and suffering humanity on the other; and this almost without redeeming circumstances — we are told. Is it so?" (1:1–2).

Her final query is a key to her intention in *William Langshawe*. Stone presents the "familiar" image of Manchester in order to estrange it. The purpose of the social novelist as Stone conceives it is not to supply the familiarity which breeds contempt but the unfamiliarity which arouses concern. This purpose is evident as the introduction continues, for she devotes much space to the "North/South" opposition, noting: "In many of the southern counties, peculiar costumes and antiquated customs present themselves on every hand, and would give the idea of habits transmitted through many generations, even if tradition and history did not attest the fact. In Lancashire this is not the case" (1:2–3). While she can acknowledge that mercantilism brings "in many instances, a degraded population," she attacks the charge of Northern immorality: "The 'hot-beds of vice,' the manufactories, are, perhaps, not more redolent of crime — in proportion to the numbers congregated — than are the potato-tracts and harvest-fields in those counties where a great proportion of out-door work is still done by females . . . With regard to the simple question of the morality of the manufacturing districts as compared with the agricultural, there is perhaps less difference than is generally imagined" (1:8–10). In a characteristic manner Stone supplies this footnote: "Some experience, both in a manufacturing town and a secluded agricultural county, has led us to form this opinion . . . but . . . as we believe, the statistical records bear us out" (1:10). One of her sources for this information could be Cooke Taylor's *Tour in the Manufacturing Districts,* which condemns "the idle tales respecting the deplorable morality and mortality of the factory operatives" compared to agricultural sections (269). This emphasis on statistics, shared with her brother James Wheeler, reflects her Mancunian disposition.

Having dealt with a preconception of Manchester in the introduction, Stone explores the idea of industry as a subject for fiction in her first chapter:

> Mr. and Mrs. Langshawe lived in the manufacturing districts. He was a cotton-man, and—
>
> "A cotton-man! the manufacturing districts!"—what a host of unpoetical, unromantic associations does the very term excite in the mind, vapoury and wearisome as was the lengthened and unwelcome vision of Banquo's descendants to the aching eye of Macbeth!
>
> "The manufacturing districts!"—"A cotton-man!" exclaims some *parvenue,* when she opens her monthly importation of novels, and glances over the first page of each—"What can Hookham have been thinking of to send this? it must go back immediately."
>
> "But," remarks a companion, "you desire him to send everything that comes out."
>
> "Certainly, everything *readable,* but who can read this?" (1: 12–13)

This passage echoes the introductory essay of James Wheeler for *Manchester Poetry.* As her brother intended to reveal a different facet of the city, so Elizabeth Stone intends to defamiliarize Manchester. Stone's practice is thus different from that of the thirties' novelists. Her aim is not familiarity but its opposite: to force the reader to recognize his easy acceptance of unjustified stereotypes.

Stone's belief that industrial fiction demands observation and factuality corresponds to the Manchester Statistical Society and its influence on Wheeler's *History.* Aware of readers' skepticism, she appeals to authentication. Whether dealing with labor issues, the nature of the town, or Mancunian social customs, this evidence is forthcoming. When she describes the hovels of the poor, she immediately dissociates them from the slums of London: "Nowhere do extremes meet more glaringly than in London, where houses that might almost vie with Alladin's palace in splendour, do absolutely touch upon dens of the utterest filth, misery, wretchedness and crime. But these are peculiarities, and are marked as such, when known; in Lancashire this contrast is so evident a consequence of 'the system' and is of such universal occurrence that it is hardly remarked" (1:156–57). No cabin in Lancashire is without its fire, unlike the similar dwellings of "the wretched Londoner." When discussing strikes, she notes: "Readers who have not happened to reside in the 'Manufacturing Districts' may be surprised to learn that, on an intimation from the leaders of the 'Spinners' Union,' who may have some cause, real or imaginary, of dissatisfaction with some of the masters, 'all hands' will strike" (2: 160). To corroborate her portrait of unions she refers the reader to E. C. Tufnell's monograph *Character, Object, and Effects of Trades' Unions* (1834), later used by Disraeli for *Sybil* in 1845. Her concern for testimony appears with the climactic murder of Henry Wolstenholme by strikers at the novel's conclusion. She states that the incident is factual. She alludes to the murder of Thomas Ashton in 1831, recorded in her brother's *History* and later used by Gaskell for the murder of young Carson in *Mary Barton*. She frequently declares, "At all events we describe what we have seen" or "This improbable-looking incident is fact" (1:56, 121). She even transcribes a letter from Samuel Bamford.

Because her brother's *History* terminates in the mid-thirties, Stone sets her novel in the period 1828–1831 rather than later in the decade or in the early forties. The accuracy of her portrait of Manchester during this time is demonstrated by comparison of her study with Kay's monograph of 1832. His emphasis corresponds to Stone's: "We have avoided alluding to evidence which is founded on general opinion, or depends merely on matters of perception; and have chiefly availed ourselves of such as admitted of a statistical classification" (72). Aspects of life at this time Stone may have drawn from Kay's report. The lack of domestic science among female operatives (1:197) is mentioned several times by Kay: "Domestic economy is neglected, domestic comforts are too frequently, unknown"; "The early age at which girls are admitted into the factories, prevents their acquiring much knowledge of domestic economy" (25, 69). Stone's observation about hand-loom weavers (2:263) parallels Kay's statements and the view of the *Report* from the Select Committee on Hand-loom Weaver's Petitions of 1835. It is likely that Stone and her brother were familiar with Kay's monograph and possibly Fielden's *The Curse of the Factory System*.

William Langshawe was conceived over several years. Describing a conversation, Stone appends this footnote: "This sketch was written some three years ago, when a periodical work was in circulation which defeated its own benevolent and honourable ends by the exaggerations of its statements. These exaggerated horrors were drawn, it is said, from a very scarce pamphlet. . . . Into the mouth of my cotton-merchant in the text I have put statements and opinions, not such as might appertain to the hero of a novel, but such as I believe a great portion of his class to possess" (1:188). The pamphlet is the *Memoir of Robert Blincoe*. Stone may be refuting Trollope's attitude to industrialists in *Michael Armstrong*. When Stone defends the employers in her novels, she mentions that the passage was written before the *First Report* of the Children's Employment Commission on coal mines. Stone's concentration on 1828–31 in *William Landshawe* reveals that for her, as it was to be for George Eliot in *Middlemarch,* the pre-Reform years were decisive in England's cultural and economic development.

Behind Elizabeth Stone's analysis of the industrial magnate in *William Langshawe* is Carlyle's mythologizing of Richard Arkwright in *Chartism.* Carlyle describes Arkwright as the man "that had to give England the power of cotton," a person who will become "mythic like Arachne" (183–84). Stone, however, is not concerned with Cotton Lords as mythological figures. She intends to explain the nature of a group, since "the industrial magnates dominated the regional scene" (J. Harrison 128). In her complete title she emphasizes both the individual character and his type, "the Cotton Lord." She may be noting Cobbett's mockery of the term in *Rural Rides.* Cooke Taylor had called the Exchange "the parliament of the lords of cotton" (10). Melada observes that the period 1830–1850 was characterized as a second stage in the depiction of the magnate, considering him as "benefactor," "enemy of the people," or symbol (49). In presenting the Cotton Lord to her readers, Stone depicts three industrialists, William Langshawe, his contemporary John Balshawe, Sr., and Ainsley. Peter Gaskell noted similar classifications of manufacturers, including "the sprinkling of men of more refined habits" among the early manufacturers, while the master cotton-spinners were predominantly "uneducated — of coarse habits" (54–55).

The type to be studied in *William Langshawe* is distinctly marked: "The magnificence of the cotton lords has become a theme for general satire, and deservedly so; still it is admitted on all hands that their magnificence, however ostentatious, is *real. . . .* The rising generation, educated in a better style and habituated from childhood to more civilized usages, may redeem this flaw in the character of the race, if, indeed—and this is the opinion of many well qualified to judge— if, indeed, gentlemanly habits, delicate feelings, and cultivated minds, are not inconsistent with success in Manchester trade. . . . And so long as the cotton trade exists, it is very possible that the gentleman will be surpassed in the race by the low-born mechanic, whose powers of calculation are not checked" (1:137–38). However, she advises, there are subdivisions of Cotton Lords: "While a great and characteristic resemblance may be traced through the whole, there are yet such varying circumstances appertaining to it as almost to divide it into distinct and separate classes. Though by the self-same steps, and in the same—to speak technically—'line of business,' all have risen from a low rank in life to one of wealth and power, and influence; yet light and darkness are scarcely more dissimilar than is the low-lived and ignorant, though shrewd, mill-owner of some outlying district, from the cultivated denizen of the town. . . . Between these extremes there is a third class, a connecting medium, partaking in some degree both of the vices of the one and the refinements of the other" (1:182–83). This interest in classification is shown in Stone's chapter titles, "Two Cotton-men," "The Hero and a Cotton-man," or "The Rise of the Cottonocracy." Stone links her three Cotton Lords, since Balshawe is an old associate of Langshawe's, and Ainsley is the uncle of Edith Langshawe's suitor Frank Walmsley.

To understand Stone's interest in the Captain of Industry and his assimilation, it is instructive to study her short tale "The Widow's Son" of 1844. In following the career of Tom Multon, albeit not in an industrial situation, she presents the course of assimilation treated extensively in *William Langshawe:* work, gradual success, final respectability. The schoolmaster Mr. Fenton expresses the credo of the upwardly mobile: "The habit, the very early habit of industry and usefulness, is what you must try to give your child; and that habit alone is the best fortune he can have." Multon eventually becomes a clergyman, even marrying Fenton's niece Rose (11). The career of William Langshawe, involving work, success, setback, renewed success, gradual assimilation, and respectability, is summarized in the few pages of this short work. In *William Langshawe* Stone's achievement is the precision with which she depicts the assimilation of her three industrialists.

The title character is a synthesis of the other two industrialists:

he has shed some of the crudity of Balshawe Senior and has acquired some taste in the manner of Ainsley. Langshawe advises his daughter not to marry a gentleman: "I've earned all my money by the sweat of my brow; I don't care who knows it; I began the world an errand boy, and not a shilling of what I've so hardly gained shall go to pamper any idle gentleman or fashionable spendthrift: so mind what you're about" (1:18). On the other hand Balshawe Senior is described as "proprietor of one of the largest mills in the country . . . a tyrant to his wife, a despot over his workpeople, and a person of no slight influence around" (1:131). Stone stresses the two men's dissimilarities so the reader avoids a simplistic association of the two: "He and Mr. Balshawe had begun life together, and he knew well that such in acquirement, in style, and in manner, as Mr. Balshawe was now, had *nearly* all the peers of the Cottonocracy been in youth; though many like himself, from circumstances of much travelling . . . and from perpetual intercourse with the intelligent inhabitants of the principal manufacturing towns, had become civilized in manners and usages; while some few had taken flight, and become in fact and in habit gentlemen. . . . Mr. Balshawe . . . oftener enacted the tyrannical despot than the considerate master. . . . Such was Mr. Balshawe, and such Mr. Langshawe knew him to be" (1:123–24).

Stone's third industrialist, Ainsley, differs from both Balshawe and Langshawe, as his differing name indicates. When his nephew Frank Walmsley reveals his attachment to Edith Langshawe, Ainsley criticizes her family: "Far be it from me to depreciate Mrs. Langshawe's actual worth . . . but with all this she is vulgarity personified. . . . Mr. Langshawe is a shrewd and worldly man; his calculating head and his busy fingers have told a golden tale for him; but his heart and soul are wrapt in his counting-house and ledger, and he looks with feeling not very remote from contempt on such a dreaming youngster as yourself" (1:65). Stone seems to be echoing Peter Gaskell's observation about the wives of Captains of Industry: "He is . . . fitted to move reputably in the rank in which his exertions and industry have placed him. Not so his wife—vulgar in speech, or its vulgarity so badly patched up as to render it still more offensive" (60). For Ainsley work and financial success were part of a program of assimilation to respectability: "I have a considerable fortune, acquired, as you know, in the trade of the times; but hand-in-hand with riches have I striven to gain those habitudes, tastes, and acquirements which alone can make riches respectable." He desires Frank to choose another bride from the Cottonocracy: "I do not want you to step out of your sphere, Frank, I merely wish that you should maintain in all respects an elevated position in that sphere" (1:66, 79).

One of the earliest examiners of assimilation, Stone in *William Langshawe* anticipates later studies of this process in novels like *Marian Withers, John Halifax,* and *North and South.* Stone's precision of observation extends to the next generation. Social historians as late as 1868 were remarking facts noted much earlier by Stone in *William Langshawe:* "[For a cotton man] the first step is to send his children away from home to boarding school, nominally to get rid of the dialect, but really to get rid of the cousins, to form genteel connections. . . . They are anxious that their sons should make no acquaintance among their social inferiors" (Aspin 84). Frank Walmsley is college-educated and destined to the bar. John Balshawe, Jr., the seducer of Nancy Halliwell, is "a low-lived libertine, carrying . . . shame and sorrow to the lowly hearths of his father's operatives" (1:124). The seducer was often the "son of a newly-rich commercial family" so that "there is frequently an undercurrent of class antagonism" in the seductions of protest fiction (S. Mitchell, "Lost" 120). *William Langshawe* prefigures a comparable situation in *Mary Barton.*

Elizabeth Stone's precision in depicting industrialists in *William Langshawe* distinguishes her from other Condition-of-England novelists. She would have dissented from the view of factory life given in Trollope's *Michael Armstrong* or Tonna's *Helen Fleetwood.* To Stone, Sir Matthew Dowling and his cruel superintendent Joseph Parsons, the mill owner Elgood Sharpton, or the callous Mr. Z. in Tonna are stereotypical presentations. On the other hand she avoids the canonizing of the mill owner Wallace in Harriet Martineau's *The Turn-out* or the similar treatment of the Cheeryble brothers by Charles Dickens in *Nicholas Nickleby* (modeled on the Grant brothers of Manchester). Since these works could have been known to Stone, *William Langshawe* may be a response to such treatments. In spirit Stone is closest to John Galt's portrait of Mr. Cayenne in *Annals of the Parish* (1821). Stone may have known Galt's novel, since her brother Charles Henry's essay in *Blackwood's* immediately preceded an installment of Galt's *The Steam-Boat* in 1821.

Stone links her study of the assimilation process to the issue of women's position through Langshawe's relationship with his daughter Edith. As Branca notes, for middle-class women during the period "the dominant problem was assimilation to a very new life-style"

(2). When his business suffers reversals, as many did in the difficult times from 1826 to 1830, Langshawe forces Edith into an alliance with Balshawe Junior. Stone heightens the consequences of this young man's seduction of Nancy Halliwell, since she is Edith's second cousin. Peter Gaskell (1833) notes the pernicious example of sexual morality set by overseers in mills and that "it was . . . upon the sons, younger brothers, and immediate male connexions, that the example set by these individuals exerted the most pernicious influence." He condemns the "organised system of immorality which was pursued by these younger men and boys" (62–63). Stone presents the result when working-class girls, believing in the tradition of the rural areas that premarital intercourse would be followed by marriage, as Gaskell records, were deluded in the new urban environments, where the expected marriage would not take place. Nancy Halliwell allows Stone to present an operative and her family. She gives point to this depiction because Halliwell was the surname of radical agitator John Halliwell of Oldham. The fact that Nancy and Edith are related is Stone's indication that assimilation is gradual and does not assure insularity from the lower classes. If, as Neff has observed, "the working woman was not independent of the female leisure class" (188), Stone demonstrates that the opposite is also true when Edith must promise herself to the seducer of her cousin. "Woman's lot is on her, and she will yet be proved by suffering. . . . This is woman's heritage," the author observes (1:21). Edith is more polished than her parents since "the rising generation enjoy advantages to which their parents had no access" (1:23). Though Edith is educated, like George Eliot in *The Mill on the Floss* Stone has little favorable to say of women's education. Ellen Moers is correct in noting that illiteracy is a woman's theme, and Stone comes to this subject very early in the social novel. Edith superintends the factory school.

In *William Langshawe* Stone pioneers the portrayal of mothers and daughters of the managerial class. Mrs. Langshawe's origin is lower than her husband's: "Her manners were *in some degree* polished by society, and by constant intercourse with others; but the calibre of her mind was precisely of its original dimensions" (1:24). This is revealed when Mrs. Langshawe confronts Edith about marrying young Balshawe:

> "Now mother," said she, "tell me what all this means: speak to your child."
> "I have nothing to tell you, love, nothing."

"Why, then, do I see you in this distress, mother?"

"Because your father's distress increases."

"And why conceal that from me? why not speak to your daughter, your own child, of that?" (2:35)

Mrs. Langshawe asks Edith to marry Balshawe "to save us from ruin":

"Mother, is your wealth really dearer to you than your child?"

"Edith!" said Mrs. Langshawe in amazement.

"You were not always rich, and yet I have heard you say you were always happy. You had once but a humble, miserable cottage, and yet I have heard you say that the day was always too short for you. . . . I am young, strong, and healthy, well-educated, not unqualified to earn some addition to our income, if it be requisite. . . . Why cannot we be happy together in a cottage?"

"And have you, Edith, you, my own child, judged of your mother thus? do you, indeed, suppose that my happiness depends on these things: How little do you know me."

Edith looked at her mother with surprise, and with a feeling of respect which she blushed to think she had hardly hitherto accorded to her. (2:37–38)

This is a bitter but sensitive commentary on both the situation of women and the familial discrepancy caused by the assimilative process.

Mrs. Balshawe fares no better with her husband, who verbally abuses her in public. When the two industrialists are conversing, Mrs. Balshawe "continued her attendance without remark, the husband expecting it as a matter of course." When they finish, Balshawe barks, "That'll do . . . Now, make thysel' scarce; go to roost, and, I say, Mag, mind the parlour's ready in good time i' th' mornin'; and stir your chalks, woman" (1:119). Stone reveals her strategy for survival: "Mrs. Balshawe's hospitality during the remainder of the year had a less conspicuous but a more valuable range. Her proud elevation of purse had not in the least affected the natural simplicity of her character; and her former co-mates were always sure of a welcome and a meal at her fireside; and her charity to the poor was, like that of numbers of her class, unwearied and unbounded. Thus she held on *her* way" (1:140). By showing the persecuted Mrs. Balshawe, Stone makes her son's seduction of an operative more plausible, since Balshawe Junior has witnessed his father's abuse of women in his own home. Stone pioneers again, here in showing the extreme difficulty of assimilation, the pressures of business on the domestic environment, and the abuse of middle-class wives, hardly ever noticed. In scenes involving women in the novel, Stone achieves the "extremely clever passages" noted by the reviewer in the *Examiner* (709).

Stone's desire to present life realistically influences the conclusion of her novel. Against the reader's expectations, she denies Edith Langshawe a happy marriage. Frank Walmsley marries Bianca, the daughter of an expatriot manufacturer Luttrell, who lives in Italy. Stone's minute observation is confirmed even in this detail, as Dodd noted that power looms were sent into Italy from England (*Factory* 143). The woman dies of consumption when Frank returns with her to England, but Stone refrains from having Edith marry Frank, although it would be possible. If one considers that Frances Trollope's wealthy heiress Mary Brotherton marries a factory hand she had herself educated and saved in *Michael Armstrong,* it is clear that Stone introduces a new honesty in industrial fiction with *William Langshawe,* which eluded Disraeli in *Sybil* with his marriage of Egremont to Sybil Gerard. She refuses to gratify a reader's "familiar" expectations.

A similar refusal to accommodate the reader is behind the fact that the seducer Balshawe Junior suffers very little. He will assume a seat in "a reformed House of Commons" (2:315). Stone shows that the double standard protects a man's reputation, even if he is in government. Jem Forshawe, the working-class lover of Balshawe's victim, ends as an incurable in a lunatic asylum. Although Stone attributes this to Jem's union initiation, the episode is not ludicrous. Stone undoubtedly used Tufnell's record of the terror of union initiations: "Every accessary device is employed to strike terror into those who go through these inaugural rites, and with such success, that workmen have sometimes been unable to recover their proper senses. . . . A London journeyman . . . was so overcome by the ceremonies he went through on his admission, that he was literally deprived of reason, and died in the agonies of raving madness" (66). Jem Forshawe would not have been so easy a prey to union agitators had not his master's son seduced the woman he loved. James Kay (1832) mentions "mental anxiety" (19) as a significant plight of the operatives, and both Jem Forshawe and Nancy's father Joe Halliwell suffer from her seduction. Stone recognizes the mental as well as physical suffering of her operatives. In this recognition she anticipates the focus on the mental suffering of workers in such later works as *Mary Barton* and *Alton Locke* and the findings of investigators like Cooke Taylor, who cited "depression of mind" (203) frequently when he studied Lancashire during the distresses of 1842, the year of the novel's publication.

On its appearance in 1842, *William Langshawe* received notice in the *Athenaeum* and the *Examiner*. The novel is valuable for its presentation of Mancunian life by a native and for its emphasis on assimilation and on the position of women of the managerial class. Its depiction of middle-class women and of second-generation industrialists is a sober advance over Trollope's *Michael Armstrong*. In differentiating her cotton lords Stone achieves some of her strongest effects, with some credible experiment in dialect. The fact that Stone read the *First Report* after writing *William Langshawe,* while it did not alter her presentation of factory life in the novel, did influence her to study a workwoman in her next narrative. It was to dressmaking that she turned her attention in 1842.

To readers of *William Langshawe* the fact that Elizabeth Stone would undertake a novel about milliners was not surprising. In that novel, when the visitor Frances Halling tours Ainsley's factory, she questions the arduous duties of the operatives. Ainsley replies that while "hands" in factories work difficult hours, other trades are worse: "I need not remind you of the proverbial endurance of the milliners, and straw-bonnet workers; they are usually apprenticed at the very age when, if ever, the youthful female requires relaxation and relief; their hours of work are said to be twelve, but for three parts of their time these young females are kept fourteen, sixteen, seventeen hours closely sewing, and they are not infrequently detained all night. For this spirit-breaking, health-consuming toil, the apprentice receives nothing, literally nothing but on the contrary frequently pays a high premium. But the business is *genteel,* and is therefore preferred to that of a factory operative" (1:193–94). Ainsley's statement comes from Cooke Taylor's *Tour in the Manufacturing Districts:* "Factory labour . . . is less injurious to either than many of the ordinary employments of females—far less so than the trade of the milliner, the embroiderer, and the straw-plaiter" (261). Cruikshank notes that so far as regards child labor "there were other working children worse off—sedentary ones like the little milliners' girls who were at the mercy of individual employers" (48).

In the Introduction to *The Young Milliner* Stone admits that her awareness of this situation is not accidental. She remarks that after the publication of her book *The Art of Needlework* in August 1840, several people noted there was an "omission" in it. While it discussed the craft of sewing, it had not dealt with the plight of the women in the trade. She declares that "The 'opportunity neglected' however, she has endeavoured to redeem in this volume" (iii). This is her avowed purpose in *The Young Milliner:* "It is an attempt to awaken attention to the miseries which a great number of people—and those often of the weakest and most unprotected portion of the community—endure in their exertions to gain their daily bread,—viz., the Milliners' Apprentices, and other Needle-workers, of London, more especially. . . . The Narrative itself is, of course, fictitious; but the circumstances adduced are unexaggerated and strictly true. The Authoress has availed herself of facts which she drew from private authentic sources; but her statements are fully borne out by parliamentary documents which have been published since her story was written" (iii–iv).

Just as she had acknowledged the *First Report* in *William Langshawe,* Stone recognizes the *Second Report* of the Children's Employment Commission, which had appeared on 30 January 1843, with its exposure of dressmakers. In 1842 there were 15,000 dressmakers in London, that number increasing to 20,000 by 1850 (Walkley 18, 14). Walkley corroborates Stone's notice of the distinction between factory and needlework: in the factory the seasonal pressures would be less and the workers would be subject, at least theoretically, to factory legislation. Although Stone wrote *The Young Milliner* without the *Second Report,* the conditions of milliners had received exposure in Chadwick's *Report,* which shows their grim death statistics (176):

Deaths from Disease of Milliners and Dressmakers, in the Metropolitan Unions during the year 1839, as shown by the Mortuary Registers

Age	Number of Deaths	Average Age	Number of Deaths from Consumption	Average Age	Number of Deaths from other Lung Diseases	Average Age
Under 20	6	17	4	18	—	—
20 Under 30	24	24	17	23	1	23
30 Under 40	11	34	6	34	1	33
40 Under 50	2	45	—	—	1	40
50 Under 60	4	54	1	58	2	55
60 Under 70	5	64	—	—	—	—
Total	52	32	28	26	5	41

[Note:] Out of 52 deaths in the year, 41 of the deceased attained an age of 25. The average age of the 33 who died of lung diseases was 28.

The same year saw the publication of William Dodd's *The Factory System Illustrated* and the Truck Report.

To understand the urgency of Stone's novel in 1843, one can contrast it with the treatment of the seamstress a decade earlier in John Galt's (1779–1839) "The Seamstress," from *Stories of the Study* in 1833. Galt's story is written not with any intention of protest or reform but as an illustration of the word "eydency" in Scottish dialect, "descriptive of . . . constancy and patience, in employments of a feminine and sedentary kind. We never say a ditcher or a drudger is eydent; but the spinster at her wheel, or the seamstress at her sewing, are eydent" (21). Miss Peggy Pingle "was a creature ordained for eydency," raised in "pinched gentility" (23). The narrator, a man who knew Miss Pingle when he was a young lawyer's clerk, distinguishes between the wheel and the needle: "We make this important distinction between the wheel and the needle, because, although we have often overheard malcontent murmurings against the former, yet we do not recollect, in any one instance, the latter spoken of either with complaint or disparagement" (23). Galt's tone is one of benevolent irony in dealing with Miss Pingle's fortunes, as she loses her father and then a suitor because she inquired about money. She develops a talent for "pyrology," reading embers for prophetic signs. She "departed this life, as she had lived, in the most methodical and quiet manner" (27). For Galt, writing ten years earlier than Stone, the seamstress is still a figure of interesting local color, not a suffering slave as she is in *The Young Milliner.*

Stone's *The Young Milliner* is distinct from most literature dealing with seamstresses because it did not use the *Second Report.* It is part of a large body of literature and painting that appeared after January 1843. Charlotte Tonna drew on the *Report* and quoted it verbatim in Part I, "Milliners and Dress-makers," of *The Wrongs of Woman* (1843–1844). As Wanda Neff observes, the significance of the *Report* was that "for the first time the non-textiles shared with the textile industries some of the public attention" (88). The challenge to novelists to present such occupations was considerable: "Non-textile workers are even more scantily represented in literature than those in the textile trades. . . . They offered more difficult technical problems to the author, their lives were equally barren of romantic interest, and were more completely hidden from public scrutiny" (114). The *Second Report* contained such quotations as these from Richard Dugard Grainger's Introduction: "No men would sustain the labour which is imposed on these young and delicate women." "No slavery is worse than that of the dress-maker's life in London." "No men work so long. It would be impossible for any animal to work so continuously with so little rest" (*Parliamentary Papers* 14:F30). Such comments led to Thomas Hood's *The Song of the Shirt* in *Punch* 1843, Camilla Toulmin's *The Orphan Milliners* in 1844, Tonna's *The Wrongs of Woman,* and Gaskell's *Ruth* in 1853. In 1844 Richard Redgrave painted *The Sempstress.* Stone could have known that the 1841 Census stated that of 106,801 persons in dressmaking, only 563 were males (Edelstein 186).

In *The Young Milliner* Stone had a specific audience in mind, the middle-class women who patronize dressmakers: "Fashionable ladies, —individually kind and good, and exemplary,—are collectively the cause of infinite misery to the young and unprotected of their own sex. Of the existence even of this misery, they are, it may well be believed, scarcely aware; of its frightful extent, utterly unconscious. . . . Should this Narrative meet their sight, it is hoped that its appeal will not be made in vain" (iv). For understanding Stone's range of characters and her emphasis in *The Young Milliner,* this passage is important. At least half the narrative is devoted not to the situation of its suffering seamstress Ellen Cardan but to its "fashionable" young lady Marian Godfrey. Although the reviewer in the *Athenaeum* (May 1843) is correct in believing that Marian Godfrey is included to interest middle-class readers, she also exists to give them a figure with whom to identify, not always in an appealing way. While good-natured, Marian is oblivious to the suffering of Ellen Cardan. At the conclusion of the novel, when Marian Godfrey discovers that she and Ellen are cousins (a situation paralleling that of Nancy Halliwell and Edith Langshawe in *William Langshawe*) Stone's symbolic linking is evident: consanguinity reflects economics.

The Young Milliner is a complementary text to its predecessor *William Langshawe.* While the latter concerns the managerial class in Manchester, the former involves the shabby "genteel" millinery trade of London. Edith Langshawe is a more admirable and observant fashionable young woman than Marian Godfrey. The misunderstandings of mother and daughter in *William Langshawe* are replaced by a young woman growing up with no mother at all. In *Cassandra* Florence Nightingale was to note that the heroine "has *generally* no family ties (almost *invariably* no mother), or, if she has, these do not interfere with her entire independence" (28). In *The Young Milliner* this condition leads to distress for both Ellen and Marian, but it is a factor in their "independence," as Nightingale shrewdly realized. Whereas Stone criticized women's education in *William Langshawe,* in *The Young Milliner* Ellen Cardan is economically an outcast because she lacks any education. Ellen's friend Bessy Lambert, seduced by Marian's father Frederick Godfrey, becomes a prostitute, unlike Nancy Halliwell, who remains in a caring family. Like Langshawe, Godfrey suffers business losses, but these have both economic and retributive consequences in *The Young Milliner.* Stone sets *The Young Milliner* in the forties, not distancing her narrative as she had in *William Langshawe.* The two novels together represent the beginning and ending of a decade of transition. Stone believes that there has been considerable change but little progress.

The artistry of *The Young Milliner* represents an advance over that of its predecessor. The intrusive narrator/author of *William Langshawe* is virtually eliminated. The only footnote to the text occurs when Stone cites Ellen's work hours: "This circumstance will no doubt appear to many readers a gross exaggeration. I beg merely to refer them to the 'Report and Appendices of the Children's Employment Commission,' lately presented to Parliament, and published since these pages were written" (289). However, it is typical of the narrator of *William Langshawe* that the one note in *The Young Milliner* concerns authenticity. *The Young Milliner* was published in a single volume, which suggests Stone's advance in condensation of narrative. Such rapid composition reveals her intention to protest abuse and to provoke reform. This objective is reflected in her characters' names. *Cardan* suggests the carding of fiber before spinning; *Godfrey* the opium-based drug administered to infants (much condemned in the *Second Report*). The beneficent Thomas Brummage, who aids both Ellen and the Godfrey family, is the half-brother of the girls' mothers. His name, suggesting the slang form of Birmingham, alludes to the upward mobility made possible by industrialism.

Orphaned at the opening of *The Young Milliner,* Ellen Cardan is without skills beyond those of her needle. As Walkley notes, this was the *one* skill possessed by nearly all women (1-2). The landlady Mrs. Baring and the curate Mulgrave discuss possible occupations for her, including that of governess: "Hard work, Mrs. Baring; hard and miserable. A housemaid is happier, more independent, and—better paid. A governess is perpetually exposed to circumstances which are torture to the soul of a high-minded woman; and, moreover, she may toil unremittingly from sixteen to sixty, without having been able to realize a home or a shelter for her last years" (6). Ellen is bereft of "accomplishments": she cannot speak French, make tapestry, or do fancy work. They decide to apprentice Ellen with the milliner Sally Minnow (now "Sarina Mineau"), sister of Mrs. Baring's friend. To Elizabeth Stone the situation of the impoverished woman is a cul-de-sac: if educated, to be a governess; if not, to be an apprentice dressmaker: "So Ellen was sent to London, that great charnel-house of withered hopes, and subdued aspirations, and tamed energies; to London, where of all the busy myriads hurrying to and fro, not one individual should be found to smile on her. . . . There, amid the constant passing of thousands, learn what it is to be lonely" (22). Ellen, because she has some experience, is quickly made an "improver," often the case, as the Parliamentary papers attested, of girls from the country. If she is lucky, her work day is twelve hours.

The seamstress's hours of labor occupy an important place in *The Young Milliner* as they were to do in the *Second Report*. Ellen tells her friends the Lamberts: "Though the season is not at the height, we have sat up three whole nights every week for some weeks past, and worked eighteen or twenty hours the other days; but Madame Mineau is not to blame: she is kind to us — kinder than most are, I believe — as much as she can. But she cannot refuse work; she dare not disoblige her customer." Echoing Stone's Introduction, Ellen declares that the fault rests with "the ladies themselves. You cannot imagine . . . how unreasonable they are; how little thought they have for us" (122). Stone conceals the worst details of the life until later in the novel, when the reader has developed sympathy for Ellen Cardan: "It was very bitter — it was almost unendurable. Sometimes, in the earlier part of the season, she had stood to her sewing throughout the night and had thereby been enabled to repel the advances of sleep more effectually; but this she could no longer do, for her ankles swelled. . . . On Sunday morning, about ten o'clock, she retired to bed, after being (for it had been a dreadfully busy week) at work for upwards of seventy hours consecutively" (288–89). Conditions even worsen: "Sometimes they sat up three nights in a week, sometimes four; sometimes they sat up the whole week, taking it in turns to lie down for two hours out of the twenty-four" (337). Such circumstances account for Dickens' notice in "The Streets — Morning" from *Sketches by Boz* of "the milliners' and staymakers' apprentices . . . poor girls! — the hardest worked, the worst paid, and too often, the worst used class of the community" (51).

Marian Godfrey is callous to her dressmakers, and even Madame Mineau reproves her. To Marian it is "the old tale — that her people are worked to death. Not that she meant me to believe that, or half of it, of course. I dare say the poor wretches have a tire-some life enough, but it is their business you know." Her brother Arthur retorts, "Their business to be worked to death!" (347). When Marian learns of the "extreme toil" and "constant deprivation of rest" that her cousin has endured, "did not every dress which Miss Godfrey, with the usual *insouciance* of spoiled vanity, had ordered to be made in an unreasonably short time — did not every one rise like an accusing spirit before her now awakened eye!" (374). This comment carries Stone's rebuke to her reader in *The Young Milliner.* This passage may have been the inspiration for the well-known *Punch* cartoon of "The Haunted Lady, or 'The Ghost' in the Looking-Glass" of 1863, which shows a lady startled by the spectre of a dead seamstress in her mirror. There is no solace for Ellen: "Her funeral was plain and simple; anything else would have been a mockery of her fate" (387). By giving Ellen a family at the conclusion, Stone rescues her from the sure anonymity of thousands, especially before the publication of the *Second Report.*

Stone does not confine her study of the urban poor to the genteel. Most establishments left their employees to their own devices on Sundays, often with disastrous consequences as the *Second Report* demonstrated. On these days, Ellen visits her friends the Lamberts, which allows Stone to show even worse states of degradation among the "ungenteel" poor. Mrs. Lambert recounts the vicious competition among middlemen (butties) that makes life hell for pieceworkers: "It is not the employers themselves, my dear; it is not the respectable employers themselves. . . . The people whom they employ take a vast deal more than they can do, and give it out to others, such as myself; and as they, of course, make their profit out of the price given to them . . . we who come second or third-hand, are ground down to the earth. . . . It can hardly be called living" (135–36). Stone uses the Lamberts to encapsulate the process of immiseration: "The most wretched of these sewing jobs was undoubtedly that of the slop-worker: the needlewoman working at home" (Basch 124). Engels noted that "the condition of the shirt-makers is worst of all" (238–39), and *Punch* as late as September 1859 noted the horrors of slop-workers' existences.

This poverty eventually drives Bessy Lambert to become the mistress of Frederick Godfrey, Marian's father. In treating this very old subject, Stone's achievement is the presentation of the gradual process of Bessy's yielding: the first notice of Godfrey, the surveillance by his servant, the worsening competition, the near starvation, and the capitulation. By the time Bessy keeps her assignation with Godfrey, Stone's London has become desolate: "No policeman was there, however; they seldom are when they are wanted" (240); "A cab would drive furiously past, and bespatter the well drest pedestrian with mud — London mud" (243–44). Mrs. Lambert keeps a vigil all night for her lost daughter: "And the hours passed — how drearily who shall tell? Morning broke: it was bright day in the open streets, but in this dingy alley the lamp had hardly begun to pale beneath the first beams of light. The inhabitants knew, however, that it was day elsewhere, and they were stirring" (249). Although Brummage rescues Ellen from the millinery trade, it is he, ironically, who calls for policemen to remove the distraught Bessy Lambert from Ellen's graveside. Stone leaves her readers the man of charity and the woman of wretchedness juxtaposed over their common friend's grave. Brummage's charity does not save Ellen and does not extend to her friend, the prostitute Bessy Lambert.

While Stone's presentation of the millinery world in the novel is convincing, her treatment of the upper class is derivative. The *Athenaeum* reviewer in May 1843 thought these scenes were added "to interest boudoir-readers in characters of 'their own class,'" but Stone's intention is to reveal the interaction of the two classes (437). Marian Godfrey, however, does not achieve the individuality of Edith Langshawe. The business reversals which develop Edith's character come too late in *The Young Milliner* to alter Marian's nature. The difficulty is in the narrative placement of these revelations, not their intention. Both she and her brother Arthur escape the consequences of her father's profligacy. In several instances, Stone seems to draw on Jane Austen. Lord Henry Woolford aids Marian's cousin (and lover) Charles Seymour to obtain a naval commission in a manner similar to the assistance given by Henry Crawford to Fanny Price's brother in *Mansfield Park*. When Marian rejects Lord Henry she does so in accents that recall Elizabeth Bennet of *Pride and Prejudice:* "I knew not myself, until yesterday, that I had no heart to give you" (219). Charles Seymour imitates Frederick Wentworth's hastily writing in a crowded room to Anne Elliot, while Marian's attending a concert with Lord Henry parallels the similar episode in *Persuasion* involving Anne Elliot and her cousin. While Elizabeth Stone's balancing of the classes is necessary for *The Young Milliner*, her artistry is strongest when depicting urban suffering.

The reviewer in the *Athenaeum* believed Stone wrote *The Young Milliner* "following the lead of the Children's Employment Commission" (437), although Stone had stated this was not so. The reviewer does place *The Young Milliner* with Trollope's *Michael Armstrong* and Dickens' *Oliver Twist*, acknowledging but not admiring the use of fiction for protest purposes. The writer compares Stone's novel to a story, *A London Dressmaker's Diary*, which had appeared in November 1842 in *Tait's Edinburgh Magazine*, preferring this anonymous tale to Stone's novel because it presents "the mind of the victim." The reviewer recognizes only this story as a predecessor of *The Young Milliner*. *A London Dressmaker's Diary* concerns the eldest daughter of a country family, identified only as Miss Wells, who records her thoughts during a seven-week period in the autumn of 1841. She works at the establishment of a Mrs. Simpson, where the other seamstresses drink brandy when the supervisor Miss Betts leaves the room. Embodied in sharp vignettes, the tale focuses on several excursions the diarist makes (to Hampstead, the theatre, St. Paul's) to contrast these with her workroom and her lodgings with the intrusive Mrs. Greaves. The narrator's reactions to nature are effective: "On the same side of the window that I sit on there is a poplar tree. I know there is! the end of some of the branches reach past the edge of the window. . . . If I knew how long the branch was, or how thick, I could guess at the size of the tree" (713). While on a Sunday excursion with the Greaves family, she takes a walk alone, and the scene becomes almost hallucinatory: "The hills stood up, and the trees, as if they were cut in iron. . . . There was a house on the left hand nearly hid by trees, but the white end of it seemed to blaze out of the darkness" (714–15). In contrast to this writer, Stone depicts the harshness of the London world rather than the drabness recorded in the *Tait's* story.

The diary form of *A London Dressmaker's Diary* allows the author considerable immediacy of representation when Miss Wells fears her mind is failing: "Sewing stitch after stitch is not work for the mind. . . . What can I do? . . . If I had sat longer I should have gone mad! . . . But the mental idleness! — must I go on so?" (716). Later she records: "A pale blue satin dress is in my eyes and fills my head. . . . I am *sick to death*" (717). This seamstress is more articulate than Stone's protagonist, and even philosophical: "Here is my life: I will ask it — Why did God make me? If I was made for the life I now lead, why have I more faculties than are needful for it? . . . I almost feel inclined to scratch out the last lines. They frighten me. They shall stand, however; for they are true" (718). While such a reflection is intriguing and immediate, it is questionable whether a seamstress in so short a time would reach such a conclusion. She wonders: "Can I be worse than I am now? Can I be worse than half alive, dead to enjoyment, sensitive to misery, without motive. . . . It may be, that other women, whom I think so wicked, are only mad, as I was" (718). Finally, she has her father retrieve her and return her to the country. Her mental prostration is shown by the fact that she miscalculates her dates toward the end of the diary. *The Young Milliner* has less instantaneous impact than *A London Dressmaker's Diary* because it is a novel. Stone presents a grimmer, more deadening situation because Ellen Cardan's plight is protracted. She experiences brutality while learning of degradation through the experience of the Lamberts. In contrast to *A London Dressmaker's Diary,* Stone depicts a much wider spectrum of society to show the complicity of the entire social organism in the downfall of her protagonist. The *Dressmaker's Diary* includes few details of specific aspects of seamstressing, unlike *The Young Milliner* with its information about hours, prostitution, and physical debility. The *Athenaeum* is probably correct that *A London Dressmaker's Diary* and *The Young Milliner* are among the first, if not the first, depictions of such conditions in their respective literary forms.

William Langshawe and *The Young Milliner* mark a transition from the protests of Frances Trollope and Charlotte Tonna to the disciplined work of Elizabeth Gaskell, and it is not surprising that her work was mistaken for Stone's. One cannot argue that Stone was an artist of the caliber of Gaskell or Kingsley, but with these two novels she responded early and earnestly to Carlyle's call for "inquiry" in *Chartism.* In a work like *The Young Milliner*, she anticipated Engels' description of millinery conditions in *The Condition of the Working Class in England:* "a group of workers in London whose conditions of work merit investigation because of the extraordinary barbarity with which they are exploited by the greedy middle classes" (237).

Stone's treatment of women's labor differs in its methodology from Charlotte Elizabeth Tonna's in *The Wrongs of Woman,* published in four installments in 1843–1844. One of these, "Milliners and Dressmakers," deals with the same subject as does Stone's *The Young Milliner*. Tonna's approach differs from Stone's not only in the use of the *Second Report* but also in her verbatim inclusion of the testimony into her fiction. The fact that Tonna wrote *The Wrongs of Woman* indicates that she did not regard *Helen Fleetwood* as conclusive. In February 1842 Tonna was exasperated with social conditions: "Look at the factories; session after session passes by, and no effectual step is taken by Parliament, no pledge to be obtained from men in power, that they will promote the sacred cause of these poor destitute ones," she exclaimed in *The Christian Lady's Magazine* (17:186). The following month she chastises her reader, stating the motive of both *Helen Fleetwood* and *The Wrongs of Woman:* "It is not that people can do nothing, but that they are not sufficiently roused to attempt doing any thing in the matter. . . . If a lady on reading your pages finds her heart moved to go to some male relation or friend who will listen kindly to her plea . . . [l]et her take pen and paper, and simply set forth the fact that the undersigned petitioners earnestly desire to call the attention of the Honourable House to the deplorable conditions of the labourers employed in our manufacturing districts." Tonna believes that "ENGLISH FEMALE SYMPATHY" may work in unison with "the noble, persevering, uncompromising Ashley" to effect reform: "Give us justice for the factories, and a TEN HOUR BILL!" (17:285, 287–88).

Toward the end of 1842 Tonna was asked by the Committee of the Christian Influence Society to write a study of the conditions of Britain, being "deeply impressed with a sense of the alarming state of the country, from the habitual grinding oppression to which the labouring classes were exposed." As a result "she was at once amply supplied with facts and information, both from parliamentary Reports and private correspondence of many who were devoting themselves to this momentous inquiry." The resulting work, *The Perils of the Nation,* appeared at Easter (16 April) 1843. The work was published anonymously, "as it was not to be supposed that legislators and those for whose perusal it was intended, would pay much attention to a work on such a subject from a woman's pen." Louis Tonna recalled after his wife's death: "The book speedily reached a second and a third edition; and that it had a marked and decided influence, not only on the tone of public feeling, but directly on the Legislature, admits of no doubt. It was quoted on platforms and discussed in private circles; three important societies may be attributed to its influence, viz., the Society for improving the condition of the Labouring Classes, the Church Extension Fund, and the Clerical Education Aid fund; and what were its effects in aiding the passing of the Mines and Collieries' Bill, and the Ten Hours Bill, and in bringing forward the Health of Towns Bill, will only be known when the secrets of all hearts are revealed" (*Personal Recollections* 374–75). If one considers the Ten Hours Bill and the Public Health Act as results of *The Perils of the Nation,* Tonna's influence was great. The work is valuable for illustrating Tonna's methodology prior to the composition of *The Wrongs of Woman.* Tonna had worked among the people about whom she wrote and, like Trollope, she had traveled. Virginia Woolf's idea of the captive female novelist in *A Room of One's Own* is not universal. When Martineau and Tonna left Norwich for London, their experiences broadened. Tonna's writing of *The Perils of the Nation* defies Herbert Spencer's later idea that "women possess and are only capable of acting according to the moral principles which govern the ethics of the family" (Delamont 72).

More than any other work by Tonna *The Perils of the Nation* relied on documentation. It begins with a quotation from Lord Ashley's speech 28 February 1843 and maintains its documentary emphasis to convince its readers that it is not fiction. Tonna's purpose and method are stated with clarity in the ninth chapter, "Want of Sanitary Regulations": "We shall follow into their dwellings the same classes that we have already glanced at in their occupations. . . . We must supply data to those who desire to investigate the evil, that they may devise a remedy. . . . It is obvious that relief does not, cannot lie within the reach of the sufferers. . . . The legislature must interfere" (127, 135–36). Tonna's practice in *Helen Fleetwood* and *The Wrongs of Woman* parallels this intention to "follow into dwellings." In her third chapter Tonna notices the prevalence of females in manufacturing: "His, do we say! *her* toil, *its* toil; for women and children form the larger portion of those who are so employed" (19–20). She observes the hazards of the moral state: "Her morals may have escaped the practical pollution of the mass, her mind cannot have continued undefiled in the daily hearing and seeing of such abominations" (24). Tonna here alludes to Lord Ashley, Martineau's *A Manchester Strike,* and the *Morning Chronicle.*

Indicative of Tonna's procedure is chapter five, "The Workshop Labourers." She draws heavily from the *Second Report,* especially the evidence collected by Horne and Grainger. (Disraeli used some of this same material for *Sybil.*) Tonna quotes extensively for three pages

from the introduction to the *Second Report,* omitting only employers' names. So rapid was the composition of *The Perils of the Nation*
that Tonna quotes this introduction verbatim, without halting to use
the complete transcript. In *The Wrongs of Woman,* she returns to
the complete transcript, using the material about the children's lack
of religion. Tonna prefers these summaries from the introduction,
since its modification of the complete accounts increases the shock
value of the testimony. Of the social novelists Kettle notes: "It was
to the conscience — not to mention the downright factual ignorance —
of the middle class that they addressed themselves" (171). Tonna in
her role of both researcher and novelist does the same. Hewitt notes
that Ashley exaggerated some of his data, for example about the number of married women in factories, but Tonna accepted Ashley's fer-
vid word and the documents' personal testimonies. In the Introduction and in Tonna (*Parliamentary Papers* 13:81; *Perils* 51, 53) there
appears: "Works at latches; has not enough to eat; his master is a-
cursing at him every day of his life; once knocked him down with
his fist. . . . His master behaves very bad. His mistress behaves worst,
like a devil; she beats him; knocks his head against the wall." In the
complete transcript (15:q35, q32) these passages are as follows: "Cannot spell his name; works at latches; has not enough to eat — very often
not enough; has a good bed; is not often beaten, but his master is
a-cursing at him every day of his life; once knocked him down with
his fist. . . . His master behaves very bad sometimes — another time
he'll be just the other way. His mistress behaves worst to him. The
master is not amiss; it is his wife — second wife; she behaves like a
devil to him; she beats him sometimes — knocks his head against the
wall." In this chapter Tonna reproduces the same sequence of quotations that exists in the *Report,* all exhibiting these cuts from the complete transcript in Volume Fifteen. Young has noted that *The Perils
of the Nation* was "hurriedly compiled . . . in the alarm following
the Chartist Riots of 1842. . . . [It] undoubtedly represents a great
body of educated opinion of, broadly speaking, a Tory-Evangelical
cast, and furnishes a link between the Sadler-Ashley thought of the
thirties and *Unto This Last* of 1860" (*Victorian* 54).

In addition to this use of evidence in *The Perils of the Nation,*
Tonna introduces another idea that will be prominent in *The Wrongs
of Woman,* the emphasis on the necessity of "female influence" to
achieve legislative reform. She devotes the penultimate chapter of *The
Perils of the Nation* to the question, arguing: "It is much to be wished

that the mighty engine of female influence were more efficiently directed. The ladies of England are famed for tenderness of feeling, for decision of mind, for firmness of purpose, and promptitude of action. Their position in society is more commanding than that of any other females throughout the world: they comprehend our political or commercial objects, share our anxieties, and assist us by their intelligent counsel, to an extent which renders their power, for good or for evil, almost irresistible; and, contrasted with the insignificance of women in foreign lands, truly marvellous. No human beings, perhaps, are so quick at detecting injustice, resenting oppression, relieving the necessitous, and soothing the unhappy. Witness their efforts in the cause of negro freedom, at a time when it may be said all the female chivalry of England was up and striving; nor did they once relax their hold of the driver's whip, till they had fairly wrested it out of his hand. In all our great national crises, has the feminine mind appeared clad with masculine energy, and evinced a fortitude, an endurance most admirable" (345–46). She does not remain content with general statement.

To conclude the chapter she concentrates on the plight of dressmakers and milliners, which will be the subject of Part I of *The Wrongs of Woman:* "And this call for interposition is especially urgent in a department principally under female patronage and control; one, where almost every lady in the land has power to interfere, at least negatively, by withdrawing her custom, and stating the reason of her so doing, where the offence is committed. Dress-making and millinery, are, with few exceptions, carried on in establishments, and by means of young females, either apprenticed to learn the business, or employed on hire. It is utterly impossible to describe what this class of operatives undergo: physically, morally, and spiritually, their condition is heart-rending" (359–60). Tonna records the grim details of the work conditions, hours, and moral corruption. At its conclusion, she anticipates writing *The Wrongs of Woman:* "To force the greatest possible amount of labour from the least possible number of labourers, is the one governing maxim; and how would the fashionable lady loathe the costume that she most delights in, were the tears, the life-blood of the poverty-stricken sempstress employed by her *artiste* in the details of its embroidery . . . made visible upon its surface: or, far more, could she there read the tale of ruin, temporal and eternal, to which the miserable sister of her nature is doomed, to swell the gains of a calculating directress! These things

ARE: to be wilfully ignorant of them, or to know that they exist, and to take no decided step towards putting them away from before the eyes of the Lord God of Sabaoth, is a matter between the English lady and Him to whom she must give account" (363). The review of *The Perils of the Nation* in *The Christian Lady's Magazine* states that "the ladies of the land are not omitted from among those required to rectify these abuses" (19:467).

The Wrongs of Woman was published in four parts between 1843 and 1844, the fictional result of Tonna's long researches for *The Perils of the Nation.* In the September 1843 issue of *The Christian Lady's Magazine,* Tonna published a letter from a clergyman under the heading "Dress-making," in which the pastor praises Part I of *The Wrongs of Woman*: "You have spoken well and boldly upon the oppressive character of the slavery which prevails among thousands of wretched women, who minister to the fashions and frivolities of the gay world, — and who spend their early days, and exhaust their precious lives in a bondage which is thankless, profitless, and often the instrument of ruin both to body and soul." The minister continues, "Oh that the ladies of England, the mothers, the daughters of England, would stand forth as with one voice, and say that such a system shall not be!" (20:244, 248).

The publication of the *Second Report* confirmed the validity of Tonna's essays in *The Christian Lady's Magazine* and convinced her to pursue *The Wrongs of Woman.* Although Tonna used evidence for *Helen Fleetwood,* she did not employ the direct quotation that appears in the four parts of *The Wrongs of Woman.* She learned from *The Perils of the Nation* that direct testimony was necessary to persuade the reader, realizing that *Helen Fleetwood* must have lacked conviction because it lacked evidence. Tonna uses such documents because they were "not likely to be read by the middle-class wives and mothers through whom she hoped to influence their voting husbands, fathers, and sons" (Kovacevic, "Blue" 156). Therefore at the end of each part of *The Wrongs of Woman* there appears a chapter of evidence: "Consequences" (Part I), "Corroborating Evidence" (Part II), "Authentications" (Part III), and "The Finale" (Part IV). Such quotation is the most conspicuous difference between *Helen Fleetwood* and *The Wrongs of Woman,* a result of the intermediate composition of *The Perils of the Nation.* Tonna's method of combining fiction and documentation anticipates the purpose of social fiction noted by Geraldine Jewsbury in her review of *Alton Locke* in the *Athenaeum:*

"The purpose is, to arouse the attention of a wider class than that which refers to blue books and official reports, and to force them to look on the social evils that are lying at their doors" (944).

Although *The Wrongs of Woman* was composed of four separately written parts, Tonna unifies her stories in several ways. By concentrating on dressmaking, screw-driving, pin-heading, and lace-running, Tonna emphasizes the nontextile industries, new emphases after the *Report* of 1843. With the exception of Part II, each part includes a chapter detailing a "typical day" at each of the employments. Tonna links her four stories by having the protagonists come from the same village "not far from a town of considerable traffic" (339). Ann and Frances King, who become the milliner and the dressmaker of Part I, are daughters of a "small farmer." Tom Clarke, a widower who works in a stable-yard, has lost his custom since a railroad bypassed the inn. He is specifically called "a grade lower in station" than King. Parts II and III concern the family of John Smith, "still worse off" than either King or Clarke (400). His wife Alice becomes a screw-worker in Part II; his children Betsy and Joe enter pin-heading in Part III. In several of these families there is no mother, and possibly the childless Tonna was fulfilling the role of surrogate mother to these characters.

Complementing these unifying devices, Tonna introduces variety sufficient to compel her reader to distinguish among these women. While *The Wrongs of Woman* focuses on nontextile industries, the occupations Tonna studies exhibit class variations. Dressmakers and milliners, frequently from the country, were usually shabby genteel rather than working class. Those engaged in pin-making, on the other hand, were frequently "drawn from the lowest classes" (Pinchbeck 276). Tonna's readers were thus introduced not only to "woman" as a group but to class subdivisions. She can depict her characters according to the class distinctions noted in the Parliamentary reports. The Parts indicate some principles of alternation. Parts I and III have two protagonists, Ann and Frances King and Betsy and Joe Smith; Parts II and IV have a single central character, Alice Smith or Kate Clarke. Part II is unusual in having for a title the consequence of industrialism, "The Forsaken Home," rather than an occupation. The title is ironic since it applies to each family both before and after its move to the industrial center: the home is forsaken twice. These structural variations reinforce the title *The Wrongs of Woman* by assuring that the group is demarcated. Tonna is dealing, she says, with "actual wrongs" (399), vowing "to repudiate all pretentions to equality with man" (397).

The premise behind her method is stated in Part II: "The abstract idea of a suffering family does not strongly affect the mind; but let the parties be known to us, let their names call up some familiar images to our view, and certain facts connected with their past lives be vividly brought to our recollection when they are spoken of, we are enabled much more feelingly to enter into their trial. For this purpose, a case of constant recurrence has been fixed on, and the same individuals have been kept in view throughout, in order to engage the reader's sympathies, while concentrating her attention more effectually than the pages of a formal report, necessarily prolix and full of repetitions, could do" (441). Tonna is compensating for the unavoidable heterogeneity of the 1843 *Report,* specifically addressing a reform-minded female audience.

Tonna wrote the first Part of *The Wrongs of Woman* about dressmakers and milliners because their plight was so brutally exposed in the *Second Report.* She may have been particularly concerned with this trade because its conditions were so bad in her birthplace, Norwich. Tonna follows the *Report* strictly; the details of the lives of Ann and Frances are precise. She lends conviction to her tale by specificity. Ann is not simply a milliner, but an improver, defined in the *Report* (14:F29) as one who has already learned some elements of the trade in the country. Ann's introduction to the shop, recorded in the chapter describing a typical day, follows Grainger. She is allowed fifteen minutes for dinner, ten for tea. Grainger records that fifteen or twenty minutes were allowed for dinner, fifteen or less for tea. Tonna selects the lowest possible time limit. Tonna culls from the *Report* the brutal work hours, the fact that no meals were served on Sunday, and the account of Ann's symptoms (14:F30, f232–f236).

In her fifth chapter Tonna returns to Frances King at the dressmaker's, reinforced by the *Report,* especially in that Frances is taught nothing and is beginning to consort with "gentlemen" (413). Tonna's final chapter is devoted to evidence from the *Second Report.* Beginning this testimony, she cites the Parliamentary papers that 15,000 women work in 1,500 establishments in London alone, emphasizing the statement of E. L. Devonald of 3 May 1841: "In no trade or manufactory whatever is the labour to be compared to that of the young dress-makers: no men work so long. It would be impossible for any animal to work so continuously with so little rest" (13:144; 14:f236).

For Tonna woman is a "beast of burthen to her own sex" (415). Tonna treats such subjects as hours, meals, workrooms, and health (416; 14:F29–32) approximately in the order in which the investigators were required to compile their data. Recounting Ann's death and Frances' slide into prostitution, Tonna concludes her first part. The work presented readers with the data of the *Reports,* with the advantage of a restricted focus and a plot. The structure of the first part — departure from home, typical day, decline, evidence — established the form of the remaining three installments.

Parts II and III of *The Wrongs of Woman,* "The Forsaken Home" and "The Little Pin-headers," concern the Smith family at two different periods, since Alice Smith, the central character of Part II, is dead when Part III begins. The theme of Part II is close to ideas expressed in *The Perils of the Nation,* the preference for female over male labor and the consequences to family life of this policy. Lord Ashley demanded in 1844, when surveying women in the work force: "Where, sir, under these conditions are the possibilities of domestic life? How can its obligations be fulfilled? Regard the woman as a wife and mother — how can she accomplish any portion of her calling? And if she cannot do that which Providence has assigned to her, what must be the effect on the whole surface of society?" (Hewitt 31). The Smiths go to Wolverhampton (W____ in the text), where John Smith speaks with Richards, a militant worker who recalls the agitator Smith of *Combination:*

> "Your wife may get work easy enough at the screws, but you won't be taken in."
> "Why not?"
> "'Cause women are all the thing there. Out of a hundred workers, you won't find over ten men, and 'tis the same rule they go by at all the shops, in business that isn't out and out beyond a woman's strength."
> "'Tis a bad rule, and one I won't agree to. Why should women be chosen before men?"
> "Oh, the masters find they work harder and take less; and that's all they care for." (420)

Peter Gaskell had stated flatly in 1836: "There is no employment to be found for adult males" (172), and like Dodd in 1842 he commented on the lack of domestic skills.

Smith finds, pursuant to the *Report* (13:16), that "the great majority of the workpeople are females, as many as ninety percent." In the second chapter Tonna records the process by which Alice is hired over her husband, rather than, as in the other parts, detailing a typical day. The outcry against women working was partially from "the fear that women were gradually displacing men" (Hewitt 23). Peter Gaskell had noted in 1833 that "a disposition is developing itself to have recourse to the labour of women and children in preference to adults. . . . The adult male has begun slowly to give way, and his place been supplied by those who in the usual order of things were dependent upon him for their support" (183–84). It is interesting to note that Gaskell implies that women workers are not "adult." He felt that the hiring of women "must of necessity lead to the neglect of all the domestic offices," devoting an entire chapter to the question, contending that "domestic avocations are those which are her peculiar lot" (167). The following figures from a Leeds spinning mill in the 1830s reveal the extent of this disproportionate employment of women (J. Harrison 52):

| Year | Men | | Women and Girls | | Children (under 14) | | Hours per Week |
	No. employed	Average weekly wage	No. employed	Average weekly wage	No. employed	Average weekly wage	
1831	139	19s 10d	385	5s 3d	250	3s 2d	72
1836	144	21s 6d	442	5s 5½d	307	2s 10¾d	66
1840	135	21s 8d	478	5s 11½d	409	2s 5¾d	66

Discrimination did underlie this practice: "Women were discriminated against by both their employers and the men with whom they worked. Manufacturers preferred them because they were cheap. . . . Manufacturers also found women more docile to manage" (Neff 30). There were insistent denunciations of the collapse of the home because of women working, as in Tonna, although Hewitt contends that "much of the condemnation . . . of the married worker as a housewife appears both misconceived and exaggerated" (83). In probing this situation in *The Wrongs of Woman* Tonna anticipated Engels, who observed that "the wife is the bread-winner while her husband stays at home. . . . Family relationships are reversed" (162).

The issues raised by women leaving home so arouse Tonna that she includes in her second and third chapters either direct quotation from or indisputable reference to the Parliamentary data. At the conclusion of the second chapter she denounces the use of Godfrey's cordial, citing a long passage verbatim from Horne's *Report* (15:Q30). As Branca notes, the use of Godfrey was not confined to the working classes, so middle-class readers knew the issue (106). Angus Reach's investigations in 1849 showed the use of Godfrey still rampant among the working classes: "The child is drugged until it sleeps, and then too often it is drugged until it dies" (25). Tonna defines and denounces the tommy shop and the truck system, introducing her middle-class readers to a new vocabulary. Acts had been passed in 1817, 1820, and even 1831 against truck but to little avail, and Disraeli was to pursue the exposé in *Sybil* the following year. Tonna condemns the neo-Malthusianism of people like Harriet Martineau, whom she had criticized in *The Perils of the Nation.* John Smith complains: "I don't repent marrying *you,* Ally, more than another; but you see, the root of all our troubles in this life is having a family; if it was not for that we might jog on well enough" (432). Tonna concludes by recording the decline of the Smiths, their drinking, the disintegration of the marriage, and the break-up of their family. In the final "Corroborating Evidence" Tonna includes much quotation from the *Report,* including a long extract from the evidence of Joseph Corbett (15:f131–f132) on the ruin of his home from his mother's absence.

During the story Alice Smith stays away from home with other female workers, and it is not accidental that the story appeared in 1844 when the Matrimonial Causes Act "decreed that a husband could not force his wife to return home" (Basch 17). "The Forsaken Home" is an important statement of a central issue of the forties, extending the first part in several respects. Tonna informs readers of issues beyond the specific trade under consideration, and she presents the process, not merely the fact, of the disintegration of the marriage, probably because of her wretched first marriage in 1813. The opening of the first day nursery in March 1850 may have been a result of the pleas by Tonna and others for an alternative to the fatal Godfrey.

"The Little Pin-headers" concerns two of the Smiths' children, Betsy and Joe. Tonna's work on *The Perils of the Nation* had exposed her to harsh evidence concerning children in pin-making. She calls the children "wretched little automata" (451). The construction of this part follows the basic pattern of Parts I and II. In its second chapter, "A Sunday Stroll," Tonna takes the reader through the filthy manufacturing district, showing that no workers are attending religious services, a detail that concerned her in *Combination*. Abandoned by their stepmother, the children are forced into the workhouse. The one practice peculiar to pin manufactories that Tonna does not use is "that of masters lending parents money, to be repaid in their children's work" (*Parliamentary Papers* 13:24). Thus, if such is possible, the children might have been worse off had they *not* been abandoned by their father and his second wife. The final "Authentications" of this part are especially detailed since Tonna is moved by the plight of these children. On the nature of the work, lack of provision, abuse, and health she draws on Grainger, then turns to Horne, citing the same passages used in *The Perils of the Nation*. Part III emphasizes the importance of religion, since Tonna regards the lack of religious training as an abuse along with other forms of neglect. Implicit in her indictment is the assumption that the final check against revolution, religion, is deteriorating.

For Part IV Tonna concentrates on the lace-runners or embroiderers. The lace-runners were of much contemporary interest since in 1840 they had organized an unsuccessful strike in Nottingham. "The lace-runner, although the most skilful, was the hardest worked and the worst paid of all the operatives connected with the lace trade"; as a result, "almost all became prostitutes" (Pinchbeck 211–12). Grainger's evidence stated that these women worked sometimes "15, 16, and even 17 hours a-day" and that married women were forced to use Godfrey because of the long hours (14:F10). Runners "become totally unfitted for other manufacturing labour, and even common household work and the discharge of domestic duties" (14:F11).

These statements form the narrative of Kate Clarke. Tonna records each detail of the *Report* in the events of Kate's life. As in Part III, she instructs the reader in specific vocabulary, like *drawing, running, mending,* and *pearling*. She links Part IV to the earlier sections of *The Wrongs of Woman* by having Tom Clarke note "They sha'n't have it to say of me as they do of John Smith, that he made slaves of his children. I know better than to put mine in a factory prison" (479). Thinking Kate is with the Collins family, he believes all will be well. In the second chapter Tonna presents a typical day in the Collins household, with graphic instances of the use of Godfrey, which links Part IV to Part II. Kate thinks of going into hosiery, but this proves even worse than lace-running. Paralleling Grainger's evidence about lace workers and prostitution, Tonna has Kate enter a brothel: "'Let them answer it,' she crosses the threshold. And here we part with her for ever" (499). In her evidence for Part IV Tonna concentrates on two elements, work hours (14:f42, F10) and Godfrey's cordial (14:f60–f61), concluding with a statement about unfair pricing and the inevitable prostitution (14:f40). She advises her readers, as she did in *The Perils of the Nation,* that prostitution cannot be concealed from female middle-class readers.

Her final remonstrance is addressed to these readers: "Ladies of England! under such circumstances as we have laid before you, are the materials of your daily attire prepared by manufacture and embroidery, the articles made up by dress-makers and milliners, and the very pins with which you secure them, formed to answer the purpose. At such a price you make your toilet — we have gone no further than that one branch of the almost numberless productions of British industry, and we will not wrong you by any appeal — if such FACTS do not speak, all language is utterly vain" (501–2). "Have we not a woman on the throne?" she asks. Tonna fears the "fiery tumult of universal insurrection." The clothing idea that informs three of the four parts of *The Wrongs of Woman* may allude to Carlyle's *Sartor Resartus,* published in book form in England in 1838. Tonna concludes: "The cruelties now heaped upon the poorest of our sex are, in the broadest, most inclusive sense, THE WRONGS OF WOMAN" (502). Both Tonna and Stone are part of "the great philanthropic awakening of the forties" (Best 29), inaugurating a tradition in women's social fiction.

The work of Stone and Tonna, especially their depiction of millinery and dressmaking, shows the concern expressed by female novelists about conditions revealed in the Parliamentary reports, especially as they affected women. Dickens created Kate Nickleby in 1837, but the tone of the depiction had altered since the revelations of the Commissions. Dickens had written: "Madame Mantalini led the way down a flight of stairs, and through a passage, to a large room at the back of the premises where were a number of young women employed in sewing, cutting out, making up, altering, and various other processes known only to those who are cunning in the arts of millinery and dress-making. It was a close room with a sky-light, and as dull and quiet as a room need be" (156–57). In contrast to Dickens, Stone and Tonna use the technical vocabulary of the trade. Dickens had earlier satirized the milliner Miss Amelia Martin in *Sketches by Boz,* where the sequestered milliner attends a dinner and develops an ambition to sing in the theatres. She makes a disastrous debut and is lost to memory. Dickens allows his fallen needlewoman Little Emily from

David Copperfield to emigrate to Australia after her desertion by Steerforth, but she can scarcely be considered a study of the conditions of needlewomen. Emigration was "an insignificant factor" in remediating the conditions of milliners and dressmakers (Walkley 125).

Stone's and Tonna's novels anticipated many later works detailing these conditions, including Camilla Toulmin's *The Orphan Milliners* (1844) and Charles Rowcroft's *Fanny, the Little Milliner* (1846). The heroines of Gaskell's *Mary Barton* (1848), *Lizzie Leigh* (1850), and *Ruth* (1853) were involved in dressmaking or millinery. Jane Eyre thought of dressmaking when she left Rochester, and Kingsley's grim tailoring scenes in *Cheap Clothes and Nasty* and *Alton Locke* are descendants of the early forties via Henry Mayhew's essays in the *Morning Chronicle* (1849–50). While in terms of characterization or dialogue Gaskell is superior to Tonna and Stone, one may admire Tonna's studious avoidance of any romance in her milliners' lives. She does not offer even emigration as a solution. Such drabness will not be reproduced until Julia Kavanagh's *Rachel Gray* in 1856. Gaskell's objectives in *Ruth* are more far-ranging than the limited objectives of Tonna and Stone in presenting female laborers. By the late forties and early fifties the plight of female workers was subsumed in larger contexts. In *Mary Barton* the girl's occupation is an issue only in the context of questions such as unions, social cooperation, murder, prostitution, and emigration.

By the late forties some groups had been formed to assist needlewomen, such as the Distressed Needlewomen's Society, founded in January 1847, and the Milliners and Dressmakers Provident and Benevolent Institution, begun in February 1849. It was to take far longer to remedy the conditions of milliners. In 1856 Grainger discovered that the apprentices suffered more than ever before. The Parliamentary reports of 1861 record continued use of Godfrey's narcotic, and those of 1864 are replete with details of the sufferings of dressmakers. Some acts passed after Tonna's death in 1846 gave impetus to reform. The 1847 Act (Ten Hours Bill), the 1850 Act to Amend the Acts relating to Labour in Factories, Palmerston's Factory Act of 1853, and the Lace Works Act of 1861 gradually provided improvement, although enforcement of a law, particularly in the case of nonfactory labor where it might be strictly inapplicable, was frequently impossible. In the September 1863 issue of *All the Year Round,* twenty years after *The Young Milliner,* an essay focused on "The Point of the Needle," complete with quotations from the *Second Report* concerning hours, conditions, and overwork. It notes that the Association for the Aid and Benefit of Dress-makers and Milliners had failed to remedy the problem. Women were being increasingly confined to needlework as machines supplanted their labor in trades like envelope-folding and shoe-binding. Then the writer adds: "The ladies of England never did, and do not yet, as a body, thoroughly perceive how much it rests with them to improve or maintain the unhappy condition of the milliners' workwomen" (36). In this protest, the writer echoes Stone and Tonna, who had initiated reform in this area two decades earlier.

Tonna and Stone, while concerned with the abuse of women in labor, concentrated on specific trades. In contrast to this approach, Frances Trollope published in 1842–1843 an indictment of the 1834 New Poor Law in the figure of her seduced seamstress *Jessie Phillips*. Trollope's indignation was aroused by the New Poor Law, which was marked by "its ferocious denial of all social responsibility for the distressed" (J. Mitchell 265). Trollope prefigures the later use of the seamstress in a novel like *Ruth* where the occupation is no longer the sole object of the study. Trollope's major purpose in *Jessie Phillips* is to criticize the New Poor Law and particularly one dimension of that Law, the bastardy clauses. Instead of focusing on better-known aspects of the Law, such as the concepts of no outdoor relief, the termination of the Speenhamland practice of subsidizing wages, and the workhouse test of less eligibility, Trollope was concerned with the changes the 1834 Law made in the previous Law by which "any pregnant spinster [could] 'swear her child' to any adult male she might choose. The result was often grievously unfair to men so accused, but they had no recourse." The emphasis of Adam Smith, Malthus, and Ricardo on "the individual ethos" was combined with a Benthamite conception of utilitarianism, less intervention with greater centralization, to produce the New Poor Law (Checkland 36, 20). The revision was based on the following recommendation: "As a further step towards the natural state of things, we recommend that the mother of an illegitimate child born after the passing of the Act, be required to support it, and that any relief occasioned by the wants of the child be considered relief afforded to the parent," with the further recommendation "that the second section of the 18 Eliz., cap. 3, and all other Acts which punish or charge the putative father of a bastard, shall, as to

ALL BASTARDS BORN AFTER THE PASSING OF THE INTENDED ACT, BE RE-
PEALED" (Checkland 479, 483). Trollope's tale recounts the seduction
of the seamstress Jessie Phillips by the callous Sir Frederic Dalton,
her pregnancy, her confinement to the workhouse, the murder of her
child, her trial and death.

The main objective of *Jessie Phillips* is to keep before the reader
the consequences of the bastardy clauses. When Dalton calculates
the seduction of Jessie, he thinks in terms of the new provisions: "The
terror that formerly kept so many libertines of all classes in check
was no longer before him, the legislature having, in its collective wisdom, deemed it 'discreetest, best,' that the male part of the population should be guarded, protected, sheltered, and insured from all the
pains and penalties arising from the crime he meditated. 'No, no,'
thought Mr. Frederic Dalton, 'thanks to our noble lawgivers, there
is no more swearing away a gentleman's incognito now. It is just one
of my little bits of good luck that this blessed law should be passed
precisely when it was likely to be most beneficial to me" (67). Various
male characters offer opinions of the new provisions. Captain Maxwell has instilled in his daughter Martha "a profound abhorrence for
that very tremendous specimen of modern legislation which, while
charily sheltering the seducer from every annoyance or inconvenience
of any kind in his licentious amours, throws with unmitigated ven-
geance the whole burden of retribution on the frail creature seduced"
(203). The attorney Lewis advises Dalton: "I should be no lawyer, my
dear friend, if I could hear you speak of this business as if you were
not aware that, whether the girl's charge be true or false, it makes
no sort of difference to you. Is it possible, Dalton, that you are ignorant of this most important clause in the new act?" The date of
intercourse is meaningless, as Lewis tells Dalton: "So, as to the date,
you see, it matters nothing. We have nothing to do with facts now
in cases of this sort, the law is comprehensive enough to do without
them" (252–53). The attorney's dismissal of "facts" in a protest novel
is its own commentary.

Lewis is severe with Jessie herself when she lays her case before
him: "I, therefore, tell you, my girl, that you may stand all day swearing that one man or another is the father of your child, and no more
notice will be taken of it than if you whistled." "If you can't maintain
yourself, it will be born in the workhouse; and if you can't maintain
your child, why then it will be bred in the workhouse. Let the father
be a king or a cobbler it will not make the slightest difference, so you

need not trouble yourself to say any thing about that. The law has taken care of them, and such as you too, in that respect, at any rate, for it won't let you tell lies, you see, however much you may desire it" (255). Trollope has perceived the fact that "so great was the stigma attached to birth in a workhouse that there were families who pawned all they had to avoid such an event" (Cruikshank 89). Trollope attributes a developing political consciousness to her heroine: "Jessie knew well enough as everybody else did, that the new law had ordained many severe enactments against women in her unhappy situation." Since this is so, Trollope fails to explain why Jessie, aware of the predatory nature of upper-class men, believed Dalton's promise of marriage. Jessie recognizes that the law intended to "spare the pocket of the fondly protected man" (255).

Trollope ignores the fact that testimony validated that innocent males were coerced into marriage. Henriques observes that "loose women would swear not to the real father of the child, but to the wealthiest man against whom the charge could stick" and that through affiliation orders "mothers of bastards frequently obtained higher allowances than widows with legitimate families." Mothers even were "instrumental in having their daughters seduced" for the purpose of obtaining money through an affiliation order (106–7). Trollope's situation in the novel would have been strengthened by supplying a character whose deceit balanced the innocence of Jessie to discriminate her indictment precisely. Peter Gaskell noted the consequences of the double standard, and it is on this issue that Trollope's protest is substantiated and substantial. Gaskell noted in 1833: "The wanderer is condemned to the persecution of a host of troubles and vexations, which in the one sex ends by its expulsion from its natural rank in the social confederacy" (79). The situation of Jessie Phillips differs from the rural ritual of "premature intercourse . . . generally between parties, when a tacit though binding understanding existed" (31). Gaskell was critical of the Old Poor Law when he wrote in 1833: "The poor laws and bastardy laws have unquestionably acted, and are still acting, as premiums for immorality and idleness" (216). Trollope has isolated a problem, as did the Poor Law Commission, but neither has solved it adequately. No one could deny the evil of the old bastardy provisions, but Trollope chooses to ignore these, albeit the 1834 solution was also inadequate. Trollope seems aware of this basic flaw in her title character when Mr. Rimmington, the clergyman, queries Jessie about her handling of the situation. She admits that she went to Lewis "in the hope . . . that I might be able to make the lawyer frighten Frederic Dalton into doing for me what I wanted him to do." When Rimmington tells her that "you must have known that the law gave you no power whatever to compel Mr. Frederic Dalton to give you assistance," Jessie replies, "Yes . . . I did know that the law left me helpless. . . . But I thought I might frighten him into doing what I wanted by threatening to expose him" (319). This conversation, on the evening of her trial for infanticide, instead of reinforcing her character undermines it.

Trollope is not above exposing other elements of the legislation that she finds distressing. Rimmington adds: "Take from the bill the hateful Frenchified principle of centralisation, in its administration, and all its bitterest — all its most *unconstitutional* faults disappear at once, and nothing would remain to complain of but what English patience on one hand, and English good sense on the other, might be able to remedy. The cruel part of the business is the having cut the tie that, throughout the whole country, bound the rich and the poor together by interests that were reciprocal, and which could not be loosened on either side without injury to both" (55). This criticism of centralization extends to the conditions in the workhouse. When Jessie arrives there, she is lodged with "some of the vilest and most thoroughly abandoned women that the lowest degradation of vice could produce" (288), including a group of prostitutes from a coastal town. The governor of the workhouse, Dempster, and his wife, are coarse and unfeeling, while the clergyman, asked if he would speak with Jessie for fifteen minutes, spurns the appeal, shocked that anyone would expect him to waste time counseling a seamstress. Jessie is acquitted on the grounds of temporary insanity, that is, she is still thought to be the real murderer, while Dalton, the slayer of his bastard, drowns attempting to leave the country. Trollope's tale is anything but a vindication of Jessie.

Trollope's *Jessie Phillips* is a compound of several forms of narrative. To interpret it strictly in terms of the critique of the New Poor Law is inadequate. Beyond being a form of social protest, the novel is a detective fiction and a romance. The detection function derives from the search by the characters for the child's murderer, and the novel concludes, as will *Adam Bede,* with a trial for infanticide. The difficulty with this dimension of the novel is that the reader knows Dalton will be the murderer because of his stereotypical portrayal as a rake. To appease the tastes of her readership of romance, Trollope adds a complicated plot involving Ellen Dalton and the young squire Lord Pemberton, whom she eventually marries after frequent separations.

Trollope, however, creates a myth in the novel, of a league of women acting as Furies against the guilty male. This striking alliance of women is unusual and is the true innovation of her revolt against the New Poor Law. The two women involved in this league are Ellen Dalton and Martha Maxwell. Ellen is abused by her brother Frederic because of provisions in their grandfather's will that might allow her to inherit his estate should Frederic die without legitimate issue. Martha becomes the object of Frederic's pursuit, to form a marriage and ensure the money to himself. Martha determines to expose Dalton for two reasons, his pressuring marriage upon her to suit his financial desires and his conduct to Jessie Phillips, which Jessie discloses to her. Ellen, who had seen Dalton embracing Jessie and guesses he is the father of her child and its murderer, suffers mental distress when she learns Jessie is indicted for infanticide. Trollope shows these two women attempting to subvert male authority by their plans. Dalton, however, ignores Martha's threat to expose him, and Ellen obtains a confession from Frederic, telling him to flee after writing a declaration. Dalton drowns without having written the confession; Ellen recovers from her delirium to marry Lord Pemberton, but she is never told of her brother's end. Jessie dies before learning of her acquittal. Martha marries an attorney, believing that Dalton was not the murderer. Dalton regards the women as Furies when he thinks of living "without control, without restraint, and with no Ellen, no Martha, and no turbulent Jessie either" (344).

Trollope's league of women fails, but this version of a female league against male authority is an important myth in the tradition of the social novel, anticipating the myths about women advanced in Charlotte Brontë's *Shirley* six years later. As a form of social protest, *Jessie Phillips* fails because of the inadequacy of its title character and the exaggeration of its seducer. Trollope is careless about narrative distance: "It is very difficult to touch on any of the most mischievous points of this ill-digested law without being led to dwell upon them till the thread of the story is dropped and almost forgotten; but this will be considered as excusable by all who take a real interest in the subject" (210). Such a disclaimer indicates the fundamental flaw of the novel, that it is "ill-digested" in its narrative stance.

While still in installments the novel was reviewed in the *Athenaeum,* and Trollope appears in her own person at the conclusion of the book version to state: "The story of Jessie Phillips would have wandered less widely from what was intended, when the first numbers were written, had not the author received, during the time it was in progress, such a multitude of communications urging various and contradictory modes of treating the subject, that she became fearful of dealing too closely with a theme which might be presented to the judgement under so great a variety of aspects. The result of the information which has been earnestly sought for by the author, and eagerly given by many, appears to be that a new poor-law, differing essentially from the old one, was absolutely necessary to save the country from the rapidly corroding process, which was eating like a canker into her strength, but that the remedy which has been applied lacks practical wisdom, and is deficient in legislative morality" (352). Trollope recognizes the partiality of her position. The novel may have had some effect on the passage of the New Poor Law Amendment in 1844, that did allow a mother to bring suit against the father if there were corroborative evidence. *Jessie Phillips,* while valuable in its depiction of the flaws in the law and the conditions of workhouse life, fails to integrate its concerns into a successful novel. This is not to say that the work is unimportant. In several respects it anticipates Gaskell's *Ruth,* including the scene of Dalton's meeting Jessie in the cloakroom. The infanticide trial suggests *Adam Bede,* as does the device of the two bedchambers in chapter seventeen, contrasting Ellen and Jessie. Trollope's assured protest, however, did not lead her to a construct with equivalent formal authority.

Between the writings of Tonna, Trollope, and Stone, and prior to the first publication of fiction by Elizabeth Gaskell in 1847, the most prominent social fiction to appear was Disraeli's *Sybil* in 1845. The previous year Disraeli had published his programmatic *Coningsby,* which established the tenets of Young England and the bases of Tory democracy as solutions to the nation's problems. Young England espoused aristocratic interventionism, as a result of the disillusionment with the Reform Bill of 1832. This idea, a form of feudal interventionism in which the lower classes would be guided by the enlightened and responsible members of the aristocracy, was a powerful social myth to Disraeli and his adherents. The alliance of Whigs and radicals would be eliminated by the newer alliance of the manor and the factory, with the guiding aristocracy of the older families allying itself with the newer aristocracy of the industrialists, the Norman aristocracy of the manor and the Saxon aristocracy of the mills. The emphasis on Norman and Saxon traits had been used prior to *Sybil,* for example in Cooke Taylor, also in an industrial and class context.

Disraeli's program was counter to the rationalism of the Utilitarians, based as it was to be on a feeling for traditional institutions and enlightened sympathy. In this respect, Disraeli differed from Carlyle, who had little use for the degenerate aristocracy and instead, in such works as *Past and Present,* called on the Captains of Industry to become the new leaders of the people. To Disraeli socialism and Chartism represented radical and violent solutions to problems that Young England believed could be resolved peacefully in a new form of social contract. This philosophy was advanced in *Sybil* in 1845. Since the work remains an important example of Condition-of-England fiction, it is appropriate to consider its place among the social novels written by women before an appraisal of the innovations accomplished by Gaskell in the later years of the decade.

Disraeli's method in *Sybil* involves the same reliance on works of research that Tonna, Martineau, and Stone had acknowledged, including the use of Blue Books and other resources. To establish a milieu for the political ideas that *Sybil* as a *roman à thèse* promulgates, Disraeli turns to Parliamentary sources. Disraeli's preface to *Sybil* contrasts with that of Gaskell's *Mary Barton* in its less forthright statements: "The general reader whose attention has not been specially drawn to the subject which these volumes aim to illustrate — the Condition of the People — might suspect that the Writer had been tempted to some exaggeration in the scenes that he has drawn, and the impressions he has wished to convey. He thinks it therefore due to himself to state that the descriptions, generally, are written from his own observation; but while he hopes he has alleged nothing which is not true, he has found the absolute necessity of suppressing much that is genuine. For so little do we know of the state of our own country, that the air of improbability which the whole truth would inevitably throw over these pages, might deter some from their perusal" (xxxii). Those who have investigated the sources of Disraeli's material in depicting the town of Wodgate and the wretched conditions of Marney have demonstrated that while Disraeli had visited the northern industrial areas in 1844 with Lord John Manners, the main body of his material is derived from a number of government documents. "The charge that Disraeli was not writing from first-hand observation is just" (Fido, "Treatment" 161).

Pre-eminent in *Sybil* is Disraeli's use of Richard Horne's material included in the *Second Report* of the Commissioners, published in 1842. As Sheila Smith has pointed out, there are extensive correlations between Disraeli's description of the condition of Wodgate and the corresponding details about Willenhall collected by Horne. The reviewer in the *Athenaeum* in May 1845 had already declared that: "*Sybil* is more largely a political treatise, a warming-up of speech materials, a transcript of blue-book incident and adventure. . . . With all his feeling for the people, Mr. Disraeli appears to have studied them in the pages of the parliamentary or statistical Reports referred to, rather than to have 'eaten with them, drank with them, or prayed with them,' as Shylock says." The reviewer continued: "Marney Abbey comes far nearer reality than Mowbray, the scene of Chartism, and all manner of popular grievances. For a more vivid notice of the latter, let us refer the reader to Mr. Horne's pictures of Willenhall and Wolverhampton . . . the source from which Mr. Disraeli's 'Wodgate' is obviously derived" (477, 478). There is in *Sybil,* for example, "a lank and haggard youth, ricketty, smoke-dried" (165) virtually quoted from Horne. Disraeli's use of sources is cautious, leading to omissions of details which would have weakened his case. Such an instance is Horne on the masters' drinking which "would have damaged his picture of the master of Wodgate as a true aristocracy of labour" (Smith, "Willenhall" 375). While Horne mentioned that Willenhall had a church and chapels, Disraeli ignores this detail to enhance the grimness of the circumstances. Many workers' dwellings were clean, but Disraeli ignores the datum. The selling of apprentices, which Horne said was unusual, Disraeli describes as common: "They are often sold by one master to another" (163). Sharp details, such as the girl with the grasshopper back from Horne, Disraeli retained.

Martin Fido has demonstrated that Disraeli was indebted to Edwin Chadwick's 1842 *Report on the Sanitary Condition of the Labouring Population of Great Britain* for his description of the town of Marney. The detail about the roof of a cottage looking "more like the top of a dunghill than a cottage" (52) Disraeli extracted from Chadwick, who had taken it from W. S. Gilly's *The Peasantry of the Border* (1840). "The whole of Disraeli's description of Marney is . . . cobbled together from Chadwick" (Fido, "Treatment" 158). Fido discounts Smith's claims of the use of the 1843 *Report on the Employment of Women and Children in Agriculture,* showing that much of this material originated in Chadwick. Disraeli did not use such documents as the *Handloom Weaver's Report* (1841) but rather William Dodd's *The Factory System Illustrated* (1842) for many details. The *First Report from the Midland Mining Commissioners* (1842), composed after the Plug Plot Riots which conclude *Sybil,* provided "Disraeli with authentic dialect phraseology for his dialogue." These details include payment once in five weeks, tommy shops, and butties. "It is clear from the clustering of the echoes and parallels that Disraeli often worked with the blue book open before him" (Fido, "Sources" 277, 283). If one compares this to Tonna's use of sources, it is apparent that Disraeli, far better known as a social novelist, scarcely differs from Tonna's verbatim quotation when fictionalizing sources. He avoids the tactic of appending evidentiary matter at the conclusion of each section. A distinction between Disraeli and Tonna is Tonna's focus on women's issues. Disraeli, condemning the apprentices' conditions, indicts tommy, truck, opiates, abuse, and housing, enlarging the range of his concerns but leaving domestic issues untouched. The *Athenaeum* reviewer noted "obvious and fierce exaggeration" in *Sybil* that "out-Trollope's Mrs. Trollope" (478).

In their practices of characterization Disraeli and Tonna differ considerably. Through the influence of the reports, Disraeli attempts to use workers' language and to reproduce the milieu of operatives like Dandy Mick and Julia, including their amusements. Tonna ignores such material to emphasize the oppression of her female workers, for whom there is no relief. Disraeli's pronouncement about the Two Nations has several precedents in the writings of Martineau and Tonna, who advocated an alliance between disparate social groups, albeit not on the lines of Young England. A novel like *The Wrongs of Woman* does not have the distortions of history that Disraeli employs to buttress the Young England politics of *Sybil* or *Coningsby.* Disraeli advances a more specific political platform in his novel than either Tonna or Stone does, although Martineau's advocacy seems clear. The integration of specific contemporary historical events into the narrative, a method not widely used by Tonna or Martineau, is important in Disraeli. The Birmingham Bullring Riots of 4 July 1839, the rejection of the first Chartist petition in July 1839, the Newport Rising where Gerard is arrested in November of the same year, and the use of the Plug Plot Riots of 1842 at the novel's conclusion enhance the context of protest. The difference from a writer like Tonna or Stone is not so much in the inclusions as in the nature of women novelists' decreased emphasis on historical grounding. The symbolic marriage of Sybil Gerard and Egremont represents one version of the alliance between the Norman and the Saxon, recalling the symbolic marriage at the end of *Michael Armstrong*. The characterization of the socialist Stephen Morley is marred when Disraeli attributes Morley's private failings to his ideology, a tendency exhibited earlier in Tonna's *Combination*. His exaggeration of Feargus O'Connor as Bishop Hatton suggests a similar tendency by Trollope. Disraeli has much in common with the practices of his female predecessors.

An important transitional author of the 1840s is Camilla Toulmin (1812–1895), a writer whose narratives *The Orphan Milliners. A Story of the West End* (1844) and *A Story of the Factories* (1846) indicate a continuity with previous protest literature and a tentative new direction of inquiry. Humphry House notes that Toulmin's work, now "forgotten," is part of the tradition of the late thirties and forties, "the period of Chartism, terrific unemployment, and angry strikes" (204). Edelstein reduces *The Orphan Milliners* to a story of "two parentless girls [who] come to London to become dressmakers; one subsequently dies of ensuing hardship, the other is saved by marriage" (189). This statement is not only misleading, it is also inaccurate, ignoring Toulmin's main tenet, the necessity of female economic independence, an idea emphasized in the later *A Story of the Factories* with its female factory manager.

The Orphan Milliners establishes the lack of foresight of the widow Mrs. Sandford, "one of those characters in whom feminine softness borders very decidedly on feminine weakness" (279). She imagines her two daughters, Henrietta and Anne, will marry and "thus be provided for, and protected. Too many mothers, who think little, think thus; and so neglect to cherish in those they love a spirit of self-reliance, or to place within their reach the means of self-dependence" (280). When Mrs. Sandford dies, leaving the girls with no education and no money, Henrietta and Anne are apprenticed to a dressmaker, Madame Dobière (Dobs). Their lack of marketable alternatives parallels the plight of Ellen Cardan in *The Young Milliner*. Like Tonna and Stone, Toulmin criticizes the women whose thoughtlessness forces seamstresses to work abominable hours: "What is so monstrous as woman with a hard heart? — and well do I believe that many who seem cruel, are only — thoughtless" (282). When Henrietta and Anne Sandford become salaried, they move out of Madame Dobière's establishment to a small apartment.

Like Miss Wells in *A London Dressmaker's Diary,* the girls take suburban excursions on Sunday, during which Henrietta meets Charles Morton, a young doctor. When on the verge of yielding to him, Henrietta sees a higher kind of love in a young bride she meets while on business. When she returns to the apartment, she learns that Morton is in fact her cousin, the son of a man who establishes the women in their own business near their home town away from London. Henrietta and Charles do not marry, but on the contrary realize that their union is impossible. Morton admits: "We know the truth — the very truth — 'tis best we part — you cannot be my wife. *I have never thought of you as my wife"* (285). As in *The Young Milliner,* the consanguinity indicates the interdependence of social classes. Toulmin notes that "Such heroines as mine measure life by the inner world of the feelings, not by moving accidents or romantic adventures. Henrietta has been three years in business" (285). Although Anne dies from her harsh experiences, Toulmin only suggests Henrietta will find a husband, "second love is sometimes a *better* love than first" (285). The story has not only the motive of exposing dressmaking conditions, which it does less incisively than *The Young Milliner* since it never examines slop-work. More significantly, *The Orphan Milliners* calls for female preparedness to face the rough economic conditions of the forties. Emphatically, it denies that the expectation of marriage can be a justification for the lack of training and education for young women. Toulmin's story argues beyond remediation of conditions in the dressmaking trade, exposing the danger of exclusive dependence on the needle as the economic solution to the plight of single destitute women.

Like *The Orphan Milliners, A Story of the Factories* reveals continuity with previous social literature while proving anticipatory of later social fictions. Toulmin describes three children from the country, Lucy, James, and David Butler, who come to Manchester to stay with their uncle William Morris after their father dies. Morris' house is a "sort of colony, in a manner not altogether unlike the old feudal system" near the factory. Morris' wife has left employment and now she can "superintend the domestic arrangements of *home*" (3–4). Toulmin describes the children as pleased to get employment in the Charlton cotton mill since they knew "the poor wages and poor living of an agricultural district." In a few pages Toulmin advances the argument about married women in the home and the distress in the agricultural districts that is as severe as in the cities, as Stone noted in *William Langshawe.* Both the issue of agricultural distress and the wife remaining at home after marriage probably came from Cooke Taylor, who noted: "Daughters from most of the houses, but wives . . . from none, worked in the factory" (32). "They told us in Dorsetshire that we were going to be white slaves; but what field labourer lives as uncle does here?" (7). This is similar to the realization Margaret Hale will experience later in *North and South.*

A Story of the Factories is an amalgamation of past and future aspects of the social novel. Toulmin believes in a combination of providence and self-help for the poor: "There is a spirit of humanity, enlightenment, and investigation abroad, which, if they will but help themselves, must, by the blessing of Providence, bring about changes conducive to their happiness and prosperity" (10–11). This is a response to the complaint registered in the National Petition that man had nullified the beneficence of providential guidance. In advancing the idea of self-help, Toulmin is in line with the argument of *William Langshawe* and anticipates fifties novels like *Marian Withers* and *John Halifax.* Her premise for writing recalls the similar objectives of Jewsbury in *Marian Withers* and Gaskell in *Mary Barton:* "Not all who hurry over some large establishment, where hundreds of men and women toil, pause to think each heart has its own mighty world of feelings, its struggles, passions, and temptations — that each has a separate soul" (20). There are several echoes of Disraeli's *Sybil.* James Butler becomes involved with a group of factory hands who as teenagers have set up independently, but Toulmin thinks this should not be touched by legislation, which would give parents even more abusive authority. This detail recalls the living circumstances of Dandy Mick and Julia from *Sybil.* The strike in *A Story of the Factories* is part of the Plug Plot Riots of August 1842, with which Disraeli had concluded *Sybil* and which Cooke Taylor had discussed in the second edition of *Notes of a Tour in the Manufacturing Districts.* As in *The Hill and the Valley,* the rioters destroy part of the machinery of the Charlton mill. Prefiguring the shielding of John Thornton by Margaret Hale in *North and South,* Margaret Brown protects Allan Douglas from the mob. Toulmin believes that "every step they take of violence or menace is a backward step, that hinders their real progress!" (32), a statement coming at the end of the tale that recalls Martineau. Toulmin's attitude that "the interests of the country so hang together, communities are so interlaced, that it is seldom indeed that one class can suffer without others participating" (15), closely suggests the preface to *Mary Barton* and Cooke Taylor's emphasis on the economic reciprocal consequences among operative, middle-class shopkeeper, and landed proprietor.

The most innovative aspect of *A Story of the Factories* is Toulmin's depiction of a female factory owner. During the winter of 1841 Charlton dies, and his wife becomes manager of the mill. The resourceful Mrs. Charlton is a positive counterpart to the helpless widow Mrs. Sandford in *The Orphan Milliners,* whose lack of self-reliance leads to the destitute condition of her daughters, who are thus compelled to become seamstresses at her death. The accountant Allan Douglas assists Mrs. Charlton through a riot, machine-breaking, and renewal. The study of a female manager is a precedent for Shirley Keeldar in Brontë's *Shirley* several years later. This is an acceptable mode of conduct for Mrs. Charlton, since she is a widow, but when Lucy marries Allan Douglas she leaves work to become a housekeeper. By showing the fluctuations, private and public, of its characters *A Story of the Factories* reflects "the anxieties of the forties" (Burn 73). Its female factory manager is an innovation. Its concentration on female factory workers is anticipated only by Tonna. Wanda Neff notes: "Disraeli does not make Sybil a worker in Trafford's mill, where in real life she would have been, and Mrs. Gaskell keeps Mary Barton from following the trade of her father, her mother, and aunt. The factory girl lacked all qualifications for the ideal Victorian heroine" (86). Despite this obstacle, Toulmin's *A Story of the Factories* does attempt to mark new areas of investigation, aspects of which will appear in Gaskell, Jewsbury, Craik, and Brontë.

In the history of the social novel, 1847, a year including the passage of the Ten Hours Bill, unemployment in textiles, and cholera, is important for the appearance of Elizabeth Gaskell's tale *Libbie Marsh's Three Eras* in *Howitt's Journal.* Married to William Gaskell, a Unitarian minister and the son of a manufacturer, Elizabeth Gaskell (1810–1865) brought to Manchester upon her marriage in 1832 experience of living in Knutsford (in actuality not far from Manchester but still "south"). This status supplied the observer's steadiness as well as the participant's ardour to her depictions of industrial life. In the tradition of the social novel, she was to be different from her predecessors both male and female. Unlike Tonna she could argue without sectarian and theological dogmatism, although she may have read her predecessor's work. Unlike Disraeli she had personal knowledge of conditions. Death was an experience she could view with a detachment alien to Dickens or Tonna, more in the manner of Stone. Without arguing from a theoretical bias, as did Trollope or Disraeli, Gaskell advocated a humanitarian, not solely legislative, interventionism that embraced individual effort and government programs. Because she knew factories, mills, prisons, and ragged schools, she emphasized personal experience and response. She wrote to Eliza Fox in 1849 about *Mary Barton:* "I told the story according to a fancy of my own; to really SEE the scenes I tried to describe, (and they WERE as real as my own life at the time)" (Chapple 82).

Unlike Dickens, Tonna, and Trollope, Gaskell refrains from indictments, avoiding the artificiality caused by overwriting. From her earliest work, it is the person rather than the occupation that is stressed. Gaskell assumes that the reader knows the technical terms of a profession like dressmaking. Her characters are no longer defined by their work but by the relationship of that work to multiple factors of daily life. By this broadening of context, she avoids the stridency of earlier social fiction, which abstracted work from a complete experience. The passage of legislation like the Ten Hours Bill and the Public Health Act permitted her to be free from the constraints of her polemical predecessors. Tonna would allow no love interest to her operatives, but Gaskell does. Unlike Tonna Gaskell alludes to evidence but never quotes it verbatim; unlike Trollope her issues are more comprehensive. She is interested in altering a state of mind, not only the conditions of a profession. Her achievement rests on two particular strengths: the ability to create a narrative voice that is not immediately identified with the author (as occurred in Tonna or Trollope), and the ability to endow her narratives with a gradual rather than episodic rhythm of revelation. In her novels the climaxes accumulate rather than surprise. Two stories published pseudonymously in 1847, *Libbie Marsh's Three Eras* and *The Sexton's Hero,* reveal the strengths of the narrative voice and this gradual rhythm of revelation.

Libbie Marsh is a solitary needlewoman changing homes in Manchester. Gaskell constructs her tale around the events of a single year, beginning in November and continuing through Valentine's Day, Whitsuntide, and Michaelmas. The story scarcely concerns Libbie's work life. For Gaskell the central concern of the story is the woman's forming a connection with a crippled boy, Frank Hall, and his mother. She emphasizes the growth in understanding between the two women, despite the latter's acerbic temperament, after the boy's death. The narrator is identified as one who speaks about "our neighbourhood" (459), which establishes her authoritative but sympathetic understanding as well as her distinction from Gaskell.

Libbie lives an anonymous existence. People do not have "leisure to think of the little workwoman, excepting when they wanted gowns turned, carpets mended, or household linen darned" (460). She is no beauty, as the narrator observes: "You can hardly live in Manchester without having some idea of your personal appearance; the factory lads and lasses take good care of that; and if you meet them at the hours when they are pouring out of the mills, you are sure to hear a good number of truths, some of them combined with such a spirit of impudent fun that you can scarcely keep from laughing, even at the joke against yourself" (461). It is this narrative position which marks Gaskell's progress in the social narrative. There is sharp detail about domestic behavior: "They were fine spinners, in the receipt of good wages; and confined all day in an atmosphere ranging from seventy-five to eighty degrees. They had lost all natural, healthy appetite for simple food, and having no higher tastes, found their greatest enjoyment in their luxurious meals" (461–62), a telling incident of "the 'improvidence' of the married operative as a housekeeper" (Hewitt 71).

On Valentine's Day, her own birthday, Libbie sends Frank Hall, whom she has noticed outside her window, a canary. The fact that the canary was taken into mines to warn of danger is never mentioned, but the idea of captivity and foreboding is suggested. The second of Libbie's eras occurs on Whitsuntide, when Libbie makes an excursion with Margaret Hall and her son to Dunham Park outside Manchester. Important events in the growth of sympathy occur. Mrs. Dixon and Mrs. Hall, formerly on bad terms, are reconciled. Dixon and his friends carry Frank to view the distant city: "You might see the motionless cloud of smoke hanging over a great town, and that was Manchester — ugly, smoky Manchester; dear, busy, earnest, noble-working Manchester; where their children had been born, and where, perhaps, some lay buried" (477).

After Frank's death Libbie goes to live with Margaret Hall. Anne Dixon comes to appreciate Libbie after calling her an old maid. She advises the girl against marrying a man who drinks, since her own father abused her mother and killed her brother in a drunken fit. Gaskell introduces this detail gradually, but it is central: it explains that Frank is both son and brother to the childless woman. "As I know I'm never likely to have a home of my own, or a husband that would look to me to make all straight, or children to watch over or care for, all which I take to be a woman's natural work, I must not lose time in fretting and fidgetting after marriage, but just look about me for somewhat else to do . . . just looking around for the odd jobs God leaves in the world for such as old maids to do" (484). Gaskell in *Libbie Marsh's Three Eras* has isolated a type of figure confirmed in the 1851 Census, which found that 30% of women were unmarried and another 13% widowed (Showalter, "Craik" 12). Libbie Marsh's significance transcends her occupation, since her portrayal is not of a comic or mocked "old maid" but of, simply, an "unmarried woman."

Later in 1847 Gaskell published *The Sexton's Hero,* which reveals some of the same strengths: the gradual growth of sympathetic understanding, and the endurance of a difficult moral lesson, this time in a male first-person narrative persona. This story Gaskell allowed F. D. Maurice and Kingsley to reprint in the *Christian Socialist.* Its aim is to redefine the term "hero," to redefine it after Carlyle's *On Heroes and Hero-Worship* (1841). The Sexton, John Knipe, now an old man, tells how he and Gilbert Dawson cared for the same woman. Knipe challenged him to fight, which Dawson refused. Ostracized by his fellows and rejected by the woman Letty, who turns her attention to Knipe, Dawson becomes an isolated man. Gaskell skillfully contrasts the two men, the cocky Knipe and the courageous but pacific Dawson, who thinks "it is wrong to quarrel, and use violence" (493).

One night after Knipe marries Letty, Dawson rescues them on the quicksands, losing his own life. Dawson tells Knipe, "You are a husband and a father. No one cares for me" (499). After Dawson's death, Knipe receives his bible, in which several texts are marked with his carpenter's pencil, suggesting Dawson's function as a Christ figure. Gaskell records a growth of feeling in the rough narrator in which the listener and the reader participate. The strength in the portrayal of male characters in this story shows Gaskell's progress in distancing herself as a narrator.

With these experiments behind her, Gaskell commenced her first extended narrative, the novel *Mary Barton* (1848). Gaskell's original title for the novel was *A Manchester Love Story,* and she retained *A Tale of Manchester Life* as her subtitle. This subtitle indicates the true concern of the novel. Mary Barton exists as a means of focusing the men's interest, that of her father, of the younger Carson, Jem Wilson, and Job Legh. With the exception of her bringing Will Wilson to save Jem at his trial, her function in the novel is more structural than contextual, although Gaskell does illuminate a working girl's consciousness. Gaskell's alternative title for the novel, *John Barton,* locates her emphasis as stated in the Preface: "I bethought me how deep might be the romance in the lives of some of those who elbowed me daily in the busy streets of the town in which I resided" (lxxix). The idea for this detail may have come from Cooke Taylor: "Every person who passes you in the street has the look of thought and the step of haste" (9). Gaskell may also be refuting the footnote Peter Gaskell added to his work in 1836: "In Manchester, Stockport, and other places similarly circumstanced, respectable females never pass along the streets during the period of [the operatives] going to and returning from work" (113). The genesis of *Mary Barton,* she asserts, was "the streets."

She believes "it is not for me to judge" (lxxx). Gaskell's idea of labor relations is that "those so bound to each other by common interests, as the employers and employed must ever be" must reach a humanitarian accord. This was a widely current idea. In 1834 Tufnell had noted: "A complete separation of feeling seems to have taken place between masters and men. Each party looks on the other as an enemy, and suspicion and distrust have driven out the mutual sentiments of kindness and good-will" (97). Angus Reach noted that for masters and men it is their "best interest . . . to be mutual friends" (*Manchester* 11), and Cooke Taylor had added: "The increasing harmony between the employers and the employed must be fostered and encouraged by every possible means" (286). Gaskell claims to "know nothing of Political Economy" to distinguish herself from Martineau, yet she had read Adam Smith. The reviewer in the *Westminster Review* specifically interpreted *Mary Barton* in terms of the theory of political economy, perceiving it in continuity with Martineau's work. The narrator's voice in the novel echoes the tone of the Preface: "So much for generalities. Let us now return to individuals" (200). This statement indicates one of Gaskell's differences from her predecessors, a concentration on individuals rather than ideologues. During 1839–1841, she notes there was much "bad feeling between working men and the upper classes." She characterizes "this feeling of alienation between the different classes of society" as "so impossible to describe . . . that I will not attempt it" (94–95). Sounding like Toulmin or Jewsbury she declares: "You cannot . . . read the lot of those who daily pass you by in the street. How do you know the wild romances of their lives; the trials, the temptations they are even now enduring, resisting, sinking under?" (69). So effective was this noncensorious narrative voice that the *Athenaeum* stated of the novel, "The truth of it is terrible" (1050).

Gaskell's accomplishment in *Mary Barton* is to locate the expression of social conditions within the consciousness of her characters. This is effected by the deliberately gradual development of John Barton and to a lesser extent his daughter. Gaskell's technique distinguishes Barton from his friend George Wilson as the two wander through the fields at the opening of the novel. The detail of walking in fields is not solely of Gaskell's observation, as Dodd in *The Factory System Illustrated* observed that workers on Sundays avoided worship and instead walked outside the city. When Barton invokes the parable of Dives and Lazarus, Wilson notes, "Thou never could abide the gentlefolk" (8). On the death of Barton's wife, the narrator comments: "One of the good influences over John Barton's life had departed that night. One of the ties which bound him down to the gentle humanities of earth was loosened, and henceforward the neighbours all remarked he was a changed man" (22). The inclusion of the detail of the neighbors relieves the narrative of any special pleading. Barton joins a trades' union, but it is the death of his wife that provides one reason for his eventual decision to be involved in the murder of young Carson, a personal rather than political motive. The reader learns that his son had died of scarlet fever during a trade depression, an additional personal detail contributing to Barton's attitudes.

Later, Barton's motivation becomes political as well as personal. He states that since labor is the workers' capital, "we ought to draw interest on that" (72). This political motivation is reinforced when Parliament rejects the first Chartist petition in 1839. In addition to these personal and political motivations, Gaskell introduces Barton's use of opium "to relieve him from the terrible depression its absence occasioned" (140). Fielden had noted that among workers "exciting drink and opium-eating are but too often resorted to for relief" (28). By the time Barton draws the lot to be Carson's assassin, Gaskell has constructed gradually a man's psyche so assailed by political, personal, and physical factors that it will accept the commission.

Mary Barton's emerging self-awareness is treated with a similar gradualness of revelation, beginning when Mary rejects Jem Wilson: "It was as if two people were arguing the matter; that mournful desponding communion between her former self, and her present self. Herself, a day, an hour ago; and herself now. For we have every one of us felt how a very few minutes of the months and years called life, will sometimes suffice to place all time past and future in an entirely new light. . . . Her plan had been, as we well know, to marry Mr. Carson, and the occurrence an hour ago was only a preliminary step. True; but it had unveiled her heart to her; it had convinced her she loved Jem above all persons or things. But Jem was a poor mechanic" (149–50). Mary's journey to Liverpool partakes of the adventure that was permitted to motherless heroines, as Nightingale noted in *Cassandra.*

It also provides Gaskell an opportunity to show mental stress: "A kind of nightmare dread and belief came over her, that every thing animate and inanimate was in league against her one sole aim and object of overtaking Will" (341). Mary's perception of the world is recorded starkly: "The gloomy leaden sky — the deep, dark waters below, of a still heavier shade of colour — the cold, flat, yellow shore in the distance, which no ray lightened up — the nipping, cutting wind. . . . She shivered with her depression of mind and body" (345). This emphasis on mental depression, frequently recorded by Cooke Taylor and other critics, exposes a working girl's inner life. The strangest metamorphosis of Mary occurs when she has learned of Jem's acquittal and becomes temporarily mad, like Ellen Cardan of *Jessie Phillips.* For a moment Mary has become a child: "She smiled gently, as a baby does when it sees its mother tending its little cot; and continued her innocent, infantine gaze into his face as if the sight gave her much unconscious pleasure. But by-and-by a different expression came into her sweet eyes, a look of memory and intelligence." (404). Mary passes from being the heroic rescuer of her lover to the tractable wife, having had her Browningesque single great moment. Gaskell will do mental prostration better with *Lizzie Leigh, North and South,* and *Sylvia's Lovers.*

To prevent an artificial focusing on the father and daughter, Gaskell constructs reflectors of her central characters. Although the reader learns of Mary's engagement by the milliner Miss Simmonds, only later, through the character of Margaret, does one learn of the hardships of needlework. Other female characters further define Mary. Alice Wilson presents the case of two previous generations. She left the farm when it could not support all the adults and came to the city for work, like the characters in *The Wrongs of Woman* or *A Story of the Factories.* She remained because she could not be a burden to her father. Gaskell portrays the woman's recollection of the rural world without criticizing the fact that Alice never returned to test her fantasies. It was known that in fact conditions were more severe in agricultural than factory districts. Cooke Taylor found workers who would endure any privation "with an iron endurance which nothing can bend, rather than be carried back to an agricultural district" (8). One woman, "being asked whether she would like to go back to the south, said she would rather be transported" (199). Gaskell creates Mary's Aunt Esther, who has gone on the streets. The object of John Barton's hatred, Esther nevertheless warns Jem Wilson of Mary's dalliance with Carson. Gaskell does not deliver a homiletic on prostitution but rather integrates the character into the narrative by having her function transcend her status.

The male characters, like the elder Carson, Job Legh, and Jem Wilson, are created with the insight already exhibited in *The Sexton's Hero.* In one of Gaskell's strongest scenes, anticipating the mother/ son confrontation of *North and South,* Jem declares his intention to marry Mary Barton. "For an instant his mother was interested by his words; and then came back the old jealousy of being supplanted in the affections of that son. . . . She hardened her heart against entertaining any feeling of sympathy; and turned away from the face, which recalled the earnest look of his childhood, when he had come to her in some trouble, sure of help and comfort" (397). Gaskell records several pages of dialogue, only gradually allowing the two to be reconciled. At the end of the novel, Carson Senior holds the dead Barton in an industrial version of the Pietà. Such an association "puts the members of the two classes in a *personal* relationship untypical of the *cash-nexus* relationship of reality" (J. Mitchell 261). Gaskell's symbolic association does not lose contact with reality because of the novel's gradual exposition.

The structuring of the novel is one of Gaskell's strongest achievements. While *Mary Barton* is criticized for becoming a *roman policier,* Gaskell integrates the presentation of working class life into her criminal drama by having the occasion of the crime be well-motivated in the case of Barton. By having the opposition of revenge and brotherhood operate in both the industrial and the criminal aspects of her novel, she effects textual fusion. When Mary discovers early that her father is the murderer, the stress of events is on mental revolution rather than on the process of detection. Gaskell presents the classes adroitly: the reader encounters Carson and his son only when George Wilson goes to ask help for a distressed worker, Ben Davenport. The structure of the novel is facilitated because Gaskell's social revelations, such as the poor housing conditions, arise with the same gradualness as the unfolding of her narrative events. For example, the filthy conditions of cellar life are depicted as a fact of the Davenports' existence, not as a statistic: "You went down one step even from the foul area into the cellar in which a family of human beings lived. It was very dark inside. The window-panes, many of them, were broken and stuffed with rags, which was reason enough for the dusky light that pervaded the place even at mid-day. After the account I have given of the street, no one can be surprised that on going into the cellar inhabited by Davenport, the smell was so foetid as almost to knock the two men down" (65–66). The reader enters the hovel with Barton, Wilson, and the narrator, not with a polemicist. While Chadwick, Peter Gaskell, Dodd, and Kay all might have contributed such detail, the effect is disciplined by the narrative strategy.

When Gaskell writes about the working woman's lack of domestic knowledge, already noted in *The Wrongs of Woman,* she introduces the subject through Jane Wilson: "If you'll believe me, Mary, there never was such a born goose at housekeeping as I were; and yet he married me! . . . And yet I'd no notion how to cook a potato. I know'd they were boiled, and I know'd their skins were taken off, and that were all. . . . [Girls] oughtn't to go at after they're married, that I'm very clear about. I could reckon up' (counting with her finger), 'ay nine men, I know, as has been driven to th' public-house by having wives as worked in factories; good folk, too, as thought there was no harm in putting their little ones out at nurse, and letting their house go all dirty, and their fires all out; and that was a place as was tempting for a husband to stay in was it? He soon finds out gin-shops, where all is clean and bright, and where th' fire blazes cheerily, and gives a man a welcome as it were" (136–37). Unlike the pleading of Tonna in *The Wrongs of Woman,* Gaskell's points are made through observation and documents but not by dependence on them. Tillotson notes that *Sybil, Yeast,* and *Mary Barton* "were more precisely documented" (78) than the novels of Dickens and Thackeray, but the achievement of such dialogue in *Mary Barton* is the structuring of that documentation into a character's consciousness.

Gaskell emphasizes this individuating strategy to explain Barton's development: "Now there had been some by-play at this meeting, not recorded in the Manchester newspapers, which gave an account of the more regular part of the transaction" (212–13). Smith criticizes Gaskell for having Barton engage in a "totally untypical murder"

(*Nation* 221), but there is not only the precedent of Ashton's slaying in 1831 but also the fact that Gaskell motivates this slaying on triple grounds, private, physical, and political, to justify its inclusion. Gaskell's work is marked by the "slow-moving, expository opening chapters" (Tillotson 214) that introduce the method of the entire text. *Mary Barton* had an impact because in 1848 the failure of the American cotton crop caused layoffs in Britain. Gaskell records a statistical datum, the dependence of Lancashire on American cotton, previously noted in Cooke Taylor for example, transforming it into a vital fact in the year of publication. Readers were not viewing past conditions as they had in *Michael Armstrong*, the *Memoir of Robert Blincoe*, or *William Langshawe*. In contrast to the contemporaneous events of *Mary Barton*, however, Charlotte Brontë the following year in *Shirley* was to revert to the Luddite years 1811–1812.

Although Asa Briggs has contended that *Shirley* "is not, of course, a social novel which falls into the same category as . . . *Mary Barton* or *North and South*" ("Private" 206), several of its themes recall preceding social fiction such as *William Langshawe, A Manchester Strike, The Hill and the Valley, A Story of the Factories,* and *The Wrongs of Woman.* As Sutherland argues, "It was the social problem novel . . . which attracted her [Brontë] when she had a completely free hand with her publisher" (80). In *Shirley,* like Stone in *William Langshawe* or later Jewsbury in *Marian Withers,* Charlotte Brontë (1816–1855) pursued an historical perspective by writing a retrospective tale, that of the Luddite rebellion during 1811 and 1812. While the recreation of an historical period in *Shirley* is valuable, it is more significant because it creates a mythos about women. By the time of its appearance the first women's suffrage pamphlet had been issued in 1847. An interest in the role of the middle-class woman, and her search for a function in the society altered by industrialism, makes the novel important beyond its historical recreation. In *Shirley* Brontë links an exploration of industrial conditions to the question of women's role in society. Although Robert Martin contends that "the concentration of the novel remains steadfastly on the individual not the nation" (136), Brontë's purpose is rather the symbiosis between them. The central theme of the novel is transition, from domestic to factory system, from woman as wife to woman as searcher. The book parallels the two subjects, the industrial and the female, achieving an uneasy synthesis.

Writing of the novel in 1850, G. H. Lewes declared: "The unity of *Jane Eyre* in spite of its clumsy and improbable contrivances, was great and effective. . . . But in *Shirley* all unity, in consequence of defective art, is wanting. There is no passionate link; nor is there any artistic fusion, or intergrowth, by which one part evolves itself from another. . . . The various scenes are gathered up into three volumes, —they have not grown into a work" (159). One may argue that Brontë has achieved greater fusion of her ideas than Lewes suggests. The principal difficulty of the text is that the industrial issue is of the book's fictive time (1811–1812), the female issue of its compositional time (1848–1849). Further complicating the problem is the fact that Brontë's attitudes about both subjects are contradictory. It is the divergence of compositional and fictive time that prevents a complete artistic integration.

The contradictions of the novel originate in the opening paragraphs, which reflect a discrepancy between assertion and practice: "If you think, from this prelude, that anything like a romance is preparing for you, reader, you never were more mistaken. . . . Calm your expectations; reduce them to a lowly standard. Something real, cool, and solid, lies before you; something unromantic as Monday morning, when all who have work wake with the consciousness that they must rise and betake themselves thereto. It is not positively affirmed that you shall not have a taste of the exciting, perhaps towards the middle and close of the meal, but it is resolved that the first dish set upon the table shall be . . . cold lentiles and vinegar without oil; it shall be unleavened bread with bitter herbs, and no roast lamb" (7–8). In working out *Shirley* Brontë did not eschew romance. She does, as the paragraph suggests, use the idea of a "meal" and hunger as a central motif throughout the novel, linking the hunger of the Luddites with that of women searching for a meaningful existence. At the conclusion she comments: "Whenever you present the actual, simple truth, it is, somehow, always denounced as a lie" (722). In dealing with her two subjects, she employs the actual to detail the Luddites, the mythic to depict her contradictory ideas about the role of women. Before a consideration of the possible resolution of the two ideas, the contradiction in each subject indicates the problem of the text.

The period of *Shirley* is the era of the Luddite Rebellion in Yorkshire and its social consequences. Asa Briggs notes of the Luddites that "their motive was not simply ill-considered hostility to machinery as such (this certainly played its part) but a desire to resist wage reductions and to demonstrate workers' solidarity *vis-à-vis* their employers." During 1811, for example, Arkwright's factory was attacked in

April and two weeks later William Horsfall, a mill-owner, was murdered. In January 1813, fourteen men were executed, including the murderers of Horsfall. The government "employed an army against them as large as that which Wellington was leading in the Peninsular War" (Briggs, "Private" 182). Brontë sent for the files of the Leeds *Mercury* for 1812–1814 to do research. She also incorporated the recollections of others, including her father. The origin of the disturbances, as Robert Moore notes in the novel, was the Continental System established by Napoleon, forbidding trade with Britain. Retaliating with the Orders in Council of 1807, the British had nearly destroyed the balance of trade by 1811. The Orders in Council were resented, therefore, by many manufacturers. The attitude toward the Luddites is embodied in Robert Moore, who brings in machinery to meet competition: "I only wish the machines — the frames were safe here, and lodged within the walls of this mill. Once put up, I defy the framebreakers: let them only pay me a visit, and take the consequences: my mill is my castle. . . . I am very rich in cloth I cannot sell. . . . America used to be their market, but the Orders in Council have cut that off" (30–31). The relationship of industry to America was not a dead issue in 1849. Cooke Taylor shows that the inaccessibility of American markets from the Corn Laws, only recently repealed when *Shirley* was published, was a bitter annoyance during the forties, which the failure of the American cotton crop in 1848 aggravated.

The narrator explains: "Not being a native . . . [Moore] did not sufficiently care when the new inventions threw the old work-people out of employ: he never asked himself where those to whom he no longer paid weekly wages found daily bread; and in this negligence he only resembled thousands besides, on whom the starving poor of Yorkshire seemed to have a closer claim" (36). This statement confuses the issue, contending that because Moore is not completely English he is unconcerned. Moore tells a workman: "If I stopped by the way an instant, while others are rushing on, I should be trodden down" (154). It is the pressure of competition, not his foreign blood, that prompts his attitude. To Caroline Helstone he admits that he is two men: "I find in myself . . . two natures; one for the world and business, and one for home and leisure. Gérard Moore is a hard dog, brought up to the mill and the market: the person you call your cousin Robert is sometimes a dreamer, who lives elsewhere than in Cloth-hall and counting-house" (287). Charlotte Brontë depicts the splitting of the personality in the managerial class in a manner that recalls the transitional formation of the managers in *William Lang-shawe*. The contradiction in the industrial sections of the novel origi-nates from events of the period itself. Briggs has noted that "men who opposed the war against Napoleon and the policies of the Brit-ish Government (symbolised in the Orders-in-Council) . . . at the same time . . . demanded stricter government intervention to suppress machine wrecking and attacks on property" (214). Brontë raises the problem of the limits of government intervention, showing the in-consistency of both its adherents and its opponents.

After the attack on his mill, Moore travels to London and Birming-ham to pursue the perpetrators. He does learn from the experience, but the contradiction remains: "While I was in Birmingham, I looked a little into reality, considered closely, and at their source, the causes of the present troubles of this country; I did the same in London. Unknown, I could go where I pleased, mix with whom I would. I went where there was want of food, of fuel, of clothing; where there was no occupation and no hope. . . . I saw many originally low, and to whom lack of education left scarcely anything but animal wants, disappointed in those wants, ahungered, athirst, and desperate as fam-ished animals: I saw what taught my brain a new lesson, and filled my breast with fresh feelings . . . I should resist a riotous mob just as heretofore: I should open on the scent of a runaway ringleader as eagerly as ever, and run him down as relentlessly . . . but I should do it now chiefly for the sake and the security of those he misled. Something there is to look to . . . beyond a man's personal interest. . . . To respect himself, a man must believe he renders justice to his fellow-men" (616). The debate about interventionism is particularly interesting because by the time of the novel's composition interven-tionism was an accepted fact of existence.

The reviewer in the *Athenaeum* was clear about one subject of *Shirley:* "Both [Caroline Helstone and Shirley Keeldar] suffer from the malady of unrest and dissatisfaction, — on the prevalence of which among women of the nineteenth century so many protests have been issued, so many theories of 'emancipation' have been set forth" (1107). *Shirley* is part of a period which saw such events as the establishment in 1847 of the first evening school for women in Birmingham, a period when women were searching for a functional place in society. Korg comments that "the feminist doctrines which the novel preaches so ardently are a form of its romantic egoism" (128), but this is not so. Brontë's novel, in the context of changes in women's status during the forties, creates instead three myths about the status of women, myths not consonant with one another.

The first, rather generalized, is the tale of the scorpion: "A lover masculine so disappointed can speak and urge explanation; a lover feminine can say nothing: if she did the result would be shame and anguish, inward remorse for self-treachery. . . . Take the matter as you find it: ask no questions; utter no remonstrances: it is your best wisdom. You expected bread, and you have got a stone; break your teeth on it, and don't shriek because the nerves are martyrized: do not doubt that your mental stomach . . . is strong as an ostrich's — the stone will digest. You held out your hand for an egg, and fate put into it a scorpion. Show no consternation: close your fingers firmly upon the gift; let it sting through your palm. Never mind: in time, after your hand and arm have swelled and quivered long with torture, the squeezed scorpion will die and you will have learned the great lesson how to endure without a sob" (117–18). Brontë introduces the same idea of starvation and hunger with which the novel opened at the clerics' dinner. In her first myth the woman is enduring, suffering.

The second myth, of the Eve-Titaness, is considerably different. In his review of *Shirley* Lewes commented, "There is a really remarkable tirade about Milton's Eve" (166). The Eve myth is actually comparable to the idea of the Female Savior found later in Nightingale's *Cassandra*. The Eve myth is one aspect of the female image in the nineteenth century, the other being the Virgin Mary. The "mutation of the Eve myth into the Mary myth . . . implied a fundamental process of de-sexualization of the woman" (Basch 8). In Brontë, this myth is spoken by Shirley Keeldar, who has a masculine name: "The first men of the earth were Titans, and . . . Eve was their mother. . . . There were giants on the earth in those days: giants that strove to scale heaven. The first woman's breast that heaved with life on this world yielded the daring which could contend with Omnipotence. . . . The first woman was heaven-born. . . . I saw — I now see — a woman-Titan. . . . Her forehead has the expanse of a cloud, and is paler than the early moon. . . . So kneeling, face-to-face she speaks with God. That Eve is Jehovah's daughter, as Adam was his son. . . . I will stay out here with my mother Eve" (359–61). Brontë is denying the account of Milton's Eve, who sinned by eating.

The third myth involves a counter to the Titaness myth, the marriage of Humanity (female) and Genius (male). This appears in one of her old exercise books, which Shirley shows to her former tutor

Louis Moore. Genius is the longed-for "Bridegroom" who takes "his dying bride . . . restored her . . . to Jehovah" (552–53). This myth contradicts the myths of the scorpion-sufferer and of the Eve-Titaness. The three myths are contradictory, albeit each is a depiction of an alternative: suffering, power, or submission. The three reflect the contradictory aspects of women's position in the decade. At the conclusion of the novel, when Shirley marries Louis Moore and Caroline marries his brother, Brontë removes but does not resolve the problems suggested in these myths, which partake of the forties rather than the second decade of the century.

Caroline Helstone is searching for a meaning to her existence and an occupation. She tells Moore: "As to the life I am destined for, I cannot tell: I suppose, to keep my uncle's house, till . . . events offer other occupations. . . . I am making no money—earning nothing. . . . I should like an occupation; and if I were a boy, it would not be so difficult to find one . . . I could be apprenticed to your trade—the cloth trade" (81). How close this is to Brontë's time is suggested by this passage from Margaretta Grey's *Diary* in 1853: "But what I remonstrate against is the negative forms of employment: the wasting of energy, the crippling of talent under false ideas of station, propriety, and refinement. . . . Life is too often divested of any real and important purpose. . . . It is time to rise out of this, and for women of principle and natural parts to find themselves something to do" (Black, *Victorian* 188–89). In a chapter entitled "Old Maids," Caroline reflects: "I shall not be married, it appears. . . . I suppose, as Robert does not care for me, I shall never have a husband to love, nor little children to take care of. . . . What was I created for, I wonder? Where is my place in the world?" (194). In the figures of the two old maids in *Shirley,* Miss Mann and Miss Ainley, however, Brontë does something "very different from the former comic spinster" (Tillotson 115). Caroline's idea of being a governess is opposed both by her uncle and by Mrs. Pryor, Shirley's governess, who turns out to be Caroline's mother. The narrator's view is not pleasant: "Men rarely like such of their fellows as read their inward nature too clearly and truly. It is good for women, especially, to be endowed with a soft blindness: to have mild, dim eyes, that never penetrate below the surface of things—that take all for what it seems: thousands, knowing this, keep their eyelids drooped, on system" (307).

In a long monologue, a protest about women's lot in the nineteenth century, Caroline speculates about her role: "I feel there is something wrong somewhere. I believe single women should have more to do — better chances of interesting and profitable occupation than they possess now. . . . The brothers of these girls are every one in business or in professions; they have something to do: their sisters have no earthly employment, but household work and sewing; no earthly pleasure, but an unprofitable visiting; and no hope, in all their life to come, of anything better. . . . The great wish — the sole aim of every one of them is to be married, but the majority will never marry: they will die as they now live. . . . The gentlemen turn them into ridicule . . . the matrimonial market is overstocked . . . Could men live so themselves?" (441–42). Lewes cited this passage, noting with some justification the "want of keeping in making the gentle, shy, not highly cultivated Caroline *talk* from time to time in the strain of Currer Bell herself rather than in the strain of Helstone's little niece" (165). The monologue does convey Brontë's protest if not artistically her character's.

Shirley Keeldar expresses a parallel concern: "If men could see us as we really are, they would be a little amazed; but the cleverest, the acutest men are often under an illusion about women: they do not read them in a true light; they misapprehend them, both for good and evil: their good woman is a queer thing, half doll, half angel; their bad woman almost always a fiend. . . . Women read men more truly than men read women" (395–96). While Briggs contends that the issue about women is "not related at all . . . to the Luddite background" (217), the two issues are connected. Both question the dependence on external authority that workers and women labor under, and the nature of occupation is significant for both worker and woman.

It is the idea of hunger that unites these two aspects of the novel. Just as Moore had become aware of the hunger of workers, the idea is introduced in relation to women in the opening chapter: men are feasting while women serve. Malone shouts at the housekeeper Mrs. Gale: "More bread." When she brings the loaf, he commands: "'Cut it woman,' . . . and the 'woman' cut it accordingly" (11). This seems to be not only symbolically effective but literally accurate. Clark notes of coarse clergymen that "there seem to have lasted well into the century a reasonable number of clerical grotesques" (*Making* 259). The narrator writes of Caroline: "She suffered, indeed, miserably: a few minutes before, her famished heart had tasted a drop and crumb of nourishment that, if freely given, would have brought back abundance

of life where life was failing; but the generous feast was snatched from
her, spread before another, and she remained but a bystander at the
banquet" (282). This idea had been introduced in the imagery of An-
dré Chénier's poem *La Jeune Captive* earlier in the novel. When
Caroline is ill, she cannot eat at all, attempting by anorexia to deny
the idea of Milton's Eve. Both women and workers starve.

In several passages Brontë links the situation of women and that
of workers. Caroline is aware that since she is a woman she is as excluded as a worker displaced by machinery. In a long debate with
Joe Scott, the overlooker at Moore's mill, Shirley discusses woman's
role, with Joe stating: "Let the woman learn in silence, with all subjection. I suffer not a woman to teach, nor to usurp authority over
the man; but to be in silence. For Adam was first formed, then Eve.
. . . Adam was not deceived; but the woman, being deceived, was in
the transgression. . . . [Women should] take their husbands' opinion,
both in politics and religion" (370–71). The use of religious sanction
for the capitalist exploitation of women is one of Brontë's insights
that remains unpursued.

At the conclusion Brontë consigns both women to marriage, despite the fact that marriage is shown to be unsatisfactory. The marriage of Caroline's uncle was difficult, and Shirley realizes that marrying would mean "I could never be my own mistress more" (242).
Caroline's own mother abandoned her. When speaking with Louis
Moore, whom she will marry, Shirley "found lively excitement in the
pleasure of making his language her own" (558), but it is in this trans-
ference of languages that Brontë's Shirley finally is married. She who
said men could not "read" women now adopts their language. Robert Moore can propose to Caroline only after the Orders in Council
are repealed. When Caroline describes Shirley's attachment to Louis
Moore, she says: "Whatever *I* am, Shirley is a bondswoman. Lioness!
She has found her captor. Mistress she may be of all round her – but
her own mistress she is not" (689). When Shirley accepts Louis Moore,
she says "I am glad I know my keeper" (711). (Keeper was the name
of Emily Brontë's dog.) "She was at last . . . fettered to a fixed day:
there she lay, conquered by love, and bound with a vow. . . . Her captor alone could cheer her; his society only could make amends for
the lost privilege of liberty: in his absence, she sat or wandered alone;
spoke little, and ate less" (729–30). The implication is that only the
man can feed her. Writing to John Forster about Charlotte Brontë's
forthcoming marriage to Arthur Nicholls, Elizabeth Gaskell com-

mented in April 1854: "She would never have been happy but with an exacting, rigid, law-giving, passionate man" (Chapple 281). Brontë's view of women in marriage in *Shirley* accords with the prevailing nature of marriage during the period. Best observes that the Victorian home "was normally a patriarchate, woman's place within it being subordinate." Only very slowly was the "woman's position . . . beginning to become a little less unenviable." The Eve myth in *Shirley* is only a remote ideal: "It was this desperate shortage of opportunity to survive socially outside the respectable home that compelled its wives, if they were wretched, to put up with their wretchedness, and . . . its daughters either to accept whatever offer of marriage they could get or to put up with lifelong dependent subservience to father and mother at home. For most middle and upper class girls who could not get married, *no other course was open*" (278, 281).

The disappointment one experiences at the conclusion of *Shirley* derives from an awareness of Brontë's different method of dealing with women's fulfillment in *The Professor,* which she had written in 1846. Although the narrator of the novel is a male, William Crimsworth, his experiences parallel some of those of Charlotte Brontë during her Brussels years. The theme of the novel is in fact work, as she declares in a Preface written after completing *Shirley:* "I said to myself that my hero should work his way through life as I had seen real living men work theirs — that he should never get a shilling he had not earned — that no sudden turns should lift him in a moment to wealth and high station . . . that he should not even marry a beautiful girl or a lady of rank" (xi).

The Professor opens with William Crimsworth's having to take employment at his brother Edward's mill in the north of England. Edward Crimsworth is the exacting, crude, unfeeling Captain of Industry, like Stone's Balshawe a tyrant to his simpleton wife. Of the valley where the mill is situated, the narrator notes that "steam, trade, machinery, had long banished from it all romance and seclusion. . . . A dense, permanent vapour brooded over this locality" (10). Edward Crimsworth is a "proud, harsh master" (14). William Crimsworth's circumstances are humiliating, and he expresses them by identifying partially with women: "I looked weary, solitary, kept down like some desolate tutor or governess" (17). Crimsworth rebels against this slavery, although he is a clerk and not a factory-hand: "Work? why should I work? . . . I cannot please though I toil like a slave" (33). William leaves his brother's establishment after being lashed with a whip and told to "get away to your parish, you pauper" (36). He declares, "I leave a prison, I leave a tyrant."

These experiences of work, although distressing, prove its value. When Crimsworth meets his future wife, Frances Henri, she is a teacher of needlework at a girls' boarding school in Brussels. Like the hero, the heroine "works." As a lace-mender "she had only her own unaided exertions to rely on" (152). Frances asks to retain her employment after their marriage. When Crimsworth observes that "You are laying plans to be independent of me," she responds: "Yes, Monsieur; I must be no incumbrance to you — no burden in any way" (199). She continues: "Think of my marrying you to be kept by you, Monsieur! I could not do it; and how dull my days would be! You would be away teaching . . . and I should be lingering at home, unemployed and solitary; I should get depressed and sullen, and you would soon tire of me. . . . I like a contemplative life, but I like an active better; I must act in some way, and act with you" (200). This Crimsworth eventually accepts: "I put no obstacle in her way; raised no objection; I knew she was not one who could live quiescent and inactive, or even comparatively inactive. Duties she must have to fulfill, and important duties; work to do — and exciting, absorbing, profitable work; strong faculties stirred in her frame, and they demanded full nourishment" (220). He realizes after several years that "I seemed to possess two wives," one the teacher, the other the wifely companion (223). In *The Professor* Brontë suggests a possible working out of dual roles for women: worker and wife. Although Crimsworth may be a fantasy of an understanding husband who recognizes his wife's needs, the novel advances an idea about women and work that *Shirley,* for all its historicism and mythic power, fails to embrace. Because Caroline and Shirley have money, work is not essential to their economic survival. An assessment of *Shirley* vis-à-vis *The Professor* indicates that the later novel is not so advanced in its presentation of actual working women as is its predecessor. Unlike Stone's seamstress in *The Young Milliner* who works for survival, Frances Crimsworth in *The Professor* works for her own fulfillment.

Shirley is the last of the significant social novels written by women during the forties. It anticipates the broadened issues of the fifties concerning women's role. It is not true that the novel remains unintegrated in its two emphases. The problem is that within each there is inherent contradiction: laissez-faire/interventionism regarding the industrial question, independence/submission in the case of women.

Brontë's novel attempted a synthesis of these two ideas and to some extent achieved it through the concepts of dependence and hunger. Each issue, however, is handled in a contradictory fashion. The uncongenial third person, adopted to universalize the range of issues, was not successful. She had been able in *Jane Eyre* to probe one lot, that of a governess, by a restricted pseudo-autobiography. Such a narrative form was too limited in implication for the issues she wished to present in *Shirley,* but her choice of method left the issues unresolved and contradictory. The affiliation of the work and the woman issues is suggested by the fact that Brontë sent a copy of *Shirley* to Martineau, whom she greatly admired. She may have known *The Rioters* from its reissue in 1842, and her mill owner has the same Christian name as Robert Wallace in *The Turn-out.* In the novel's industrial sections Martineau is a predecessor, and Lewes noted that in Caroline's monologue she "takes a leaf out of Miss Martineau's book" (166).

The last of the important social fictions of the decade, published just prior to and following *Shirley,* were written by Charles Kingsley (1819–1875). A comparison of *Yeast* (1848) and *Alton Locke* (1850) to *Shirley* indicates the transitional nature of the latter, for Kingsley's novels in their methodology look back to the period of the thirties and early forties. There are several similarities between the intentions of Kingsley and Brontë in *Shirley.* Most prominent is the place Kingsley gives to the idea of vocation in *Yeast,* particularly as it applies to Argemone Lavington and Lancelot Smith. Like Brontë, Kingsley is critical of the clergy in *Yeast* and especially in *Alton Locke.* The two novels, one written in third person, the other a fictive autobiography, demonstrate the use of different techniques, as do *Jane Eyre* and *Shirley.* Kingsley was at school in Bristol during the Reform riots of 1831, and later, having come under the influence of Carlyle like Lancelot Smith in *Yeast,* he joined forces with F. D. Maurice to promote Christian Socialism. As Buckley notes in *The Victorian Temper,* Kingsley's novels are "sociological fiction," unions of apocalyptic literature and social fiction (27). The two novels represent the transition of the social novel from the forties to the fifties.

Although revised and published as a book in 1851, *Yeast* was first serialized in *Fraser's Magazine* beginning in July 1848, the year of the final submission of the Chartist petition to Parliament (used in *Alton Locke*). The characters partake of the spokesman quality of persons in Tonna or Trollope. The son of a merchant, Lancelot Smith undergoes a commitment to social reform through acquaintance with Tregarva, the gamekeeper, and the socially-conscious Argemone Lavington. Recalling Martineau's practice from the thirties, the novel is a series of debates involving a sequence of characters who educate or miseducate Lancelot. As Smith notes in *The Other Nation,* his name symbolically embraces that of the old chivalric ideals and the common man, which suggests Kingsley's intention in the novel. Lancelot's cousin Luke with his Puseyism, his uncle Smith the banker with his Mammonism, the painter Claude Mellot with his aestheticism, Lord Vieuxbois with his policies about Young England, and Argemone's father with his traditional ideas about the squirearchy are all inadequate as Lancelot undergoes his pilgrim's progress in this *Bildungsroman.* Lancelot reads Blue Books, studies *Chartism,* and learns about the conditions of the poor. The narrator reflects that "the finest of us are animals after all, and live by eating and sleeping: and, taken as animals, not so badly off either — unless we happen to be Dorsetshire labourers — or Spitalfields weavers — or colliery children — or marching soldiers — or, I am afraid, one-half of English souls this day" (34). It is about that half that Lancelot becomes educated.

Some of Kingsley's most vivid writing in *Yeast* concerns depictions of conditions previously dealt with by women like Tonna. He disarms the reader, contrasting the superficial placidity of the country and its reality, for his purpose is to expose the conditions of the agricultural poor of England: "Of all the species of lovely scenery which England holds, none, perhaps, is more exquisite than the banks of the chalk-rivers — the perfect limpidity of the water, the gay and luxuriant vegetation of the banks and ditches, the masses of noble wood embosoming the villages, the unique beauty of the water-meadows, living sheets of emerald and silver. . . . There, if anywhere, one would have expected to find Arcadia among fertility, loveliness, industry, and wealth. But, alas for the sad reality! the cool breath of those glittering water-meadows too often floats laden with poisonous miasma. Those picturesque villages are generally the perennial hotbeds of fever and ague, of squalid penury, sottish profligacy, dull discontent too stale for words" (40–41). Tregarva disabuses Lancelot about the misleading placidity of rural Great Britain: "But the oppression that goes on all the year round, and the want that goes on all the year round, and the filth, and the lying, and the swearing, and the profligacy, that go on all the year round, and the sickening weight of debt, and the miserable grinding anxiety from rent-day to rent-day, and Saturday night to Saturday night, that crushes a man's soul down, and drives every thought out of his head but how he is to fill his stomach and warm his back, and keep a house over his head, till he daren't for his life take his thoughts one moment off the meat that perisheth — oh, sir, they never felt this" (47). While attending a rural festival, Lancelot begins to comprehend the devastation: "Everywhere waste? Waste of manure, waste of land, waste of muscle, waste of population — and we call ourselves the workshop of the world! . . . No wonder you have typhus here . . . with this filthy open drain running before the door" (191–92). Kingsley draws on several passages of the *Report on Agriculture* (1843) for his information.

Kingsley's studies of women in *Yeast* are not progressive but rather denigrating. Honoria Lavington is criticized for her charity, which is well-meant but uninformed: "She is an angel of holiness. . . . She sees people in want, and thinks it must be so, and pities them and relieves them. But she don't know want herself!" (47). Argemone Lavington, her sister, is shown to have intellectual pretensions: "But what was Argemone doing all this time? Argemone was busy in her boudoir . . . fancying herself, and not unfairly, very intellectual. She had four new manias every year; her last winter's one had been that bottle-and-squirt mania, miscalled chemistry; her spring madness was for the Greek drama" (28). Kingsley notes that Tennyson in *The Princess* (1847) "shows us the woman, when she takes her stand on the false masculine ground of intellect, working out her own moral punishment" (32). Once Argemone comes to understand Lancelot Smith, "she was matched, for the first time, with a man who was her own equal in intellect and knowledge; and she felt how real was that sexual difference which she had been accustomed to consider as an insolent calumny against woman" (127). In contrast to the female industrial novelists before him, however, Kingsley associates his women with poetry. Argemone authors a poem entitled *Sappho,* declaring that the poetess should find the universe "a dead picture, unsatisfying, unloving — as I have found it." Kingsley then adds: "Sweet self-deceiver! Had you no other reason for choosing as your heroine Sappho, the victim of the idolatry of intellect . . . ?" (33). Kingsley uses poetry to mock his visionary woman in *Yeast,* both distancing and demeaning his portrayal of women. Gaskell's *Mary Barton,* published in October 1848, used working-class poetic song, inadvertently thereby reproving Kingsley. Argemone's final poem, with its echoes of Shelley's *Epipsychidion,* elevates her in the reader's regard, despite Kingsley's appraisal of women in the novel. Argemone is a descendant of Frances Trollope's Mary Brotherton from *Michael Armstrong,* sabotaged however by her creator. Kingsley acknowledges the hunger of women for learning only to mock it from a masculine preserve. Later, when Kingsley has ceased to mock, Lancelot learns of the common wife-beating in the rural districts from Tregarva, who tells him there is no "escape" for the poor from a brutal alliance: "It's only you gentlefolks who can afford such luxuries; your poor man may be tied to a harlot, or your poor woman to a ruffian, but once done, done for ever" (187).

Kingsley focuses on sanitation in his indictment of the entire society, an effective tactic since typhus and cholera had returned to Britain in 1846–1847. Argemone Lavington dies from having visited a fever-ridden cottage, no longer wondering why men turn Chartist. The class issue is prevalent throughout *Yeast.* Tregarva tells Lancelot that there is an unpassable advantage for him in being a gentleman: "When you've lost all you have, and seven times more, you're still a gentleman. No man can take that from you. . . . Why should not the workman be a gentleman, and a workman still. . . . I had to curse the state of things which brings a man up a savage against his will." "All poor-laws, old or new either, suck the independent spirit out of a man; how they make the poor wretch reckless" (217–18, 174). The disadvantages of birth, he tells Lancelot, affect morality. "I think sometimes, if [Honoria] had been born and bred like her father's tenants' daughters, to sleep where they sleep, and hear the talk they hear, and see the things they see, what would she have been now?" (68). Lancelot is converted to a form of Christian socialism, following "Jesus Christ — THE MAN" (264) as the great social reformer. *Yeast,* like the novels of the thirties and the early forties, concentrates on a specific sector of abuse, the agricultural counties, using documents as Tonna did earlier and containing some of her apocalyptic rhetoric.

The year after the serialization of *Yeast,* the letters in the *Morning Chronicle* by Mayhew influenced Kingsley. In January 1850 he published *Cheap Clothes and Nasty,* an indictment based on some of Mayhew's material about conditions in tailoring. These included such subjects as sweating, the lowering of prices, and filthy conditions of labor. He associates the abuse of tailors with slavery: "We have, thank God, emancipated the black slaves; it would seem a not inconsistent sequel to that act to set about emancipating these white ones. . . . But indeed, if, as some preach, self-interest is the mainspring of all human action, it is difficult to see who will step forward to emancipate the said white slaves; for all classes seem to consider it equally their interest to keep them as they are" (lxxiii–lxxiv). The rich should fear wearing the garments made in disease-ridden dens: "Diseases numberless are carried home in these same garments from the miserable abodes where they are made" (lxxvii). Kingsley will use such an incident in *Alton Locke.* Recalling the opening paragraph of *Chartism,* Kingsley states that reform must be accomplished quickly, "for if it be not done by fair means, it will surely do itself by foul" (lxxxv). The tone of *Cheap Clothes and Nasty* is that of Tonna and Trollope from the thirties and early forties, and even of *The System* from the twenties.

Alton Locke is a complementary text to *Yeast.* The story is a *Bildungsroman* concerning a tailor-poet, Alton Locke, based on Kingsley's knowledge of persons like Gerald Massey, a working-class poet; and Thomas Cooper, the atheist Chartist poet and lecturer. Kingsley regarded the book as a revelation: "I have hopes from the book I am writing, which has revealed itself to me so rapidly and methodically that I feel it comes down from above," he wrote in February 1849 (xxv). Politically Alton is caught between two men, Mackaye and Crosswaithe, representatives respectively of moral-force and physical-force Chartism. In the course of the novel Alton, like Cooper, is imprisoned, in this instance for participating in agricultural rioting in 1845. When he is released he participates in the events of 10 April 1848, the third submission of the Chartist petition. Alton has a visionary conversion that leads him to see Jesus as the true demagogue, the reformer of Christian socialism.

In depictions of both urban and rural distress the novel is strong. Alton goes to St. Giles, as had Dickens, Tonna, and Engels before him: "It was a foul, chilly, foggy Saturday night. From the butchers' and greengrocers' shops the gas lights flared and flickered, wild and ghastly, over haggard groups of slip-shod dirty women. . . . Blood and sewer-water crawled from under doors and out of spouts, and reeked down the gutters among offal, animal and vegetable, in every stage of putrefaction. . . . Go, scented Belgravian! and see what London is!" (95). Kingsley presents the chamber of wretched seamstresses: "There was no bed in the room — no table. On a broken chair by the chimney sat a miserable old woman" whose daughter has become a prostitute: "I hate myself, and hate all the world because of it; but I must — I must — I cannot see her starve, and I cannot starve myself. . . . They never gave us out the work till too late on purpose, and then they lowered prices again" (98, 100). The portrait of these slopwork-ers is only slightly more dire than the circumstances shown by Stone in *The Young Milliner*. Unlike Stone, Kingsley has his protagonist travel outside the city, where he learns that conditions in the country are just as bad: "As we came up to the fold, two little boys hailed us from the inside — two little wretches with blue noses and white cheeks . . . 'Turmits is froze, and us can't turn the handle of the cut-ter'" (292–93). Later Kingsley depicts the Jacobs Island slum in Ber-mondsey that Dickens had used in *Oliver Twist,* and Alton learns that the "sewer is your only drinking water" (380). In these scenes, Kings-ley is the descendant of Tonna, giving the same attention to evidence. Kingsley in *Yeast* had praised Dickens as "our most earnest and genial novelist" (25), possibly because he perceived Dickens as a sincere so-cial critic. His real predecessors in the tradition of the social novel are, however, Stone and Tonna.

The treatment of religion in *Alton Locke* is similar to that in Ton-na's much earlier *Combination* with its skeptical workingmen. Alton realizes that "the burning thought arose in my heart that I was un-justly used; that society had not given me my rights" (52), and he proceeds to repudiate religion: "Religion? Nobody believes in it. The rich don't; or they wouldn't fill their churches up with pews, and shut the poor out, all the time they are calling them brothers. They believe the gospel? Then why do they leave the men who make their clothes to starve in such hells on earth as our workroom?" (58–59). Burn notes that the urban population included numbers who "were conscious secularists . . . or were estranged from organized religion" (273). Be-cause the protagonist's existence is linked through historical events to that of the nation, Kingsley's condemnation is extensive. It em-phasizes oppression of the mind, not merely oppressive occupations.

Although the first important social novel of the fifties, *Alton Locke* is the culmination of a tradition. Its emphasis on sources and on po-litical ideology are characteristic of the forties rather than the new direction the social novel would take in mid-century. Kingsley sum-marizes the practices of the female industrial novelists who preceded him in his narrative experimentation, use of data, focus on sanitary conditions, and exposure of specific trade abuses. His use of women as visionary figures, with Argemone Lavington in *Yeast* and Eleanor Staunton in *Alton Locke,* is derived from characters like Trollope's Mary Brotherton in *Michael Armstrong,* Martha Maxwell in *Jessie Phillips,* and Edith Langshawe in *William Langshawe.* As Thomson notes, Eleanor Staunton develops "from feudal queen to social worker" (27), but nevertheless she bears a closer similarity to Plato's Diotima than to a Charlotte Tonna pounding the streets of St. Giles. Kingsley emphasizes the contrast between those who are gentlemen by birth (Lancelot in *Yeast,* Lord Ellerton in *Alton Locke*) and those who are morally gentlemen (Tregarva, Alton), endorsing the upward mobility suggested by Stone. Like Disraeli, Kingsley uses fiction to advance specific political platforms. Unlike Tonna and Brontë, Kingsley is not concerned with women's role in society as functional individuals; instead, he regards them as priestesses. George Eliot recognized this difference. Although she praised the first volume of *Alton Locke* (among other novels) for doing "more . . . towards linking the higher classes with the lower, towards obliterating the vulgarity of exclusiveness, than . . . hundreds of sermons and philosophical dissertations," she criticized the "feebleness of his *dénouements*": "We prefer a partially borrowed beauty to an original bathos, which was what Mr. Kingsley achieved in the later chapters of 'Alton Locke' and 'Yeast'" (Pinney, 270, 128). Kingsley could sympathize nevertheless with acute distress in fiction, as he later wrote to Gaskell on the publication of *Ruth:* "I never heard but one unanimous opinion of the beauty and righteousness of the book and that, above all, from real ladies and really good women" (P. Thomson 134).

Reviewing *Alton Locke* in the *Athenaeum* Geraldine Jewsbury noted a marked change: "'Association' is the watchword of the new order of things which is beginning. The age of individualism is passing away" (946). Women novelists in the fifties were to be concerned with the consequences of "associationism" on the individual. The female social novel in the next decade broadened its contexts of inquiry beyond specific occupation. It is doubtful, however, if such progress would have occurred if works like *The Wrongs of Woman* and *The Young Milliner* had not been written. The character of Edith Langshawe in *William Langshawe,* of Mrs. Charlton in *A Story of the Factories,* and the mythopoeic intention of *Shirley* show in the forties some of the tendencies developed in the next decade. This development beyond the presentation of harsh conditions was caused by an ideological shift in the next decade, for as Burn notes "things could be said in print and topics publicly discussed in the 'forties which would have met with much stronger resistance a few years later" (Burn 79). The novelists of the fifties found it not only desirable but also necessary to advance to new positions.

4   The Eighteen Fifties

For the social novel in Britain, the decade of the fifties represents a development of material and technique before the gradual dispersion of the form by the mid-sixties. This condition is not unrelated to the alterations in British society and legislation that occurred during the decade. Several issues of the forties, such as the purpose and scope of government intervention, were being resolved *de facto* and *de jure* by the 1850s. "There are certain characteristics which one would expect to find in the 'fifties and 'sixties: a concentration on minor rather than on major reforms; a slackening of interest in domestic politics after the general election of 1852 had made Free Trade secure, and a decrease in political tension; . . . a somewhat brittle complacency but certainly not apathy or indifference—rather, a lively, critical, argumentative, political attitude" (Burn 82). The 1850 Factory Act limited working hours to ten and one-half hours per day, or a maximum of sixty hours per week. This was succeeded in 1853 by Palmerston's Factory Act which provided workers a free Saturday afternoon. The Penal Servitude Act and the Smoke Nuisance Act the same year altered the nature of employer-employee relations and the condition of the environment. In 1853 the abolition of the soap tax ensured basic sanitation in all social classes, while compulsory vaccination for infants added to the gradual improvement of infant care. In 1853 the Nine Hours Movement initiated further modification of work conditions. The revisitation of cholera in 1853–1854 produced health reports on sanitation and water. The founding of the Working Men's College in 1854 represented a step toward enlarged possibilities of self-improvement. The abolishing of the newspaper tax in 1855 increased readership of the daily press among the lowest classes. These examples of legislative intervention influenced the details of domestic life.

Although the Great Exhibition of 1851 might have obscured the consequences, the decade experienced considerable labor activity. In 1851–1852 there was a builders' lockout for the nine-hour day, and in 1853–1854 occurred the Preston Strike that influenced Dickens to write *Hard Times*. The 1855 riots against the Sunday Bill led to the passage of the County and Borough Police Act of 1856. The establishment of the National Miners' Association in 1858, the strike in 1859 by London builders, and the deficient harvests of 1859 and 1860 illustrate the range of events that affected all social classes. The Molestation of Workers Act of 1859, which allowed peaceful picketing, showed the legitimation of labor action. Since the 1851 Census had shown that 54 percent of the population was urban, Britain by mid-century exhibited the demography it was to follow for the remainder of the century. Pike contends that superficial reforms "put the public conscience to sleep for another generation" (*Victorian* 109), but if the decade was less violent, it was certainly not less active in reform than its predecessor.

The condition of women began to receive the attention and provoke the agitation that would lead to greater legal independence. The first petition of women for the franchise was submitted to the House of Lords in 1851. Harriet Taylor published her essay on the subject in the *Westminster Review*. Barbara Lee Smith's *A Brief Summary in Plain Language of the Most Important Laws Concerning Women* (1854) provided basic legal information and cause for argument. Caroline Norton's *Open Letter to the Queen* (1855) was followed by changes in marriage legislation in succeeding years. The Divorce and Matrimonial Causes Act of 1857, establishing civil procedures for divorce, mandated that divorced women need not give income to their former husbands, while the Amendment the following year claimed that women could recover income obtained by lawful industry. The pleas of Charlotte Brontë's Caroline Helstone in *Shirley* for a significant place in society anticipate the theme to be emphasized by Jewsbury in *Marian Withers* and Gaskell in *North and South,* reinforcing the demands for legislative reform that would make work meaningful and profitable. "In the fifties England was becoming keenly aware of the narrowness and meagreness of her middle-class tradition" (Young, *Victorian* 87–88), and the incipient interest in legal reform, as well as the new range of inquiry by female novelists, reflects this attitude.

One of the earliest of social fictions to appear in the decade, and one espousing a strong personal if not political independence for women, was *Lucy Dean; The Noble Needlewoman* by Eliza Meteyard (1816–1879), published in *Eliza Cook's Journal,* March and April 1850. The tale is indicative of two tendencies in social fiction of the fifties: the broadening of social issues beyond occupation; and the specific development of a myth about women, suggested by *Shirley.* The *Journal* was "mainly concerned with social conditions, specially so far as they affected women and children," and Meteyard was a steady contributor. "Sober realism" in a "modern setting," fictions dealing "with themes other than romantic love" and centering on middle-class and lower-class characters mark Meteyard's subjects and are consistent with the intentions of the magazine (Dalziel 57). The main subject of *Lucy Dean* is the value of emigration for starving and destitute seamstresses: "There are blessed lands in this wide world, for them as'll strive and work, and not cling to the pauperism o' the needle . . . because it's 'ginteel'" (315). Lucy is the iconographic seamstress: lonely garret, sputtering candle, wintry moon, prostitute sister. Meteyard's focus on emigration indicates the rapidity of response by women to social reform, as it was only in December 1849 that Sidney Herbert's emigration proposal was presented to the public. Although Kingsley uses emigration at the conclusion of *Alton Locke,* he was anticipated in this by the conclusion of *Mary Barton* in 1848 and by Meteyard, whose tale preceded *Alton Locke,* which appeared in August 1850. Meteyard shows emigration as a function of self-realization, not as a component of empire expansion as had Carlyle in *Chartism* a decade earlier.

Lucy meets Mary Austen, loosely suggested by Caroline Chisholm of the Family Colonization Loan Society (1848), who espouses the ideas of emigration, self-help, and sisterly mutual concern for women. A woman should "go forth to the colonies, with the determination to work, not only for herself, but to pave a way for others of her sex, less fortunate, or less courageous. . . . As to life in the new world, it is one of hope to a resolute and good woman . . . what *one* woman, resolute of heart, can do to help her sisters here" (329). Women must become responsible for their own fates: "If we, as women, despair of helping our sister woman, what can men do? No! it is only through labour—honest self-help, that those standing can raise the fallen" (331). This sisterly concern cuts "across the ordinary barriers of class and respectability" (S. Mitchell, "Lost" 119). It is thus that women contribute to "the mighty progress of the ages." "Charitable aid for my own sex can be but a palliative," declares Lucy, emphasizing women's necessity to work for mutual improvement (342–43). It is a process of "self-redemption" (394). *Lucy Dean* reflects the numerous organizations formed to promote emigration or employment of distressed women: the British Ladies Female Emigrant Society (1849), the Society for Promoting the Employment of Women (1859), and the Female Middle Class Emigration Society (1862).

It is within a situation of urgent contemporaneity that Meteyard develops a myth of the sisterhood of women. *Lucy Dean* began serial issue on 16 March 1850, and it was on 25 February that "the first shipload of needlewomen left for Australia" (Walkley 115). Meteyard is particularly interested in addressing impoverished middle-class women: "This is the true, if new, spirit of our times. If one fraction of our middle class women could but think as you do, could but only act up to the half of such thoughts . . . instead of wearing out a wretched existence here, as ill-paid governesses, musicians, artists, or else wasting life in the mean frivolities, and half starvation of 'gentility'" (343). Mary Austen is transformed during the tale into a literal Genius: an inspiriting force. To maintain a positive focus, Meteyard does not mention that candidates for emigration might have been one step away from prostitution, as did "The Needlewomen's Farewell" in *Punch* in January 1850 (14):

> The past looms dark behind us, the future rises fair,
> > Though ne'er so bleak the shore we seek, across this waste
> > of waters;
> Hard step-mother, O England, and niggard of thy care,
> > Still hast thou been, great Island Queen, to us thy hapless
> > daughters!
>
> As to the vessel's side we throng to look our last at thee,
> > Each sunken eye is dead and dry — what cause have we for
> > weeping?
> We leave no homes behind us, no household ties had we;
> > In one long coil of heavy toil our hours went creeping —
> > creeping.
> >   .   .   .
>
> Now speed thee, good ship, over sea, and bear us far away,
> > Where food to eat, and friends to greet, and work to do
> > await us —
> Where against hunger's tempting we shall not need to pray —
> > Where in wedlock's tie, not harlotry, we shall find men to
> > mate us.

After meeting Mary, Lucy "knelt as a disciple might before the holiest teacher" (330). Mary advises Lucy: "Be truthful and serviceable to our own sex; for they need it, they do indeed" (343). Lucy becomes a totemic super Angel in the House in the Australian outback, embodying the traits — domesticity, purity — that Meteyard considers female attributes. "It was a touching, sacred thing, as their rude nature visibly softened under the pure and blessed influence of this noble woman" (378). Meteyard's depiction accords with the fact that "the civilising mission could also be used to urge women to leave their homes and undertake a perilous emigrant's journey overseas to civilise pioneer male colonists" (Hammerton 24). When Lucy decides to return to render an account to Mary Austen, Meteyard describes it in sacerdotal terms: "This was accomplished in one year's time from the time of commencement; and now she prepared for a voyage to her own country, there to whisper to the dear ear and heart of genius, what woman's promise unto woman yet shall be" (393).

Just before embarking and immediately before receiving a proposal of marriage, Lucy has a vision of an apotheosized Mary Austen: "From that hour, hope growing, she tracked [her life] onward, step by step, one bright and shining face ever being a portion of it; till, like her eyes, her soul went onward with the light she tracked, and resting on the far-up mountain crags, were one within the glory settled there." When Lucy sees Mary in London, it is disciple to master: "She pressed forward, knelt beside Mary" in "convulsed respiration" (394). Meteyard, in the parameters of a realistic account of emigration, incorporates a myth of the triumphant priestly woman, perhaps Nightingale's female Savior. Meteyard could not know in the fifties that "emigration was ultimately an insignificant factor" (Walkley 125) in solving the problems of needlewomen. Its program of self-improvement and the accompanying mythos, however, are striking. Since Gaskell and Meteyard knew one another, and both published in *Howitt's Journal,* it is possible that *Lucy Dean* might have encouraged Gaskell to develop the seamstress concept beyond occupation, linking it to illegitimacy in *Ruth.* Meteyard's conception of the sisterhood of women is a nascent Amazonian image that may have suggested the first chapter of *Cranford* in December 1851.

Published before the beginning of *Lucy Dean* and extending beyond its date of completion was *The Seamstress* by George M. W. Reynolds (1814–1879), serialized in *Reynolds's Miscellany* from March to August 1850. Reynolds' *The Seamstress* provides an interesting contrast to Meteyard's treatment of the distressed needlewoman. Instead of advocating emigration and espousing independence for women, Reynolds' tale reflects his Chartist/radical hostility to the aristocracy as well as his sentimentalizing of the heroine Virginia Mordaunt. *The Seamstress* combines social protest with the *roman policier*, wavering between bathos and social criticism. Unlike the sober treatments of Stone or Meteyard, and eschewing the middle-class origins of its author, Reynolds' tale moves between the working classes and the aristocracy, and the links are forced: the young Marquis of Arden falls in love with Virginia the seamstress; the Marquis' stepmother, the Duchess of Belmont, is discovered to be Virginia's mother; Julius Lavenham, the trusted confidant of the Duchess, is really her former lover and Virginia's father. Virginia discovers these lost parents only on her consumptive deathbed.

Reynolds' sources would seem to include Richard Redgrave's painting *The Sempstress* as much as any Parliamentary material. The tale, commencing in 1844, is set in the same year as the first version of Redgrave's canvas and the month after the publication of Thomas Hood's *The Song of the Shirt*. "Reader, picture to yourself a pale and pensive girl of about eighteen—with a countenance as beautiful as the utmost perfection of features could render it . . . full of sylphide grace,—a hand of the most delicate shape . . . an appearance of virginal artlessness calculated to inspire the most tender interest" (129–30). Reynolds mentions "the chastity of her morals" and "artlessness bordering upon infantine simplicity" (130). Virginia believes herself an orphan, friendless with the exception of Julia Barnet. Julia is the kept mistress of the young Marquis, her fallen state contrasting with Virginia's purity. It is through Julia that Reynolds condemns the economic system that enslaves seamstresses.

Reynolds' opposition to the aristocracy and its artificiality recalls the diatribes of Thomas Day in the eighteenth century. Of young men at a soiree, "the vainest and most frivolous . . . were sure to be Members of Parliament" (378). Virginia's morals were not "mere negative virtues, such as those which are ascribed to a female sovereign and yet are so fulsomely lauded. . . . There is no merit in virtue when it has never been tempted. All persons commence life in that negative condition which may be termed virtuous." The "wealthy classes ought to be the most perfect patterns of virtue . . . yet the British Aristocracy, male and female, is the most loathsomely corrupt, demoralised, and profligate class of persons that ever scandalised a country" (369–

70). Reynolds reiterates that Virginia is a working-class "angel" deserving of "worship" by her lover, the Marquis. "Oh! how sublime is the disposition of the working classes, not only in this country but in every other; — and it is because they are thus generous, thus noblehearted . . . that the writer of this tale loves them so well — devotes himself so fervidly to their interests" (357).

The Marquis' mistress Julia Barnet denounces the system that enslaves needlewomen. Reynolds' story reveals the class antagonism in stories of seduction involving the upper and lower classes, a convention as old as Richardson's distressed heroine in *Pamela*. After Virginia discovers the insidious practices of middlewomen (Mrs. Jackson, Mrs. Pembroke), by which she is drained of her rightful income, Julia explains the reasons for this oppression:

> "Madame Duplessy employs a middle-woman because it saves trouble in the first instance — and secondly because the result is to keep down the price of the work thus put out to be done. The middle-woman whom Madame Duplessy employs, contracts with sub-agents constituting a second grade of middle-women; — and from these last do the needlewomen receive their work and their pittances. . . . By thus keeping down the wages of the needlewomen, the great houses . . . can from time to time reduce the prices paid to the middle-women." (163)

Reynolds indicts the slop system as Stone had done earlier in *The Young Milliner*. However, he goes beyond Stone in providing a detailed explanation of a needlewoman's "fall," when Julia describes her situation:

> "I did not make society as it is: I was born into it such as it is — I was compelled, willing or unwilling, to yield to the circumstances arising from its false, its vitiated, its unjust condition and influence. . . . Poverty — cold — disappointment — hunger — crushing toil — and rags, — these are enemies which strike at the most rigid virtue. . . . I, too, have experienced the hardship of oppressive labor, and the horrors of starvation! . . . Already — yes, already — are you advancing at a headlong pace towards the precipice. . . . These wages are better than starving virtue — and human nature is too frail to hesitate long between the alternatives. Let those who blame me, act justly and blame the system of society. I am one of its victims — not one of its modellers. The modellers of society are the rich, the wealthy, and the indolent great." (227–28)

In such passages Reynolds exhibits the influence of the first-hand testimony gathered by Henry Mayhew and Angus Reach in *The Morning Chronicle* and used by Kingsley in *Cheap Clothes and Nasty* and *Alton Locke*. Virginia's plight leads Reynolds to an indictment of society after she is reduced to slop work:

> This costly structure, we say, is a mighty monument which capital has raised in honour of the Genius of Competition. But to view it morally, its aspect is hideous in the extreme. Its foundations are built with the bones of the white slaves of England, male and female: the skeletons of journeymen tailors and poor seamstresses, all starved to death. . . . What right has any set of men to make this country an earthly hell for all the rest? . . . She was perishing by inches — dying by slow famine — as so many thousands of British females are ever pining and fading away into early graves. (341)

Reynolds wonders about the effect if "the thirty thousand pale, spectral, wasted needlewomen of London" were to demand an audience with the Queen. "Virtue in the poor seamstresses is almost an impossibility," he concludes (356).

Interspersed with the study of the conditions of the seamstress is Reynolds' portrayal of the aristocracy, which is adulterous, profligate, and ultimately murderous. Although Virgina dies of consumption, the aristocracy suffers as well: the Duke of Belmont commits suicide, the corrupt French maid is murdered, the Duchess dies of "brain fever," the unscrupulous lawyer Collinson is killed in a duel with the Marquis, who is also killed. Unlike Meteyard, who uses emigration to suggest alternatives for distressed needlewomen, Reynolds offers no solution except interference by a government which he detests. Although Reynolds' audience was made up of middle- as well as working-class readers, without specific alternatives his indictment loses conviction in the climate of the fifties. He regards the suffering classes as helpless pawns in the hands of a ruthless economic system and an immoral aristocracy. Although *The Seamstress* is typical of radical literature in denouncing the aristocracy to emphasize proletarian superiority, this superiority does not lead to the possibility of independent action by the working classes.

The accounts of prostitution in *The Seamstress* and the possibility of emigration noticed in *Lucy Dean* recur in shorter narratives at the beginning of the decade. *Ellen Linn, the Needlewoman,* published anonymously in *Tait's Edinburgh Magazine* a week after the completion of Reynolds' *The Seamstress,* uses both emigration and prostitution in describing the plight of its heroine. Ellen Linn is left in a garret to support an imbecile grandmother while her lover, Tom Cripps, is away in Australia. Cripps occasionally forwards money, but Ellen becomes so destitute that the delay in her lover's letters leads to her destruction. Ellen Linn is unusual because the author relates that she had attended "the National School in the village of ———, kept by Mrs. Cripps, the mother of Ellen's lover. . . . Ellen being an apt scholar, soon read, wrote, and *spoke* better than most girls of her station in life" (465). This knowledge, however, avails her nothing in her present crisis.

When she and her grandmother are reduced to starvation she is forced to beg. This brings an offer to become a prostitute: "She heard a voice saying to her, 'It is a pity that such a fine-looking girl as you should be begging.' She turned quickly round, not understanding the purpose of the words; and at the same moment a gentleman (at least he had the dress of one) whispered something in her ear" (468). Ellen flees the temptation, hoping for a letter from Cripps to relieve her. Desperate, she goes to Exeter Hall and finds Mr. Fishlock, who had been making inquiries "about Ellen's obtaining a free passage to Australia" (470). His aid, however, is futile, since he and Ellen find the grandmother dead on returning to the garret. Ellen goes mad, and "to the day of her death she remained an idiot!" (470). The author notices the emigration schemes written of by Meteyard but finds them unavailing. A letter from Cripps with money for her passage arrives the day after. *Ellen Linn* thus encapsulates *Lucy Dean* and *The Seamstress,* less sober than the former and less radical than the latter. Appearing eight years after *A London Dressmaker's Diary, Ellen Linn* indicates the persistent interest *Tait's Magazine* maintained about the conditions of seamstresses.

The ideology of self-help and assimilation in *Lucy Dean* was central to *Marian Withers* by Geraldine Jewsbury (1812–1880), revised and published in 1851 after serial publication (5 January to 18 May 1850) in the *Manchester Examiner and Times.* It had two subjects, both of major concern to the fifties: the status of women and their legal situation, and the assimilative processes of the industrial era. Jewsbury disliked Lewes' idea, expressed in a review in the *Leader,* that "Miss Jewsbury was writing an answer to *Mary Barton*" (825). The novel is in reality much more like *Shirley.* Like Brontë, Jewsbury

distances her story, specifically focusing on the era of the speculations mania of 1825–1826. The issues she raises remain contemporary, particularly the concern about woman's role. *Marian Withers*
is concerned not only with the industrial situation but also with the
idea of "vocation" for women, which Jewsbury had already treated
in her 1848 *The Half-Sisters.* Jewsbury structures her three volumes
around a small number of themes: the idea of self-help, the process
of assimilation, the role of women, the nature of marriage. Both industry and women are in transitional situations in *Marian Withers.*
The reviewer in the *Athenaeum* recognized the two dimensions of the
story, noting the account of Nancy and Hilda Blair and their disap-
pointing marriages, but preferring "to introduce to the notice of our
readers the story of John Withers" since "there is in the tale here told
an understratum of actual fact." The review noted: "What we have
extracted belongs to the graver portion of Miss Jewsbury's book. The
reader for excitement will find many gayer scenes and more attractive descriptions:—but we like Miss Jewsbury best on ground like this"
(920–21).

This opinion was shared by Lewes, who declared that John Withers was "a fine type, and well studied" and that his insignificance in
the remainder of the novel was a "mistake" (825). While one might
object that Withers remains an important influence through all three
volumes, there is no denying that Lewes' opinion has validity. Lewes
praised the fact that the novel was "preserving the *realities,* not ideals."
Jewsbury herself notes in the text: "If the personages in this story do
not appear equal to the true heroic or romantic standard, let the reader
recollect that 'there is no dressing in them' . . . and that they really
were such as they are shown" (1:268), a statement recalling the opening paragraphs of *Shirley.* There is conjunction of the woman's issue
with the industrial: Marian Withers must choose between Albert Gordon, the dissolute scion of the gentry, and Mr. Cunningham, an in-
vestor and manufacturer who joins forces with John Withers. Marian
elects a life affiliated with the forthcoming era rather than with the
idle upper class whose time, the narrator believes, is finished. In making this decision, Marian looks toward Margaret Hale of *North and
South.* She aligns herself with those undergoing the transition to a
new industrialized England. By devoting a third of the texts to the
protagonists' fathers, Gaskell in *Mary Barton* and Jewsbury in *Marian
Withers* deliberately integrate the female and the industrial issues of
their novels, avoiding an artificial polemicizing of their arguments.

Jewsbury presents the concepts of work, industry, and assimilation through the figure of Marian's father John. Among the strongest pages in *Marian Withers* are those recounting the early life of this manufacturer when he was picked up in the streets of Manchester. The first three chapters of the novel, which Jewsbury considers a "Prologue," are among its strongest. She may have used this Prologue to obviate criticism that *Marian Withers* was a woman's novel, since she had said, apropos of her novel *Zoe*, "that I myself have a general sort of prejudice against women's novels, with very few exceptions" (Showalter, *Literature* 59). She opens the novel by evoking Manchester, near which she lived as the daughter of a merchant: "It was a regular Manchester wet day, of more than ordinary discomfort! The rain came down with a steady, heavy determination, aggravated from time to time to an emphatic energy by gusts of wind, which swept down the streets. . . . Nothing could be discerned beyond the distance of a few yards, the sky and the earth being seemingly mixed together in a disorganised fog" (1:5–6). John and his friend Alice are cared for by Miss Fenwick, who "had never before realized the horrible conditions of these outcast children lying in wickedness" (1:15). John eventually is sent to be an apprentice in the mills of Staffordshire. Jewsbury refutes the account of apprentices in the *Memoir of Robert Blincoe* and *Michael Armstrong*: "Parish apprentices and children working in factories were not always victims to ill-treatment. The apprentice system had many faults—too much was in the power of the masters, who were irresponsible," she notes, but she does not indict the entire process (1:22). John Withers enters the mill at the same time as did Blincoe, so she is criticizing the *Memoir* directly. This represents a balanced attitude that a writer of the thirties or early forties would have found untenable. John suggests an improvement on the machinery where he works, gets paid for it, and marries the daughter of his old master, achieving a gradual upward mobility. This woman marries because a friend tells her a woman thrown into the world is helpless. The narrator notes of Emily: "John might have done worse—she made him a good little insignificant wife" (1:55). This statement integrates the discussion about marriage into the presentation of self-reliance and mobility. Alice Withers, meanwhile, having been a servant, comes to work in John's house, becoming Marian's surrogate mother upon Emily's death.

For Jewsbury John Withers exists to prove the validity of assimilation and self-reliance several years before Samuel Smiles published

Self-Help (1859). In addition to presenting the ideology of self-help, later explored in *North and South* and *John Halifax,* Jewsbury inherits from Stone's *William Langshawe* a precision in depicting the degrees of assimilation of industrialists. Lewes detected: "She serves to bring out the characteristics of the two classes of manufacturers: the coarse rusticity of the one, and imitation of metropolitan elegance of the other" (825). Withers views Marian from a perspective truthful to his type: "John Withers was proud of his daughter, and he was proud, too, that his child began the world under such different circumstances to what he had done himself. She seemed a high-water mark which showed how much he had risen. . . . He had sent her to a very expensive school near Liverpool. . . . Like all men of his class who have raised themselves from the ranks, he set an immense value upon book learning and cultivated manners" (1:81–82). This emphasis on cultivated daughters as a sign of upward mobility recalls the situation of Edith Langshawe in Stone's *William Langshawe,* a novel which Jewsbury may well have known.

Other families had risen as well: "Mr. Vivian had been a large woolen-manufacturer, but had retired from business on inheriting a large fortune. . . . Mr. Sefton had risen from nothing, and was now a partner in some large printworks in the neighbourhood" (1:230–31). "The Wilcoxes belonged to the old race of spinners; by industry and saving they had risen from the ranks, and their housekeeping was on a most frugal scale. . . . Although Samuel Wilcox was now a rich man, and the owner of two large mills, their style of living continued to be what it had been twenty years previously" (2:6–7). Jewsbury shows versions of the upward mobility and assimilation of Captains of Industry. While it is not always possible to detect sources in *Marian Withers,* one clear influence is Cooke Taylor's *Notes of a Tour in the Manufacturing Districts.*

Jewsbury, like Stone, sees the 1820s as a turning point in British history. The speculations mania caused distress during 1825 and 1826, all classes suffering. John Withers thinks: "Though the idea of doubting God's providence never crossed his mind, still it was very difficult to feel any comfort in trusting to it" (3:101), an attitude of self-reliance differing from facile belief. Jewsbury may have taken this detail from Cooke Taylor, who includes a study of a laborer who criticizes a Methodist preacher for saying the sufferings of the working classes are a punishment from God: "No, said I to the Methodist, if Providence wanted to punish the sinful in the land, Providence would have made a great mistake in coming to the working classes. I tell thee, man, that if I believed what thou sayest I would turn Atheist" (159).

It is Cunningham who accounts for Jewsbury's emphasis on the twenties: "Social questions had not then begun to be put with the startling emphasis they have since assumed, but his recent travels amongst the manufacturing districts had given a shape and direction to his thoughts. He saw that the condition of the working-classes was daily becoming of more importance,—their ignorance, their sufferings, their strength, and their number, inspired him with the most profound interest, and he earnestly desired to devote himself to the amelioration of their condition." Society must see "where the interests of the masters and workmen cross each other" (3:103–4). Such a reflection echoes Elizabeth Stone and the Preface to *Mary Barton:* "The working classes need men of character at their head to guide wisely the movement which has begun, and which it is in vain to repress. Education is the grand thing they need. . . . A struggle has commenced already between the past and the future, which must be fought out in the battle of the present" (3:107, 109). Again, Cooke Taylor is a source for the inexorable advance of industrialism: "It would be well to recognise the Factory system as what statesmen call *un fait accompli;* it exists, and must continue to exist; it is not practicable, even if it were desirable, to get rid of it. . . . It cannot be overthrown" (5,9). Influenced by Carlyle's *Past and Present,* Jewsbury believes that in this antagonism of interests, "both sides . . . have right on their side" (3:110). Withers and Cunningham effect many changes within the two years of their association.

The alliance of Cunningham and Withers permits Jewsbury to include her own beliefs about social progress. Cunningham and Withers tour a factory, providing an opportunity for both Cunningham and the reader to learn, a device familiar from Stone. "Most of the workpeople in this room kept bits of cotton in their mouths to prevent the dust passing down their throats. But their pale, emaciated looks showed that, in spite of this precaution, it was an unhealthy branch of the occupation" (2:41). The sober tone contrasts with the embodiment of this condition by Disraeli in the character Devilsdust in *Sybil.* Words like *sliver, mules, devil,* and *throstle* are introduced, educating the reader about specific processes. This is effected not externally, as in *The Wrongs of Woman,* but internally within the character of Cunningham. Jewsbury recalls Martineau in Withers' defense of machinery: "Though at first it may seem to deprive them of some branches of employment, yet eventually it brings more hands into work" (2:46). Cooke Taylor had noted: "Every new invention does, at its first introduction, deprive a certain number of persons of their peculiar occupation, and produce some perturbation in the labour-market. . . . But when the factory system has once taken firm root, mechanical invention must every day exercise less and less of pertur-bating influence" (122).

Cunningham expresses Jewsbury's mid-century belief in self-help: "A spirit of self-help does lie at the bottom of all success. Self-reliance is the backbone of all heroism of character. . . . But we must beware how we allow our view to centre in ourselves. We are none of us alone in the world. . . . Co-operation will gradually take the place of com-petition. A great social question is opening up [which] has created a new order of men in this country. . . . Masters and men, capital and labour, are beginning to stand in antagonism to each other. It is an immense question that is lying before us. . . . Labour will be organized and its forces disciplined. . . . Side by side with this grown ANTAGO-NISM of interests, there is arising the idea of ASSOCIATION, which will mature and develop itself gradually, till, in the fulness of time, it will have strength to gather together the conflicting interests into one" (2:22–25). These ideas echo Jewsbury's attitude expressed in her re-view of *Alton Locke* about the age of "association" superseding the age of "individualism." Cooke Taylor noted the "transition" would be "very slow and gradual" (122).

A major part of this process of assimilation involves women. Marian's choice of whom to marry is not superficial. She must com-mit herself either to moving forward or stagnating in the empty futil-ity of lives like those of Nancy Blair, bored and married to Thomas Arl, or of Hilda Blair, who marries the dissolute old Glynton for financial security. In *Marian Withers* Jewsbury is concerned with the role women must find for themselves even as men are finding accom-modation in the transitional society. This was a particularly difficult problem for the middle-class woman: "Urban society was the only life for the new middle-class woman and in this she shared many of the problems of urbanization with the working-class woman. But in contrast to the ability of many working-class wives to recreate a sup-portive family network, the middle-class woman was more on her own" (Branca 146). The narrator observes that "the women of Eng-land of the present day are eaten up with *ennui* to a much greater extent than is suspected . . . they find no adequate employment"

(1:247). Withers declares, "To my mind women had better come and work in a factory than do nothing but sit all day with their hands before them. . . . I don't want her to be a fine lady, with all her schooling" (1:238).

In a passage recalling Caroline Helstone from *Shirley* and anticipating Maggie Tulliver from *The Mill on the Floss,* Marian recognizes: "I have nothing to occupy me; nothing to interest me. . . . My whole life is stagnating. . . . I feel as if I were buried alive. I am good for nothing. . . . I am stunned and stupid — nothing seems real, not even I myself. . . . I suffer all the more from having nothing of which I ought to complain" (3:124–25). This interest was a strong one in Jewsbury. In *The Half-Sisters* one character had noted: "Women in general have no settled occupation. . . . Those who have families have indeed a legitimate occupation, enough to employ all their energies. Those women, too, who have to gain their own living have their hands pretty full. . . . Look . . . at the great body of unmarried women, in the middle-classes. . . . They want an object, they want a strong purpose, they want an adequate employment, — in exchange for precious life" (189). Another character wonders: "I hardly know. . . . I have nothing to do that seems worth doing. I am depressed under a constant sense of waste, a vague consciousness that I am always doing wrong, and yet I can find out nothing that I ought to do" (204). Marian's idea reflects the uselessness of the lives of Nancy Arl and Hilda Glynton. The year following *Marian Withers* Florence Nightingale in *Cassandra* was to condemn the idea that "it is a thing *so* accepted among women that they have nothing to do" (34). The accuracy of Jewsbury's recognition of this situation is reflected by attempts during the decade to improve circumstances, as in the founding of the Society for Promoting the Employment of Women in 1857.

Jewsbury's study of marriage in *Marian Withers* suggests Nightingale's further observation that "marriage is the only chance (and it is but a chance) offered to women for escape from this death; and how eagerly and how ignorantly it is embraced" (38). Marian travels from Manchester to encounter various women who educate her about roles she will *not* choose. This travel, as Moers suggests, derives from the excursions of Gothic heroines toward self-knowledge, but it is also comparable to Lancelot Smith's encounters in *Yeast. Marian Withers* might be regarded as a female version of Kingsley's fable. In the first volume Marian visits Carrisford in Knutsford where the Arls

reside. Her friend Hilda is contracting a loveless marriage, supported
by her sister who states she can regard her husband as a "sort of uncle"
(1:176). To Glynton "marriage was in his eyes a solemn atonement
for all the irregularities of his past life" (1:283). Marian advises Hilda
against the match: "You will be miserable! do not go on with this
match — it will be quite wicked" (2:247). Nancy Arl, however, believes:
"A single woman has no standing in society, and it is a great advantage to be well married. . . . Every woman is bound to make the best
bargain she can" (3:73). In each volume Jewsbury focuses on the issue, presenting a variety of attitudes.

Jewsbury makes it clear that women are not responsible for this
situation through the character of Lady Wollaston, unhappily married to an officer and cousin to Cunningham, who had once loved
her. Women must survive in a situation not of their making. In the
third volume she declares:

> "[Hilda] is helping to degrade her own sex; for she shows that she
> has no [more] belief in her own value [than] . . . the wretched
> women who, from their necessities, sell themselves for a piece of
> silver and a morsel of bread. . . . You men *are* cruel, every one of
> you. You crush us down with a morality which you yourselves will
> not lighten with one of your fingers! . . . If women *knew* what they
> were doing when they, as you say, 'sell themselves into bondage' to
> a man they do not care about, for the sake of a position in life, —
> they would NOT do it. They commit an irrevocable deed before they
> know all it involves. . . . Believe me, that no man, with the free-
> dom and outgoing activity which is his birthright, can know or imag-
> ine what is endured by a woman shut up within herself, with no
> outlet for her feelings. . . . Love cannot be compelled by any amount
> of vows." (3:32–35)

Women receive no emotional satisfaction from enforced marriages
and have no legal recourse if dissatisfied. Having no occupation compels women, "the young women of England, who having left school,
are waiting to be married," into settlements (3:80). "Men look on us
women as so much property, to be laid out as it pleases them to have
us, not as it is good for us to be" (2:172). Lewes praised the final confrontation between Lady Wollaston and the faithless Albert Gordon
as "the most deeply interesting portion of the book" (825) after the
story of John Withers. It is a blistering exposure of the man's essential cowardice.

Jewsbury was aware of this situation herself. She wrote Jane Carlyle: "I do not think that either you or I are to be called failures. We are indications of a development of womanhood which as yet is not recognised. . . . The present rules for woman will not hold — that something better and stronger is needed. . . . There are women to come after us, who will approach nearer the fulness of the measure of the stature of a woman's nature" (Woolf, *Reader* 179). She advised: "Half your loneliness comes from having no outlet for your energies, and no engrossing employment" (Basch 282). In showing Marian's choice between a retrogressive and a progressive marriage, Jewsbury depicts the assimilative process as it related to women. While one might wish that Marian had had sufficient independence to remain single, she does choose correctly if she had to marry. Lewes commented that in Jewsbury "Observation and Sentiment were about equal; but . . . she does not work them harmoniously together" ("Lady" 140), but as he declared in his review, *Marian Withers* is predominantly "straightforward [in] dealing with *realities*" (826). Jewsbury does not offer a mythic independence for Marian like Brontë's Titaness. She grants her the "association" that accorded with her era, as she had recognized in reviewing *Alton Locke*. The gradual assimilation of Withers and his daugher in the novel suggest the compromise of economic groups that marked the fifties. Jewsbury's influence was extensive during the period, as she was both a reader for Bentley and Sons from 1858 to 1880 and the author of over sixteen hundred reviews for the *Athenaeum*. *Marian Withers* was a novel by a woman accomplished as an author, reviewer, and critic. The integration of the industrial and the female issues permitted Jewsbury to avoid a problem later noted by George Eliot in 1855, "that she is not equal to herself." Eliot criticized the superficial morality of *Constance Herbert* where "almost all the women are models of magnanimity and devotedness" while "there is not a man in her book who is not either weak, perfidious, or rascally." "She forces us to consider her book rather in the light of a homily than of a fiction" Eliot concluded (Pinney 133, 135). Rooted in Manchester, *Marian Withers* avoided such hazards.

Elizabeth Gaskell's major work of the fifties, *North and South,* appeared after *Marian Withers* but shares several of its concerns. It studies assimilation, begun with Elizabeth Stone, and the question approached in *Shirley* of women's function in the transitional society. Before writing *North and South* Gaskell produced two works that have a bearing on the social narrative in that they study illegitimacy, one concerning a seamstress. Set in the earlier decades of the nineteenth century, *Lizzie Leigh* and *Ruth* are related in that the former can be seen as a forerunner of the social question analyzed in the latter. *Lizzie Leigh,* like *Mary Barton, A Manchester Strike,* and *William Langshawe,* occurs mostly in Manchester. *Ruth* is a derivation of fictions like *The Young Milliner* that dealt with this occupation. The narratives are further connected because they represent Gaskell as "a more self-consciously professional writer" who could write her publisher Chapman that "he was not advertising her work sufficiently" (Sutherland 96–98), citing both *Lizzie Leigh* and *Cranford.*

Elizabeth Gaskell's interest in a seduced girl named Pasley and the emigration scheme for prostitutes of Angela Burdett-Coutts underlies her treatment of illegitimacy in *Lizzie Leigh,* published in the first number of *Household Words* in 1850. The story bears some resemblance to Tonna's *Combination:* the father dies at the beginning, the two sons Will and Tom Leigh have the same Christian names as the brothers in Tonna, both sets of brothers go to Manchester, and Tonna and Gaskell both use the story of the Prodigal Son. On Christmas Day, 1836, James Leigh forgives his daughter Lizzie, who has been seduced. After the father's death, Tom Leigh reads the story of the Prodigal Son, which Gaskell uses as a prototype of her story of the Prodigal Daughter, illustrating the difference between a man who "falls" and a woman who experiences the same situation. Gaskell refers to the Prodigal Son in 1853 when she depicts another Prodigal Daughter in *Ruth.* Mrs. Leigh decides to search for Lizzie in Manchester, vowing a quest-like one year for her search.

Will Leigh has fallen in love with Susan Palmer, who keeps a school to support her alcoholic father. Will fears Susan would not marry him if she found out the truth about Lizzie: "Can I ask her to marry me, knowing what we do about Lizzie, and fearing worse?" (220). Susan is compassionate when Mrs. Leigh tells her about Lizzie. She has adopted a little girl who is in fact Mrs. Leigh's grandchild Nanny, who dies in a fall. When Susan reproaches Will for his hardness, he tells her: "Thou hast spoken out very plain to me; and misdoubted me, Susan; I love thee so, that thy words cut me. If I did hang back a bit from making sudden promises, it was because not even for love of thee would I say what I was not feeling; and at first I could not feel all at once as thou wouldst have me. But I'm not cruel and hard; for if I had been, I should na' have grieved as I have done" (238). Gaskell records a shift in sensibility in this passage, as William rejects his father's intolerance. This moral change is accompanied by a social alteration, as the younger brother Tom becomes a school-master. Mrs. Leigh and the recovered Lizzie retire to a cottage, where the girl spends her time in charity, like Hester Prynne in *The Scarlet Letter*. The change in moral attitude by Will Leigh is a commentary on the male attitude toward the fallen Esther in *Mary Barton*. Gas-kell's strength in portraying the male mind was not better exhibited until her study of John Thornton in *North and South*.

Gaskell was to consider the question of illegitimacy in her novel about a seduced seamstress, *Ruth,* in 1853. Unlike the portrayal of Ellen Cardan in *The Young Milliner* or the King sisters in *The Wrongs of Woman,* Gaskell's seamstress is viewed in a context larger than her occupation. As the *North British Review* observed, Ruth Hilton is a casualty of the industrial system: "Penitentiaries are needed for the increasing numbers of poor creatures whom our depraved social state, and especially the growth of the manufacturing system, are con-stantly throwing about the streets" (156). The novel opens evoking dressmaking conditions in the early nineteenth century: "I call it night; but, strictly speaking, it was morning. . . . And yet, more than a dozen girls still sat in the room into which Ruth entered, stitching away as if for very life" (3). The mistress, Mrs. Mason, forces the girls to work "for fear . . . it might fall into the hands of the rival dress-maker, who had just established herself in the very same street" (7). As in the cases recorded in the Parliamentary papers Ruth cannot return home since her family has paid her premium. Ruth is typical of women in millinery with her background as the daughter of a "respectable farmer" (35). After she is seen by Bellingham at the Shire-hall for the hunt ball, she goes with him on a free Sunday to her old home. Gaskell, like Tonna and Stone before her, records the hazards of the "free Sunday." Ruth is discharged by Mrs. Mason, "severely intolerant if their conduct was in any degree influenced by the force of these temptations" (53). Pregnant, Ruth is abandoned in North Wales and taken in by Thurston and Faith Benson, early examplars of mid-Victorian philanthropy.

Passed off as Mrs. Denbigh, Ruth secures a position as governess in the Bradshaw family. Gaskell is concerned in *Ruth* with defining female as well as male gentility: "Whereas, six or seven years ago, you would have perceived that she was not altogether a lady by birth and education, yet now she might have been placed among the high-est in the land, and would have been taken by the most critical judge for their equal" (207). Gaskell undermines the stereotype of the Angel in the House, as Ruth becomes this although she is not strictly innocent. Gaskell shows the constraints on a governess when Ruth is forced to spy on Jemima Bradshaw by her father. Bradshaw is similar to Balshawe in *William Langshawe* in abusing his wife: "When he was there, a sort of constant terror of displeasing him made her voice sharp and nervous" (229). The similar name may indicate that Gaskell had read *William Langshawe* after writing *Mary Barton.* As Jewsbury had discussed in *Marian Withers,* men are cruel, especially in *Ruth.* Bradshaw's marriage, an exercise in patriarchal tyranny over his wife and his daughter Jemima, is camouflaged by a veneer of respectability. Its inadequacy prepares the reader for Ruth's rejection of an offer of marriage from her seducer. Bellingham reappears in Ruth's life when he canvasses the district as Mr. Donne. In their meeting on the shore, Ruth repudiates him: "I do not love you. I did once. Don't say I did not love you then! but I do not now. I could never love you again. All you have said and done since you came with Mr. Bradshaw to Abermouth first has only made me wonder how I ever could have loved you. . . . If there were no other reason to prevent our marriage but the one fact that it would bring Leonard into contact with you, that would be enough" (299–300). "It is only women who can help women, and it is only women who can really raise those that have 'fallen'" (476) Lewes noted in his review. Ruth's defiance is striking considering the fact that the "child, whether legitimate or not, belonged of legal right to the father" in the early nineteenth century (288).

In *Ruth* the role of religion is ambiguous. Ruth adheres to it; the gargoyle's patient suffering makes her able to endure the world. For Benson the situation is more difficult: "Formerly, if I believed that such or such an action was according to the will of God, I went and did it, or at least I tried to do it, without thinking of the consequences. Now, I reason and weigh what will happen if I do so and so — I grope where formerly I saw" (358). Gaskell echoes *In Memoriam* closely both in expression and intent. Although this is not specifically doctrinal doubt, it anticipates the anxiety of Margaret Hale's father in *North and South.* As Burn observes, by mid-century "it does not seem that the 'divine will' was greatly used as an anaesthetic to still the social conscience" (101). Ruth dies after nursing Bellingham through an epidemic of typhus. Davis the surgeon does not believe such a man is worth Ruth's life: "To be sure, what fools men are! I don't know why one should watch and strive to keep them in the world. . . . What was this sick fine gentleman sent here for, that she should run a chance of her life for him? or why was he sent into the world at all, for that matter?" (443). That the surgeon is himself illegitimate makes Gaskell's questioning of providence in the context of gentility the more serious.

Benson tells Bèllingham at the conclusion of the novel: "Men may call such actions as yours youthful follies! There is another name for them with God" (450). Gaskell appears to echo directly the denunciation of the double standard expressed by the Unitarian industrialist Greg, who wrote in his essay about "Prostitution" in the *Westminster Review* in 1850: "*Hers* is innate depravity, hopeless degradation, unworthiness . . . *his* are the venial errors of youth, the ordinary tribute to natural desires, the common laxity of a man of the world" (251). Gaskell uses the situation of the seamstress to condemn a social attitude. *Ruth* emphasizes Greg's argument that society makes it impossible for a woman to regain her position after her seduction. He noted; "What makes it impossible for them to retrace their steps? . . . Clearly, that harsh, savage, unjust, unchristian public opinion which has resolved to regard a whole life of indulgence on the part of one sex as venial and natural, and a single false step on the part of the other as irretrievable and unpardonable. . . . Is it not notorious that, of a hundred fathers who would fall upon the neck of the prodigal son, . . . there is scarcely one who . . . would not turn his back upon the erring and repentant daughter?" (250). In *Ruth* Gaskell's protest inextricably links economic with sexual exploitation. Greg had said that in changing public opinion "ethical writers may do something; writers of fiction may do much" (266), and significantly he had cited *Mary Barton* in this essay. Gaskell uses the seamstress aspect of *Ruth* to query the ethics of economics — and the economics of ethics.

Charlotte Brontë and Elizabeth Barrett Browning both protested Ruth's death. More women than men were against the book when it was published, but the outcry was partially because "the unmarried mother, who had lurked in the background of so many novels, was not only brought into the light of day but . . . was attired in robes till then sacred to the virgin heroine" (P. Thomson 132). In contrast to a novel like *Jessie Phillips,* where the woman is fallen (in the sense that she was aware of the circumstances), Ruth is seduced, an innocent victim. Unlike the depictions of Frances King or Kate Clark in

The Wrongs of Woman, in Gaskell the seduced woman is given a life extending beyond her occupation, a fact noted in the *North British Review*: "Its [*Mary Barton*'s] interest lay in those terrible class-rivalries, and class hatreds . . . which are the direct outgrowth of the manufacturing system. . . . But in *Ruth* the occasional element occupies the very smallest possible space." The range of the novel was especially broad since it showed "the social relations between the poorer and richer members of the middle class" (163–64). Although Gaskell distances the chronology of *Ruth* (chapter 37 alludes to Waterloo, 1815, and the typhus outbreak, 1817) and while she overemphasizes Ruth's beauty and lady-like demeanour, the text is a forceful protest against harsh social judgment in her own time. Because its range of implication was so extensive, particularly as it remained within the middle class, its argument was not only persuasive but threatening.

Gaskell's focus in *North and South* (1855) is on transition and assimilation. Unlike *Lizzie Leigh* and *Ruth,* this novel examines issues in a contemporary context. Gaskell's concerns in *North and South* are similar to Jewsbury's in *Marian Withers:* the role of woman in a changing society and the process of assimilation of the managerial classes. Assimilation is the concept uniting the stories of Margaret Hale and the manufacturer John Thornton, as well as most of the remaining characters in the novel. Some cannot assimilate at all, like Margaret's mother; others, like her father, can do so only painfully. Despite Gaskell's dissatisfaction with the method of writing the novel, for serialization in *Household Words* soon after Dickens' *Hard Times,* the work exhibits unity not only of focus but of construction. Gaskell "found it impossible to develop the story in the manner originally intended, and, more especially, was compelled to hurry on events with an improbable rapidity toward the close" (xxvii). The novel, however, does not suffer greatly from these problems.

North and South is a mid-Victorian text in that it confronts two questions close to the mid-century consciousness: religious doubt and the nature of progress. By confrontation with one or the other of these the characters achieve self-realization. Religious doubt is the catalyst for the Hales' removal from the comforts of Helstone to Milton-Northern (Manchester). Hale believes he "must no longer be a minister in the Church of England" since to accept a new position "I should have had to make a fresh declaration of conformity to the Liturgy . . . strangling my conscience" (35, 38). Hale cannot tell his wife of these misgivings, a failure of communication between husband and wife that Nightingale noted in *Cassandra:* "There is nothing in her for him to have this intimate communion *with.* He cannot impart to her his religious beliefs, if he have any, because she would be 'shocked'" (45). Margaret herself is subject to these same doubts: "She looked out upon the dark-grey lines of the church tower . . . seeing at every moment some farther distance, and yet no sign of God! It seemed to her at the moment, as if the earth was more utterly desolate than if girt in by an iron dome . . . shutting in the cries of earth's sufferers, which now might ascend into that infinite splendour of vastness and be lost — lost forever, before they reached His throne" (46). In Milton Margaret encounters the workman Higgins, who is a descendant of the religious skeptics of Kingsley and Tonna: "I'll not have my wench preached to. She's bad enough, as it is, with her dreams and her Methodee fancies, and her visions of cities with goulden gates and precious stones. . . . I believe what I see, and no more. . . . The world [is] bothering itself wi' things it knows nought about, and leaving undone all the things that lie in disorder close at its hand — why, I say, leave a' this talk about religion alone, and set to work on what yo' see and know. That's my creed. It's simple, and not far to fetch, nor hard to work." "If salvation, and life to come, and what not, was true . . . dun yo' not think they'd din us wi' it as they do wi' political 'conomy?" (104–5, 268). Religious doubt has become an element common to both the working class and the middle class. With Higgins, who realizes that economics has been substituted for religion, Gaskell develops the nascent awareness of the young protagonist of Kingsley's *Alton Locke.*

Like Marian Withers and Mary Brotherton before her, Margaret Hale in *North and South* travels, to resolve both social and religious doubts. One needs to recall, as Young observes, that "industry was a wonder, and almost a terror, to strangers from the leisurely South" ("Victorian" 155). She becomes a social explorer, an image familiar from Kay's 1832 monograph or Cooke Taylor's *Tour in the Manufacturing Districts.* Manchester even in the fifties could still seem "the shock city of the age" (Briggs, *Cities* 96). Gaskell integrates the industrial and the female issues of the novel because the exploration is as much about the condition of women as the condition of workers. Only through the struggles provoked by the industrial era does Margaret grasp the nature of her mother, the sufferings of working-class girls, and the indeterminacy of women's position. The issues of progress and assimilation are central to this exploration. In the beginning Margaret dislikes the Gormans "who made their fortunes in trade at Southampton. . . . I don't like shoppy people." "I give up the cotton-spinners; I am not standing up for them, any more than for any other trades-people. Only we shall have little enough to do with them" (18, 50–51). When Margaret calls the industrialists tradesmen, her father cautions: "Don't call the Milton manufacturers tradesmen, Margaret. . . . They are very different" (73). Gaskell shows there is no "south" at all — it is all Manchester and what it symbolizes. The idle world of the Shaws, indicated in the opening sentences with Edith Shaw asleep on the sofa, is a fading one, like that of the Arls in *Marian Withers*.

Margaret's attitudes about the north and south appear to be derived from Cooke Taylor and *Yeast*. Early in the novel she tells Henry Lennox that Helstone "is about as perfect a place in the world" as is possible (29). But when Bessy Higgins says she wished she lived in the south, Margaret declares: "There's a deal to bear there. . . . There are sorrows to bear everywhere. There is very hard bodily labour to be gone through, with very little food to give strength" (156). This passage recalls Kingsley's study in *Yeast*. Margaret advises Higgins against going south: "You must not go to the South . . . for all that. You could not stand it. You would have to be out all weathers. It would kill you with rheumatism. The mere bodily work at your time of life would break you down. The fare is far different to what you have been accustomed to. . . . You would not bear the dulness of the life; you don't know what it is; it would eat you away like rust. . . . They labour on, from day to day, in the great solitude of steaming fields — never speaking or lifting up their poor, bent, downcast heads. The hard spade-work robs their brain of life; the sameness of their toil deadens their imagination; they don't care to meet to talk over thoughts and speculations, even of the weakest, wildest kind, after their work is done; they go home brutishly tired . . . caring for nothing but food and rest" (364). Cooke Taylor noted of suffering workers "that they had rather endure anything, in the hope of some manufacturing revival, than return to the condition of farm-labourers. . . . I am forced to say, as the result of my labours, that the state of the agricultural labourer is worse than that of the operative. There is the same amount of destitution — greater there could not possibly be; but there is not the same amount of respectability. . . . The stern endurance, the moral power . . . of Lancashire . . . are wanting in the midland and southern counties. There mendicity and demoralisation are advancing with rapid strides" (80–81). Gaskell provides the final summation of attitudes about the agricultural and urban sectors that had been investigated by Stone, Kingsley, and Cooke Taylor, integrating these into the consciousness of a middle-class woman. Margaret realizes that if "I live in a factory town, I must speak factory language when I want it" (281). When she goes to London after the death of her parents, she finds it deadening, "a strange unsatisfied vacuum" (445). With her experience of both the northern and the southern counties, Margaret Hale functions as a reader surrogate in evaluating cultural differences. By this strategy, Gaskell locates such comparisons in her character's consciousness rather than in the narrator's, as had been the case in *Mary Barton* with the narrator evaluating the diverse social positions.

Gaskell registers these changes by a unifying image of the rose. She remarks early that the roses grow all over the cottages. Margaret is shown picking roses, but the change comes when Margaret sees the cheap paper on the walls in Milton: "You must prepare yourself for our drawing-room paper. Pink and blue roses, with yellow leaves!" (73). That these roses are associated with Margaret is apparent in Mrs. Thornton's hostility to her for snubbing her son: "Her sharp Damascus blade seemed out of place and useless among rose-leaves" (374). When Margaret visits Helstone again she sees "the garden, the grass-plat, formerly so daintily trim that even a stray rose-leaf seemed like a fleck on its exquisite arrangement and propriety, was strewed with children's things; a bag of marbles here, a hoop there; a straw hat forced down upon a rose-tree as on a peg, to the destruction of a long, beautiful, tender branch laden with flowers" (469). At the novel's conclusion Thornton gives her a dead rose from Helstone, marking her assimilation to a new order, the dominance of agriculture by industry. The assimilation of Margaret Hale in *North and South* is part of a tradition including Mary Brotherton of *Michael Armstrong,* Edith Langshawe of *William Langshawe,* and the protagonist of *Marian Withers.*

If Margaret Hale's growth in self-awareness leads to assimilation, Gaskell is equally concerned with the corresponding process in her factory owner John Thornton. Margaret and Thornton have a significant discussion in the chapter "Men and Gentlemen":

> "I am not quite the person to decide on another's gentlemanliness, Miss Hale. I mean, I don't quite understand your application of the word. But I should say that this Morison is no true man. . . ."

"I suspect my 'gentleman' includes your 'true man.'"

". . . A man is to me a higher and completer being than a gentleman."

"What do you mean? . . . We must understand the words differently."

"I take it that 'gentleman' is a term that only describes a person in his relation to others; but when we speak of him as 'a man,' we consider him not merely with regard to his fellow-men, but in relation to himself. . . . I am rather weary of this word 'gentlemanly,' which seems to me to be often inappropriately used." (194)

In the scene of his first declaration of love to her, Margaret notes he is not a gentleman, to which Thornton replies: "And the gentleman thus rescued is forbidden the relief of thanks! . . . I am a man. I claim the right of expressing my feelings" (232). Thornton believes the industrial system allows a man to "mount, step by step, on each wonder he achieves, to higher marvels still" (93). He uses the language of social mobility to express inventive capacity. These confrontations with Thornton do compel Margaret to wonder about her own situation in this progress. After the deaths of her parents, she reflects: "I am so tired—so tired of being whirled on through all these phases of my life, in which nothing abides by me, no creature, no place; it is like the circle in which the victims of earthly passion eddy continually" (478). "She had learnt, in those solemn hours of thought, that she herself must one day answer for her own life, and what she had done with it; and she tried to settle that most difficult problem for woman, how much was to be utterly merged in obedience to authority, and how much might be set apart for freedom in working" (497). When she gives Thornton the money to keep the Marlborough Mills operating, Margaret participates in the future. This episode demonstrates Gaskell's sharp perception of the entrepreneurial attitude of the manufacturer/investor, who was reluctant "to seek funds outside his own company and his own friends, for this would have involved him in undesirable obligations to strangers" (Deane 166). Gaskell uses the historically accurate datum for symbolic purposes.

In *North and South* Gaskell introduces a small number of references that broaden her analysis of the gentleman. The two most significant are the names of the manufacturing city, Milton-Northern, and John Thornton's defense of Oliver Cromwell, which telescopes the rose imagery of a dying tradition and Lancastrian individualism: "Rose water surgery won't do for them. Cromwell would have made a capital mill-owner, Miss Hale. I wish we had him to put down this strike for us." Margaret replies, "Cromwell is no hero of mine" (145). During the nineteenth century, Cromwell's reputation underwent considerable alteration from its ambiguous status in the Enlightenment, for example in David Hume's *History of Great Britain* (1754–1761). Carlyle's lecture "The Hero as King" in 1840, his *Letters and Speeches of Oliver Cromwell, with Elucidations* in 1845, and the lectures of Thomas Cooper (a model for Kingsley's Alton Locke) on Cromwell to Chartist groups in the forties, reestablished Cromwell. "Evangelical in religion, a self-made man, anti-aristocratic and anti-establishment, a reformer of passionate moral conviction, Cromwell had all the ingredients to make him the hero of the reformers, liberals and new men of nineteenth-century Britain" (Strong 149). It is from this perspective that he is viewed by Gaskell's Thornton. The expansion of British maritime power during the Protectorate parallels the importance of the Empire and foreign trade to the manufacturer of Lancashire during the nineteenth century. For Thornton, Cromwell is the opponent of ignorant, oppressive government, the champion of popular sovereignty. To Margaret this adulation is an "admiration of despotism" (145). As the defender of Cromwell, John Milton stands for the classically-trained man who embraces progressive policies, a prototype of Thornton himself, who studies the classics while participating in the industrial and reformist era. The name of his mills, Marlborough, alludes to the Duke of Marlborough, Governor of the Hudson's Bay Company. The Cromwell-Milton nexus of *North and South* aligns its self-made manufacturer and social reforms with political developments several centuries earlier, giving the novel a strong historical continuity.

Gaskell's study of the masculine mind, already a strength in *The Sexton's Hero* and *Lizzie Leigh,* is marked in *North and South.* It is this ability to portray the masculine as well as the feminine consciousness that gives the novel its tension. Thornton is immediately attracted to Margaret when he meets her: "She had a bracelet on one taper arm, which would fall down over her round wrist. Mr. Thornton watched the replacing of this troublesome ornament with far more attention than he listened to her father. It seemed as if it fascinated him to see her push it up impatiently until it tightened her soft flesh; and then to mark the loosening—the fall. He could almost have exclaimed—'There it goes again!'" (91). The subtlety of Gaskell's detail is exemplary. By such a device, Gaskell realized Thornton as both man and manufacturer, as she had wished: "I want to keep his character consistent with itself, and large and strong and tender, and *yet a master"* Gaskell wrote in October 1854 (Chapple 321). After Margaret's first refusal of him, the narrator explores Thornton's reactions:

> When Mr. Thornton had left the house that morning he was almost blinded by his baffled passion. He was as dizzy as if Margaret, instead of looking, and speaking, and moving like a tender graceful woman, had been a sturdy fish-wife, and given him a sound blow with her fists. He had positive bodily pain—a violent headache, and a throbbing intermittent pulse. He could not bear the noise, the garish light, the continued rumble and movement of the street. He called himself a fool for suffering so; and yet he could not, at the moment, recollect the cause of his suffering, and whether it was adequate to the consequences it had produced. . . . He said to himself that he hated Margaret; but a wild, sharp sensation of love cleft his dull, thunderous feeling like lightning, even as he shaped the words expressive of hatred. His greatest comfort was in hugging his torment; and in feeling, as he had indeed said to her, that though she might despise him, contemn him, treat him with her proud sovereign indifference, he did not change one whit. She could not make him change. He loved her, and would love her; and defy her, and this miserable bodily pain. (245–46)

Thornton and his mother quarrel about Margaret, and Gaskell allows the factory owner to reveal his torment publicly, a radically different treatment from the portrayals of industrialists by Trollope or Tonna:

> "Mother!" said he hurriedly, "I cannot hear a word against her. Spare me—spare me! I am very weak in my sore heart;—I love her yet; I love her more than ever."
>
> "And I hate her," said Mrs. Thornton, in a low fierce voice. "I tried not to hate her, when she stood between you and me, because —I said to myself—she will make him happy; and I would give my heart's blood to do that. But now, I hate her for your misery's sake. Yes, John, it's no use hiding up your aching heart from me. I am the mother that bore you, and your sorrow is my agony; and if you don't hate her, I do."
>
> "Then, mother, you make me love her more. She is unjustly treated by you, and I must make the balance even. But why do we talk of love or hatred? She does not care for me, and that is enough —too much. Let us never name the subject again. It is the only thing you can do for me in the matter. Let us never name her." (250)

Margaret and Thornton unite against the background of class antagonism; his initial laissez-faire attitude is modified by a new sense of responsibility to the workers. *North and South* depicts the power of a woman's influence (emphasized by Tonna), as John Thornton becomes a Carlylean enlightened Captain of Industry partly as a result of knowing the "southern" Margaret Hale. Their union indicates there are no longer the Two Nations of Disraeli but the single industrialized Britain of Gaskell.

North and South illustrates that "any hard-and-fast distinction between Individualism and Collectivism is not merely useless but harmful" (Burn 150). As in *Mary Barton,* the two classes are dependent: "I suppose because, on the very face of it, I see two classes dependent on each other in every possible way, yet each evidently regarding the interests of the other as opposed to their own; I never lived in a place before where there were two sets of people always running each other down" (138). Thornton initially objects to government intervention, with its ordinances about smoke pollution: "Mine were altered by my own will, before Parliament meddled with the affair" (94). Later he believes institutions must "bring the individuals of the different classes into actual personal contact" (515). The novel illustrates that by the mid-Victorian period "at every turn the interventionism of the State and individual energy met, occasionally in the way of conflict, more often in the way of mutual assistance" (Burn 287). The same process occurs in private life as Margaret and Thornton's marriage indicates. There is transition, reordering, redefining. Unlike the marriage in *Shirley,* in *North and South* marriage even with abrasion is progress. Margaret's interaction with her brother and her lying to save him have taught her a toleration that leads to a Thornton equally chastened but strengthened. More than in *Mary Barton* or *Ruth,* in *North and South* protest has become a function of reform, a recognition that interventionism is the evolving order.

In a consideration of the fifties and its tradition of the social narrative, the position of *Hard Times* by Charles Dickens (1812–1870) is important for illustrating the achievement of the female writers who preceded and succeeded him. *Hard Times* appeared in *Household Words* from 1 April to 12 August 1854, immediately preceding *North and South.* Just as Disraeli had used the Plug Plot Riots of 1842 in *Sybil,* or as Toulmin had used them the following year, Dickens used a contemporary incident as a basis for his novel, the Preston strike. There had already been an engineering strike in Britain in 1852 when the Preston weavers, in the summer of 1853, refused a 10 percent wage increase. Most were striking by September. In October the owners closed all the mills in a general lock-out, with about 20,000 out of work. In January 1854 Dickens visited Preston, publishing "On Strike" in February. When Irish workers were brought to Preston in March, the strike was undermined, and it collapsed in April. Dickens had first visited Manchester in 1838, recording: "I went, some weeks ago, to Manchester, and saw the *worst* cotton mill. And then I saw the *best*. . . . There was no great difference between them" (M. House 483). In *The Old Curiosity Shop* Dickens described the factories as nightmarish wastelands, but Preston proved less engrossing in 1854 than Manchester in 1838: "I am afraid I shall not be able to get much here. Except the crowds at the street-corners reading the placards pro and con; and the cold absence of smoke from the mill-chimneys; there is very little in the streets to make the town remarkable" (Forster 567).

There are several consequences of this unprofitable research for *Hard Times*. Dickens was "imperfectly acquainted with the groups he detested" (Cazamian 154), and "the effects of inadequate knowledge and class prejudice are reinforced by the very qualities which give *Hard Times* its vitality" (Carnall 48). Although he was a friend of Lord Ashley and Southwood Smith, Dickens infrequently relied on documents. Dickens used the *Second Report* of the Children's Employment Commission for the account of Meg Veck in *The Chimes* (1844) not "to argue a case, but to create an emotional tableau" (Cazamian 156). Questions arise about the seriousness of *Hard Times*. The book is a compound of hyperbolic characters: Bounderby, the self-made man and proponent of laissez-faire; Gradgrind, the classical economist, with sons named Adam Smith and Malthus; Harthouse, the dilettante canvasser; Blackpool, the proletarian saint. One might conclude that Dickens has written not a serious piece of Condition-of-England fiction but a parody of the material that has preceded him. If the work is serious, it is behind the times, partaking of the manner of Trollope in the late thirties. Gradgrind and Bounderby are not far removed from Dowling and Sharpton in *Michael Armstrong* or the cruel owners in *Helen Fleetwood* or the *Memoir of Robert Blincoe*. "*Hard Times* is outstanding only in the power and consistency of Dickens's vision, not in its uniqueness" (Kettle 173). If the novel is considered as a serious work, it is in the manner of an earlier tradition, not in the most developed form of that tradition in Jewsbury and Gaskell. Female novelists had advanced beyond this form of expression by the fifties. If one conceives of the work as serious criticism, then one must believe that its machinery and exaggeration result from a failure to confront its subject, a result not of engagement but of evasion. As one reviewer noted of Dickens' accusations against the government in *Little Dorrit,* "the burlesque manner and extravagant language in which they are made are at once Mr. Dickens's shield and his sword" (Stephen 68). Even if one strike leader, Mortimer Grimshaw, was like Slackbridge, he was not typical (Carnall 34). Giving Dickens the benefit of the doubt, one might consider the novel a parody of its own sub-genre, of Tonna and Gaskell. The novel then might be viewed as a satire of the characters originally treated in an earlier era.

Dickens' earlier ventures into the criticism of specific social abuses are instructive for assessing the stature of *Hard Times.* Many of its practices are similar to those of *Oliver Twist,* with characters like the Bumbles undermining its intention to criticize the New Poor Law and not far removed from the Trollope of *Michael Armstrong.* In *Hard Times* Dickens so insistently abandons the fantasy justice of *Oliver Twist* that the repudiation is as incredible as the former indulgence. Dickens was able to recreate the urban milieu of Jacobs Island in *Oliver Twist,* but "he gives far fewer details of the horror of the place than does Kingsley" (Smith, *Nation* 67). *The Chimes* includes characters like Filer, a satire on political economists, and Alderman Cute, equivocator, or Joseph Bowley, M.P. In Meg Veck and Lillian Fern, Dickens presents in the visionary third quarter a picture of distressed seamstresses: "Such work, such work! So many hours, so many days, so many long, long nights of hopeless, cheerless, never-ending work — not to heap up riches, not to live grandly or gaily, not to live upon enough, however coarse; but to earn bare bread" (108–9). Lillian becomes a prostitute, returning to die in Meg's arms. The death of Ellen Cardan in *The Young Milliner* was stark and thus more effective in its presentation; the fact that Dickens cancels this "vision" is evasive rather than effective. One key to Dickens' method in *The Chimes* and in *Hard Times* is the pervasive use of tripartite sentence structures, which reveals the narrator observing rather than reproducing the consciousness of his characters.

The same stylistic peculiarity appears with similar consequences in *Hard Times.* The satiric portrait of Bounderby is effective: "A man who could never sufficiently vaunt himself a self-made man. A man who was always proclaiming . . . his old ignorance and his old poverty. A man who was the Bully of humility" (18). But Dickens becomes excessive in describing Gradgrind: "The emphasis was helped by the speaker's square wall of a forehead, which had his eyebrows for its base, while his eyes found commodious cellarage in two dark caves, overshadowed by the wall. The emphasis was helped by the speaker's mouth, which was wide, thin, and hard set. The emphasis was helped by the speaker's voice, which was inflexible, dry, and dictatorial. The emphasis was helped by the speaker's hair, which bristled on the skirts of his bald head, a plantation of firs to keep the wind from its shining surface, all covered with knobs, like the crust of a plum pie, as if the head had scarcely warehouse-room for the hard facts stored inside. . . . All helped the emphasis" (3–4). The initial paragraph of the novel, with Gradgrind calling for "Facts . . . nothing but Facts" is effective, but the second paragraph, on Gradgrind's physical features, veers into meaninglessness. The comparisons that became extreme in the second paragraph are reproduced in the celebrated description of Coketown in the image of the elephant, where ingenuity is undercut by excess. Dickens' depiction of owners' attitudes to intervention is marked by the same narrative voice: "Surely there never was such fragile china-ware as that of which the millers of Coketown were made. . . . They were ruined, when they were required to send labouring children to school; they were ruined when inspectors were appointed to look into their works; they were ruined, when such inspectors considered it doubtful whether they were quite justified in chopping people up with their machinery" (131–32). After the presentation of interventionism in *Mary Barton* or of the self-made man in *Marian Withers*, Dickens' accumulation of detail in self-conscious phrases is retrogressive. As the narratives of Jewsbury and Gaskell indicate, by the mid-fifties topics like fencing machinery and educating factory children were no longer focal issues. The fact that Dickens canceled a manuscript passage, recording that Rachael's sister lost her arm in a factory accident, indicates that he knew such material was dated. It is an example of his "prudent retarding" (P. Thomson 104).

This narrative style, however, is not confined solely to the narrator but invades the consciousness and the dialogue of the characters. The following examples illustrate the parallel and tripartite clauses that prevent rather than prompt credibility:

Narrator on Harthouse: This gentleman had a younger brother of still better appearance than himself, who had tried life as a Cornet of Dragoons, and found it a bore; and had afterwards tried it in the train of an English minister abroad, and found it a bore; and had then strolled to Jerusalem, and got bored there; and had then gone yachting about the world, and got bored everywhere. (148)

Blackpool himself: "Look how we live, an wheer we live, an in what numbers, an by what chances, and wi' what sameness. . . . Look how you considers of us, an writes of us, and talks of us. . . . Look how this ha' growen an growen, sir, bigger an bigger, broader an broader, harder an harder, fro year to year, fro generation unto generation." (177)

Louisa on workpeople: Something to be worked so much and paid so much, and there ended; something to be infallibly settled by laws of supply and demand; something that blundered against those laws, and floundered into difficulty; something that was a little pinched when wheat was dear. . . . (186)

Harthouse on Bounderby: "If I might venture to remark that it is the least in the world deficient in that delicacy to which a youth mistaken, a character misconceived, and abilities misdirected, would turn for relief and guidance, I should express what it presents to my own view." (204)

Gradgrind to Louisa: "When I consider your character; when I consider that what has been known to me for hours, has been concealed by you for years; when I consider under what immediate pressure it has been forced from you at last; I come to the conclusion that I cannot but mistrust myself." (263–64)

Sissy to Harthouse: "I have no other trust, than that I have been with her since she came home, and that she has given me her confidence. I have no further trust, than that I know something of her character and her marriage." (275)

The accumulation of tripartite expressions characterizes everyone in the novel, Blackpool, Louisa, Gradgrind, Bounderby, Harthouse, and the narrator, a lack of differentiation that is fatal to *Hard Times*. Writing in 1856, George Eliot noted that Dickens was "gifted with the utmost power of rendering the external traits of our town population." Nevertheless, she added: "If he could give us their psychological character — their conceptions of life, and their emotions — with the same truth as their idiom and manners, his books would be the greatest contributions Art has ever made in the awakening of social sympathies," noting especially "his frequently false psychology" (Pinney 271). In *Hard Times,* however, the failure of the idiom becomes the failure of the psychology, revealing the inadequacy of its protest. Fielding and Smith attempt to defend Dickens, ignoring literary history in the process: "We have also to consider how extraordinarily confined up to this time had been the imaginative understanding even of Dickens and certainly of most of his readers when faced with the results of the industrial revolution. Industrial life was a new experience for the imaginative writer" (426–27). This apologia is untenable after the depictions of Jewsbury, Kingsley, Disraeli, Stone, and Gaskell, even of Toulmin, Tonna, and Trollope. Stephen Blackpool's problems are more marital than industrial, a fact Dickens fails to grasp in the dominance of the text by the narrative voice. Humphry House may well be correct that *Hard Times* expresses "the Southerner's dismay at what he could not assimilate" (211), but a creative writer must be judged not only by what he could not but also by what he would not incorporate. By the mid-fifties the amalgam of government philosophy had been formed of a compound of laissez-faire, interventionism, and Utilitarianism, all of which Dickens anachronistically studies in the novel. Dickens' narrator is his shield in *Hard Times.*

Hard Times recalls practices of a writer of a lower order, such as Paul Pimlico in a work like *The Factory Girl* of 1849. Pimlico intended to advance the "Radical charge of using the law as an instrument of the rich against the poor, for whom justice is not to be had" (Melada 63). Pimlico recounts the story of William and Esther Mansfield, who on their father's death are left destitute because of his speculations. Forced to go to Bradford, Esther is warned by Mrs. Unwin about the attempts on a factory girl's virtue. The closeness of the brother and sister seems to be refuting Peter Gaskell's belief in 1833 that in the mill "brother and sister lose that connexion which ought naturally and properly to exist between them" (148). Through the influence of Esther's fiancé, Frederick Flockton, William obtains a position in the firm of Julius Arnheim, while Esther goes to work at Alston's factory under the sensual overlooker Judas Bromley. Pimlico criticizes factories as "labour-harems," with the loss of domesticity among female operatives and the "women overstepping the bounds of our civilised nature and doing the work of men" (203). Pimlico criticizes the Worsted Act, by which an employer could compel a worker to finish a warp, an instance where the "law is turned into an engine of oppression,—the dispensers of *law,* not *justice*" (218).

Esther's attorney Shakechaff defends her chastity when Bromley gives her a bad warp because she resisted his advances.

Maria Edgecombe, previously seduced by Bromley, turns evidence against him: "Know, then, what it is to draw down the hatred and revenge of a wronged and indignant woman" (219). Alston, Bromley, and Arnheim all try to seduce Esther. She retorts: "Your audacity and insolence, sir, . . . are such that I can endure your presence no longer. . . . Wretch . . . take not the word *virtue* in your polluted lips. . . . Give me virtue with honesty and peace of mind, though clad in rags, and in a hovel" (235). Pimlico ignores the fact that immorality in factories, as Hewitt argues (57–60), was no greater than in society at large. Pimlico's depiction recalls William Dodd's appraisal of factory seduction in *The Factory System Illustrated* in 1842: "I regret to be compelled, in justice to the work-people, to state, that the example set them by their masters, in many instances, has not a tendency to raise, but rather to lower and debase their moral character" (68).

Pimlico manages to observe something of significance in his narrative: "Esther's virtue was . . . like a commercial material, the subject of interest and debate" (249). When the three men decide to seduce her, Pimlico indicates that women have become commodities subject to the same laws of competition and self-interest that pervade the social fabric. One should read the remaining three chapters of *The Factory Girl* as something beyond melodrama. It is satire on the competitive ethic, of the *quid pro quo* of commercial success and the concept of self-interest. Through the aid of Ellen Jowett, who works with Esther, she is taken to Mrs. Timpson's brothel, with pictures of Nell Gwynn and Fair Rosamond on its walls. This episode was probably inspired by Peter Gaskell's comment: "Houses were established in some localities by parties of young men purposely for the prosecution of their illicit pleasures, and to which their victims repaired—nothing loth, it is true, to share the disgraceful orgies of their paramours; and in which scenes were enacted that even put to the blush the lascivious Saturnalia of the Romans, the rites of the Pagoda girls of India, and the Harem life of the most voluptuous Ottoman" (64). Esther is rescued by Flockton and her brother, who marry each other's sisters and start their own businesses. While the violent language is inappropriate, Pimlico's presentation of women as commodities advances a point as could no discussion of classical economics. His exaggerated method does not pretend to loftier motives than to present the radical attitude in the style condoned by this tradition. Dickens in *Hard Times* is not consciously working in that tradition, and therefore the lack of independence of the characters from the narrator undermines his objectives. In *Hard Times* there is an echo of a writer like Pimlico, filtered through Carlyle and Cobbett. As Himmelfarb observes, "Some thought him as low as Reynolds" (457).

The year preceding the publication of *Hard Times* Fanny Mayne published *Jane Rutherford; or the Miners' Strike* in *The True Briton* from 1853 to 1854. This novel presents strike conditions in the town of Horsely during 1844 and "reflects the mood of reconciliation that is characteristic of mid-century" (Melada 142). Mayne's intention is to demonstrate a ratification of the improvement of conditions since the forties, since her story concludes in 1850. It notices the processes of legislation and reform that had affected the mining community, a commentary on *Sybil*. Mayne describes reforms like the payment of wages in money rather than tickets, that is, the elimination of the truck system and the system of tied cottages. While to some extent these reforms were actualized by 1853, they were very tentative during the dramatic period of the work, 1844. Mayne attributes fifties reforms to a period when they were at best initiated. She alludes to the 1842 Coal Mines Act which excluded women from the pit as bringing reform, but the enforcement of this and other acts against mining abuses was still being pursued in mid-century.

In the presentation of the situation of England, Mayne attempts a balanced view. Describing the conditions of a striker, she notes: "Though he may succeed in getting the required increase in his wages, which is still problematical, he is compelled to look forward to months of difficulty and even of privation before he gets over the consequences of his present conduct" (46). She criticizes the local parson, Mr. Jones, for being too ready to take the workers' part:

> This 'parson', like many another parson, was thoroughly taken in by that side of the question which he heard, and did not open his eyes wide enough to see the other. . . . He saw . . . the rich becoming very rich, and he quite forgot that by far the greater part of these very rich men had either raised themselves, or their fathers had raised themselves and their families, by frugality, economy, hard work, foresight, providence, rightmindedness, and a proper employment of their talents, joined to rigid self-denial. . . . He imputed the greater part, if not the whole, of the sin and misery which in times past, and in times present especially, was so rampant in Hors-

ley, to the system and to the individual rich; he forgot all the improvidence, all the dirt, all the domestic extravagance, all the indulgence of the animal passions . . . which urged and animated the
leaders of these strikes (61–62).

Mayne's attitude is similar to Gaskell's in *Mary Barton:* "We deny
to either class the pre-eminence in moral feelings, tender affections,
or of the higher or lower qualities. . . . It is in the individuals of the
classes, not in the classes themselves, that we find the difference" (850).

Mayne is aware of writing in a specific tradition. She deliberately
deemphasizes the exotic and emphasizes the ordinary. The narrator
addresses the reader on her seamstress heroine: "Now, don't laugh,
reader, at my talking about whether a plain needlework girl, the
daughter of a collier, is awkward or not" (810). Assuming the attitude of an observer, Mayne describes herself as getting a makeshift
"capital reporter's desk" (867). When Stephenson ejects the miners
from his cottages, she reports, "None of them liked the idea of being
turned out of their houses; and yet none of them could assert that
Mr. Stephenson was doing them any wrong in requiring them to leave
his houses, when they had voluntarily quitted his employment" (79).
Mayne attempts to be even-minded about her characters, although
her dislike of Jonathan Rutherford, strike agitator and Jane's father,
leads her to say "he resembled Jacob the dissembler somewhat in
spirit" (810) and she comments on "the littleness of the man!" (882).
Mayne's awareness of a tradition of industrial literature is indicated
in her references to previous writers, possibly including Gaskell, Disraeli, and Dickens. She echoes Disraeli's idea of the Two Nations:
"'One half of the world knows not how the other half lives' was the
talismanic key that opened out at once the brotherhood of humanity, and 'what can I do for my neighbour?' is now the cry of the neigh-
bourly in all classes. . . . All will meet together now on the common
ground of working for their neighbour's weal. Therefore, 'one half
of the world knows not how the other half lives,' is no longer true,
although it is still re-echoed by the maudlin sentimentalist, and the
radical socialist, to uphold the theories of the latter, or to make a
happy turn to the rhapsodies of the former" (867). Attributing fifties
conditions to forties contexts, she implies that the situations depicted
by Disraeli have been improved.

She may be thinking of Dickens in her comment about sentimen-
talists, since in 1851 she had criticized *Household Words.* She wrote

of that periodical: "There is scarcely a work in the land that tends more to separate class from class, or to make the poor man feel that he is oppressed and overborne by the rich, and that the laws and institutions, and authorities of the country are *against him* and *for them*" (Dalziel 52). Her radicals would include writers like Pimlico. It is possible that she criticizes Gaskell in this commentary: "Somehow or other men and women are very different. . . . The very failings and sins that are passed over and forgiven by the world in a man, are never passed by or forgiven by that same world in a woman; though we nowhere read that the Almighty has two measures for the two sexes. However, we wish it not to be otherwise! . . . We [are] persuaded that the code of earthly morality should not be altered, or, if altered at all, altered with a view to the equalization of punishment by the outlawry of both the offenders, without distinction of sex, — in brief, the putting out also of the man who transgresses, and not the tolerating of the woman who sins, as some of our fellow-authors would now advocate" (851). This statement could be an allusion to *Ruth,* which had been published 24 January 1853.

Like the stories of Martineau, Mayne's *Jane Rutherford* uses time compression to enforce the urgency of events. Set primarily in April and May, 1844, the tale commences on Maundy Thursday evening. Half the novel (chapters one to twenty-two) occurs within forty-eight hours, including the initiation of the strike and the development of Jane's affair with William Norman. At the beginning of the second volume, the narrator forgets 1844 and seems to think her tale concerns 1849: "At the last strike in 1844, five years ago, though it had lasted only a fortnight, they had been left penniless; and now it would be the same again" (3), although later she quotes evidence of the 1844 strike. She marks the deaths of several characters as occurring on 30 and 31 May 1844, and on 15 June. The slight slip by the narrator shows her telescoping present remediation and past distress. To emphasize the historical background, the narrator alludes to the cholera of 1832 (appropriate since there was cholera in Britain during the serialization of the novel, discussed in *The True Briton*), the 1842 Mines Act, the Plug Plot Riots, the improvements in cemetery locations from the 1848 Public Health Act and the 1849 Amended Nuisances Act, and the reports of Dr. John Simon. The Burial Acts in 1850 and 1852 had begun to remove cemeteries from metropolitan areas to regions outside the urban environment by the time Mayne's readers were perusing *Jane Rutherford.*

Mayne's material recalls precedents set by other novelists. Like Tonna and Jewsbury she takes her reader to industrial scenes, here a mine, which she claims to have studied underground herself, acquainting the reader with specific technical vocabulary. Like Tonna, Martineau, and Jewsbury, she emphasizes that women learn domestic science: "It is a woman's rightful sphere to make the home bright and happy"; "The women in a factory town . . . have no home occupation. Their house-work is always performed in the smallest possible time" (62). Following the examples of Stone, Tonna, and Gaskell, Mayne has a needleworker rather than a factory worker as a protagonist. Mayne is not sentimental about needlework. She quotes Hood's *Song of the Shirt,* and in March 1854, the final year of its publication, she published in *The True Briton* an essay, "Slaves of the Needle," about women "working until consumption shall end the wretchedness that social tyranny began" (533). In the novel she notes that Jane did not make "shirts for three farthings apiece, as it is reported some of the hard-worked daughters of our land are obliged to do" (810). In the same issues as her serial she includes poems like "The Trapper's Petition" or "The Miners' Complaint" despite the fact that the novel claims abuses are remedied. As in Martineau, women are shown particularly to be opposed to strikes. Mayne speaks of charity as an act of "womanity" (63), a concept she otherwise does not explore, albeit an intriguing coinage.

Like Jewsbury and Stone, Mayne is concerned with the assimilation of laborers, particularly in the figure of Henry Stephenson: "Yet time was when he had been a common labourer . . . only a bargeman's boy." When he secured money to purchase a horse, "this was Henry Stephenson's first upward step in life" (30–31). The fact that Jonathan Rutherford is the same age and began as a trapper, but never elevated himself, is a criticism not of the factory or the industrial system but of himself. As Burn notes, "Large numbers of people had to be forced to compete freely" (112). Rutherford is an example of this incapacity to adjust to circumstances. Stephenson tells Lord Westerland about his son that "if he is to rise in life, he must work his own fortune, I say, as I have done" (47). This accords with the general philosophy of *The True Briton,* which was "that it is the responsibility of working-class people to help themselves" (Dalziel 166). Mayne, like Craik later in *John Halifax,* accepts the fact that "a Christian man cannot be otherwise than a courteous, well-behaved gentleman" (47). As does Stone in *William Langshawe,* Mayne shows the assimilation process that vindicates the industrial system, although unnaturally she presents Lord Westerland as "the model of an English nobleman . . . rendered almost majestic by the maturity of mind and form . . . his long iron-grey hair floating in the breeze" (867). The illustrator shared this hagiography, for the sketch illustrating this episode shows Westerland as all of twenty-five. Mayne aims at a gradualness of narrative suggesting Gaskell in her early stories. Like them she uses a range of characters to create a credible milieu, a community: the Wesleyan Methodist Pearces, the exacting Stephenson, the more liberal Westerland, the unbelieving Rutherford, the nondoctrinal William Norman. Mayne's depiction of Methodism among the laboring classes anticipates *Adam Bede:* hers is one of the few industrial fictions after Tonna in which the novelist takes religious belief into account as a social force.

The novel, perhaps because of its serialization, displays some crudities of construction. One structural difficulty is that Mayne fails to dramatize the past life of her characters. Such events as Rutherford's accident, the death of Jane's mother, Abraham Pearce's accident, and the account of Stephenson's rise are awkwardly introduced into the narrative. Occasionally the narrator echoes the dogmatism of Martineau: "It now became a struggle between the powers of endurance and of capital. True, the masters were great losers, but, on the other hand, were not the wages of the workpeople their daily bread? the very life of themselves and their families? . . . If the poor man's capital — his labour — be unused but for a week, his position is vastly different from that of the merchant or the banker" (45). "The science of political economy is sufficiently studied or understood by all classes to prove that, as in all cases the demand creates the supply, so also, in an equal degree, the supply creates the demand" (785). Such asides and the rhetoric of Rutherford's speeches, while recalling Martineau, are not persistent. Mayne attempts to reproduce workers' dialect with some success, and she does attempt to enter her protagonist's mind: "She trembled as she took up the knife. It seemed quite certain that it must be covered with blood. But no, that was not the case. The handle she could not be mistaken in. . . . What did it mean? But there is her father at the door" (142). This passage, recounting the abrupt departure of the Rutherfords to America, reproduces Jane's shock at finding evidence of her father's destruction of the shaft-rope.

Jane Rutherford should be read as a text of the fifties despite its forties subject matter. It is a response to *Sybil* without a specific political position. Mayne does not speciously elevate a "daughter of the people" or create a myth, like Carlyle or Disraeli, about England's past. The novel also displays interesting differences from *Hard Times*. Mayne had visited Preston and wrote about it in *The True Briton*. That she recognizes improved conditions, as Dickens does not, indicates the difference in approach. Mayne is not unaware that more is to be done: "The misery and hunger of thousands of our fellow-beings is the source of happiness to millions" (883). Mayne avoids hyperbole, excessive metaphors, and stereotypical characterization, achieving a muted presentation more akin to Julia Kavanagh's *Rachel Gray* in 1856. This sombre tone possibly contributed to the failure of *The True Briton:* "The *True Briton* failed, probably because it pleased nobody. Less dogmatically evangelical than periodicals like the *Sunday at Home,* it certainly offended some of the unco' guid. . . . Those who wanted marvellous tales must have found the fiction in The *True Briton* sad stuff indeed" (Dalziel 68).

In the essay, "What I Saw and Heard in the Manufacturing Districts," January 1854, Mayne studied the consequences of the Preston Strike. She makes a key point about the intersection of industrial and domestic discord, comparing the relations of employers and employed to the relations of husband and wife: "And where once bitterness and rancour prevails between employers and employed, who can say where it is to end? It is in a wider degree much the same as the growth of bitterness in a nearer and dearer relation of life" (385). As the Editor of *The True Briton* Mayne included essays in her journal about emigration, cholera, self-improvement, suffrage, women's domestic duties, redundant women, hospitals, and cotton lords. Such exposure to these issues made her a cautious advocate of gradualism, perhaps because Mayne in her journal showed "real knowledge of the poor" and emphasized "deliberate realism" (Dalziel 166, 133). It also steadied her attitude, leading her to create in *Jane Rutherford* "no pining, dreamy heroine of a fanciful romance" (810) but a relatively unheightened study that looked toward George Eliot, Julia Kavanagh, and the sixties.

In 1856 two social novels by women appeared, each with a different focus: one presenting a myth of successful upward mobility and assimilation, Dinah Mulock Craik's *John Halifax, Gentleman;* the other an unvarnished account of two persons neither mobile nor assimilated, Julia Kavanagh's *Rachel Gray. John Halifax,* as its title indicates, records the validation of the idea of self-reliance and its result. The novel echoes the redefinition of "gentleman" undertaken earlier in such works as *William Langshawe, Jane Rutherford,* and *North and South.* This novel by Craik (1826–1887) is a textbook of the rise of the successful worker to a position of wealth and affluence, similar to the account of John Withers in Jewsbury's *Marian Withers,* "the evolution of a working-class orphan into a captain of industry" (Brantlinger, *Spirit* 119). More than twenty years earlier, Peter Gaskell in 1833 had observed that "the men who did establish themselves were raised by their own efforts" (45) and that "many of the first successful manufacturers were men who had their origin in the rank of mere operatives" (52). "Many of the masters have raised themselves from the very humblest rank of labourers . . . [and] have gradually [been] converted . . . into respectable and even handsome families" (171). Even if, as J. F. C. Harrison contends, "self-help was a myth" because of the wide social gap, "the ideology of mobility" could be motivational (176). The rise of Halifax parallels the rise of the nation to a new democratization; he *is* England in the transition between the eighteenth and the early nineteenth centuries. His surname, that of "a capital of the worsted trade" (Fielden vii) shows the commercial direction of the nineteenth century. The novel is narrated by Phineas Fletcher, from his diary and from memory. The son of a Quaker tanner, Fletcher has already achieved the higher status of the second generation. Since he is lame, his revolt against his father's trade is tolerated. (He may be a prototype of Philip Wakem in *The Mill on the Floss.*) Craik embodies her observer in a male persona, but throughout Phineas describes himself as womanish. His suppressed love for Halifax causes him to identify Halifax as David to his Jonathan throughout the narrative.

The time scheme of *John Halifax* shows the intersection of personal with national events. Like *Marian Withers, John Halifax* opens in 1794 when Fletcher finds Halifax. By 1800 he goes to live at Enderley, commuting to work at Norton Bury. In 1812 Halifax introduces power looms to his mill, in conjunction with the Luddites, the battle of Badajoz, and the assassination of Perceval in the Commons. As in Jewsbury's novel, which Craik certainly read, the 1825 speculations mania plays a significant part in Halifax's life. Catholic Emancipation in 1829 is given particular point by Craik's creation of the Luxmore family. The pre-Reform elections anticipate the analogous scenes of *Middlemarch.* Halifax and his wife die on 1 August 1834, the date of the termination of slavery in the colonies. (The novel recalls the program advocated by Tonna in *The System*). These events mark stations in the nation's progress that parallel Halifax's own progress.

Craik's two main considerations are upward mobility through self-help and the assimilation of her tradesman into gentility. As Briggs notes, the concept of self-help and that of the gentleman were two central aspects of mid-Victorian sensibility. "The idea of the 'gentleman' is the necessary link in any analysis of mid-Victorian ways of thinking and behaving" (*Age* 411). Halifax when very young states: "If I get one foot on the ladder, perhaps I may climb. . . . It's a notion of mine that whatever a man may be, his trade does not make him — he makes his trade" (27–28). "It isn't trade that signifies, it's the man" (101). John expands his trade after receiving his wife's inheritance, so his success is a combination of character and luck. "John's fortunes grew rapidly — as many another fortune grew, in the beginning of the thirty years' peace, when unknown, petty manufacturers first rose into merchant princes and cotton lords" (294). *John Halifax* describes the origins of an attitude that by the 1850s had become a creed.

One of the dimensions of this mobility is the advent of respectability in industry. "The existence, in fact, of some kind of relation between gentility and economic circumstances added to the difficulty of defining that all-important being, the gentleman" (Burn 255). The basis of Halifax's transformation is his birth, where he was listed as having a father who was "a scholar and a gentleman. . . . For since it is a law of nature, admitted only in rare exceptions, that the qualities of the ancestors should be transmitted to the race, — the fact seems patent enough, that even allowing equal advantages, a gentleman's son has more chances of growing up a gentleman than the son of a working man" (5). As one reviewer noted, this antecedent gentle birth undermines the validity of Craik's idea of self-help: "All his moral excellence and intellectual worth were derived from *ladies* and *gentlemen* who had been his remote ancestors. . . . She does depict a noble nature and an unselfish life; but seeing that John Halifax did begin the world as a poor friendless boy, she might have allowed us to think that such a development was possible to man as man" ("Author" 42–43). When John speaks of putting on the gentleman, Phineas responds: "You couldn't do that, John. You couldn't put on what you were born with" (90).

Craik's ambivalence, espousing the gradual rise of her workman while endowing him with gentle birth, represents her caution, perhaps her anxiety about the connection between economics and gentility. Halifax tells his future wife Ursula March: "The world says we are not equals, and it would neither be for Miss March's honour nor mine did I try to force upon it the truth — which I may prove openly one day — that we *are* equals" (143). This ambiguous statement obscures the issue of natural versus acquired gentility, reflected later when Halifax's son Guy states "We are gentlefolks now" and his father replies "We always were, my son" (301). Fletcher records the "great change in manners and morals, that intemperance, instead of being the usual characteristic of a 'gentleman,' has become a rare failing — a universally-contemned disgrace" (237). The basic doctrine of the novel is one of progressive though gradual improvement. About God's plan for the human race, Halifax comments: "So far as we can see, He means [it] like all other of His creations gradually to advance toward perfection" (245). *John Halifax* records a key change: "In the moralistic climate of mid-Victorian England the superiority arising from high rank or great wealth was not quite enough; certain moral attributes had to be annexed to it" (Burn 317). Thus, "a Christian only can be a true gentleman" (163).

Dinah Craik reinforces this belief in gradual improvement and assimilation by several interrelating devices. The sequence of settings reflects the gradual upward progress of Halifax, as he moves to Enderley in 1800, to Longfield in 1812, and to Beechwood Hall in 1825. Each year marks a national crisis as well: hunger and fear of war in 1800, Luddism and war with America in 1812, and the financial crash in 1825. Craik emphasizes the necessity of persistent effort for social elevation; the rise of Halifax is definitely not one of overnight success. The cautiousness of this attitude is emphasized by the visit Phineas Fletcher and Halifax make to a performance of *Macbeth* with Sarah Siddons in 1798. In the crowd at the theatre Halifax loses his money. This symbolic incident indicates the danger of complacency regarding one's financial stability. The play *Macbeth* reinforces the necessity of a careful upward progress rather than an impulsively rash change of situation. Craik manipulates the obligatory "riot scene" for her own purposes. During the riot at the flour mill on the first and second of August 1800, Halifax restores order by distributing food to the starving workers, dividing provisions from the Fletcher household, thereby suggesting Christ's division of the loaves and fishes. After this incident, a workman states, "You was born for a gentleman, sure-ly" (81). The matrix of such incidents in *John Halifax* constitutes a dogma of gradual upward mobility through Christian endurance, emphasizing the morality of gentlemanliness.

A reviewer in 1864 noted a flaw in Craik's novel: "John Halifax is another type of young man — such a type as one may find among the saints whom young ladies of High Church tendencies are fond of painting and contemplating. But ordinary life benefits little from the example of John Halifax" ("Novels Purpose" 33). When the novel was published, the *Athenaeum* noted that the protagonist "is much too idealized" (520). This may be the result of female novelists using "their heroes . . . to think out their own unrealized ambitions." Phineas Fletcher, crippled and "womanish," may be a representation of a "different kind of female experience, much closer to Craik's own." Craik may have derived this idea from the hunchbacked Thurstan Benson of *Ruth*. "Fletcher and Halifax represent the two sides of her self-image: the crippled looker-on at other people's happy marriages and lives, permanently disbarred from such joy; and the energetic, successful, and admired leader" (Showalter, "Craik" 17–18). This argument, however, ignores the most prominent woman in the novel, Ursula March, who is characterized, as a reviewer noted, by the fact that her "first attitude is always one of resistance" ("Author" 45).

Craik's treatment of women in *John Halifax* is unusual. Several of the women, like Ursula March or the governess Louise d'Argent, are strong and self-reliant, yet the roles they perform are not progressive: within the role, they are assertive, but Craik does not grant them the mobility or progressive attitudes of her males. The most defiant woman in the novel, close to Lady Wollaston in *Marian Withers,* is the adulterous Lady Caroline Brithwood, who tests the conventional role. Married to the brutal Richard Brithwood, she asks Ursula Halifax: "What constitutes a man one's husband? Brutality, tyranny — the tyranny which the law sanctions? Or kindness, sympathy, devotion, everything that makes life beautiful — " (228). Ursula responds: "I think a wife is bound to the very last to obey in all things, not absolutely wrong, her husband's will." "Beyond all maternal duty, is the duty that a woman owes to her husband" Phineas pontificates (369). If Phineas is a negative image of womanhood, Craik is then criticizing women who accept this belief. She may be responding to George Eliot's statement in the *Leader,* in October 1855, that "men pay a heavy price for their reluctance to encourage self-help and independent resources in women" (Pinney 204). For Craik self-help as an ideology for men does not extend to married women. This idea is not different from Craik's essays in *Chambers's Journal,* later collected in *A Woman's Thoughts about Women* in 1858, or in her essay "Concerning Men" in 1887. In the former she declares that "society's advance is usually indicated by the advance, morally and intellectually, of its women," but she regards as "blasphemous" and "harmful" "the outcry about 'the equality of the sexes,'" stating that "equality of the sexes is not in the nature of things." "The difference between a man's vocation and a woman's seems naturally to be this—the one is abroad, the other at home" (10–13, 20). Neither Halifax nor his wife supports Lady Caroline, "a woman false to her husband" (226). In her late essay, Craik discusses how rapidly men fall "into the nets spread by a bad woman" (375), and it is presumably to this category that Craik consigns Lady Caroline. With Jewsbury's study of Lady Wollaston in *Marian Withers,* this is one of the strongest portraits of an adulterous woman in the decade. Inadvertently undermining her thesis, Craik shows Lady Caroline dying unrepentant. Jewsbury, reviewing *A Woman's Thoughts about Women* in the *Athenaeum,* thought its content "verging on common-place" but indicating a "progress of opinion" over previous treatises about women (177).

John Halifax is part of the ideology of upward mobility, self-help, and success that formed part of the mid-century consciousness, which had found expression in the Great Exhibition of 1851, the doctrine of "the ever-advancing tide of human improvement" (302). If as Brantlinger contends the novel "leaves the problem of the masses unresolved" (*Spirit* 123), it nevertheless promulgates a myth of self-development that was potentially powerful. Narratives like *William Langshawe, A Story of the Factories, Marian Withers,* and *North and South* reveal the development of interest in this subject among female novelists. George Eliot was indignant when a reviewer compared her to Dinah Craik, then Miss Mulock: "The most ignorant journalist in England would hardly think of calling me a rival of Miss Mulock—a writer who is read only by novel-readers, pure and simple, never by people of high culture. . . . We belong to an entirely different order of writers" (Haight, *Letters* 3:302). Craik did, however, write the novel that summarized the ideology of the mid-century.

Despite the fact that many were able to subscribe to this myth of assimilation, self-help, and upward mobility, and perhaps to realize it, there were thousands who could not or would not. *Rachel Gray* by Julia Kavanagh (1824–1877) was published in 1856 just before the appearance of *John Halifax.* In the tradition of women's social fiction, the conjunction was fortuitous, for *John Halifax* expressed a myth that *Rachel Gray* undermines and refutes. On the publication of the novel, George Eliot reviewed it for the *Leader:* "*Rachel Gray* is not a story of a fine lady's sorrows wept into embroidered pocket-handkerchiefs, or of genius thrust into the background by toad-eating stupidity. It does not harrow us with the sufferings and temptations of a destitute needlewoman, or abash us with refined sentiments and heroic deeds of navvies and ratcatchers. It tells the trials of a dressmaker who *could* get work, and of a small grocer, very vulgar, and not at all heroic, whose business was gradually swallowed up by the large shop over the way. Thus far *Rachel Gray* is commendable: it occupies ground which is very far from being exhausted, and it undertakes to impress us with the every-day sorrows of our commonplace fellow-men, and so to widen our sympathies . . . in that most prosaic stratum of society, the small shopkeeping class; and here is really a new sphere for a great artist who can paint from close observation, and who is neither a caricaturist nor a rose-colour sentimentalist" (19). George Eliot was correct that *Rachel Gray* marked a new sphere.

The novel is the descendant of the seamstress stories of *The Young Milliner* or *The Wrongs of Woman,* yet as in *Ruth* the protagonist's occupation is not the major concern. Like her sister novelists of the fifties, Gaskell, Craik, and Mayne, Kavanagh is concerned with assimilation, but from the perspective of one who barely manages to achieve a place. *Rachel Gray* is defiantly a story of nonsuccess. This may have been because of reviewers' adverse reactions to her earlier novels: *Daisy Burns* was considered too indulgent by the *Westminster Review* and *Grace Lee* was condemned for its "phantasms." *Rachel Gray,* said the *Athenaeum,* is "wrought from the humblest and simplest of materials. . . . There is neither love nor the shadow of a lover in the whole book — the heroine begins and ends unmarried" (40). *Rachel Gray* defies the conventions by its drab subject, suggested by the protagonist's surname. Kavanagh mentions that Rachel Gray is not intelligent, only sympathetic.

The subtitle of the novel, *A Tale Founded on Fact,* recalls Tonna. It is explained in the Preface: "This tale, as the title-page implies, is founded on fact. Its truth is its chief merit, and the Author claims no other share in it, than that of telling it to the best of her power. . . . I do not mean to aver that every word is a positive and literal truth, that every incident occurred exactly as I have related it, and in no other fashion, but this I mean to say: that I have invented nothing in the character of Rachel Gray, and that the sorrows of Richard Jones are not imaginary sorrows. . . . I wished to show the intellectual, the educated, the fortunate, that minds which they are apt to slight as narrow, that lives which they pity as moving in the straight and gloomy paths of mediocrity, are often blessed beyond the usual lot, with those lovely aspirations towards better deeds and immortal things, without which life is indeed a thing of little worth; cold and dull as a sunless day" (iii–v).

In the novel, Kavanagh discussed her subject in a passage objected to by George Eliot: "Oh! miserable and unpoetic griefs of the prosaic poor. Where are ye, elements of power and pathos of our modern epic: the novel? A wretched shop that will not take, a sickly child that dies! Ay, and were the picture but drawn by an abler hand, know proud reader, if proud thou art, that thy very heart could bleed, that thy very soul would be wrung to read this page from a poor man's story" (314–15). George Eliot commented: "To scold a reader for not feeling is a way of trying to make him feel which is more feminine than felicitous" (19). George Eliot is mistaken. Kavanagh is not using a "feminine" ploy to control a reader's response. She is instead commenting on the genre as she knew it, one which ignores the humblest subject, the actuality of prosaic existence. In *Rachel Gray* she is concerned with two of the faceless proletariat, Rachel the seamstress and Jones the failed shopkeeper.

Kavanagh is recording social history, since between 1851 and 1881 the number of shopkeepers and street sellers increased by 69 percent (Clark, *Making* 121). Kavanagh shows foresight in the 1850s by selecting this group to study. The drabness of her main characters, along with the fact that neither of them is depicted solely in terms of occupation, makes *Rachel Gray* an important social novel. Kavanagh does not focus on the working existence of her seamstress but rather on the other elements of her life: her relationship with her stepmother, her unloving father, a distressed neighbor. Kavanagh cites Milton's "they also serve" to describe the challenge of the novel. Kavanagh's model for this focus on the ordinary, the prosaic, is Dutch painting. In a passage clearly anticipating chapter seventeen of *Adam Bede* three years later, the narrator records Rachel's observation of the poor neighbor, Madame Rose, living in a cellar: "She looked with the artistic pleasure we feel, when we gaze at some clearly-painted Dutch picture, with its background of soft gloom, and its homely details of domestic life, relieved by touches of brilliant light. Poor as this cellar was, a painter would have liked it well" (61). Kavanagh's comment must surely have been an unconscious if not conscious source of George Eliot's pronouncement in *Adam Bede*. Reviewers of other novels during the period invoked Dutch painting to describe authorial effects. Reviewing *Ruth,* one critic commented on the practices of women novelists, of which there were two groups, one which emphasizes the "harsher passions," the other the "Dutch painter's accuracy in describing the surfaces and outer aspects of social or domestic life" (Ludlow 170). Lewes had noted in *Shirley* one scene "worthy of a Backhuysen" (162). The *Athenaeum* reviewer of *Ruth* concluded by saying: "The above is a bit of honest, unlicked, unpainted nature; as good, after its kind, as the sturdiest Flemish housewife to whose thick legs and blunt features Maas did full justice" (78). *Rachel Gray* represents Kavanagh's participation in this tradition, which was to culminate in *Adam Bede*. It was probably this sombre quality that prompted Elizabeth Gaskell to comment, "I think it very interesting" (Chapple 784) when she read the first part of *Rachel Gray*. By invoking Dutch painting, Kavanagh may well have intended to revise literary history. In the first volume of *Modern Painters* (1843) Ruskin had adversely criticized the Dutch school, and Kingsley in *Alton Locke* had associated it with Dickens and *Boz*. Kavanagh rehabilitates Dutch painting in opposition to Ruskin's censure and Dickens' distortion.

Rachel Gray is a novel less of assimilation than of accommodation, and a meager one. Kavanagh shows the drab suburb where Rachel lives. Not even a suburb of London, but only a street, is her focus. Kavanagh differs from writers like Dickens on London or Gaskell on Manchester, who conceive of the entire city as impinging on the characters' lives. Rachel suffers from night work and long hours enough to notice the Chartist events of 10 April 1848, which Kingsley had used in *Alton Locke:* "Ah! poor things . . . I saw them — they passed by here. How thin they were — how careworn they looked!" (71). Richard Jones tries to endure the competitive ethic in opening a small grocer's shop, but a rival has other ideas: "Smithson had seen that he might find it profitable to cut the ground under Jones's feet. Why should he not do it? Is not profit the object of commerce? and is not competition the fairest way of securing profit?" (254–55). "Business requires a cool head; competition has its limits, beyond which yawns the bottomless pit of ruin" (270). Kavanagh defends her prosaic world: "We deal not with pitiless political economy, with its laws, with their workings. The great shop must prosper; 'tis in the nature of things; and the little shop must perish—'tis their nature too. We but lament this sad truth, that on God's earth, which God made for all, there should be so little room for the poor man; for his pride, his ambition" (273). Jones tells Rachel in his distress: "I wronged none; I did my best; a rich man steps in, and I am beggared—and you tell me God is good—mind, I don't say he aint—but is he good to me?" (298).

Rachel's society is starkly limited to relationships on her street, particularly with Jones and her stepmother, and with her father. The stepmother, having lost her own daughter, expects Rachel to compensate. Rachel endures with Christian tolerance, believing it is God's will, tending the woman on her sickbed as Kavanagh herself did her own invalid mother. The woman's outrage is increased because Rachel tries to keep in contact with her father, Thomas Gray, a carpenter who reads Paine. When he suffers a stroke, she must nurse him. When one day he acknowledges her, it is the climax of her life, albeit meager: "'Oh! why have I not too a father to love and know me, not imperfectly, but fully—completely,' a sweet and secret voice replies: 'You had your heart set on human love, and because you had set your heart upon it, it was not granted to you'" (335–36). She must be resigned, even though she had recognized that "her father wronged her—perhaps he knew it not; but he wronged her" (221). Although Rachel thinks of herself as the Prodigal Son, it is the father who is derelict.

In Rachel, Jones, and Thomas Gray, Kavanagh displays degrees of adjustment to the ruthlessness of the mid-Victorian ideology of success, concentrating on "unsuccess" and on unloving relationships. Kavanagh is registering facts more than a protest. When Rachel decides to make one more attempt to move her father, she concludes: "If he rejects me now . . . I shall submit, and trouble him no more" (223). The characters are sufficiently contrasted to show the omnipresence of drabness and failure: Richard Jones loves his daughter, Thomas Gray does not; Jones is a religious skeptic, Rachel a simple adherent. Although the widower Jones could be a prospective husband for Rachel, Kavanagh never permits the possibility to be realized. Rachel, like her creator, remains single. *Rachel Gray* is a repudiation of the Cinderella myth: the harsh stepmother is inescapable, the Prince never appears, the numbing tasks remain. "Nineteen-twentieths of the women of England earn their bread," Harriet Martineau recorded (*Autobiography* 2:149).

Kavanagh has written a novel eliminating the "career" of mother-hood for her protagonist. John Stuart Mill was to ask later, "What of the greatly increasing number of women, who have had no oppor-tunity of exercising the vocation which they are mocked by telling them is their proper one?" (239). Rachel Gray is one of the legions recorded in the 1851 Census, which showed that "three-quarters of unmarried women worked, or lived on their own earnings." By 1855, just prior to the appearance of *Rachel Gray,* "there was an excess of half a million women over men" and by 1865 "a third of the women over twenty-one were independent workers" (Basch 105). *Rachel Gray* is the study of one of the "redundant" women W. R. Greg would notice in his essay in the *National Review* in 1862. Even George Eliot yielded to Lewes and had Dinah Morris marry Adam Bede. Julia Kavanagh defied the traditions of the social novel in many ways: her protago-nist is unlovely and unloved; she lives rather than dies a pathetic death (Ellen Cardan) or an heroic one (Ruth Hilton). Kavanagh's novel as-sails the ethic of mobility, gentility, and success by which mid-century England justified itself. It is the female version of *Great Expectations,* without the colonial financial success of Dickens' Pip. For him the myth is functional, for Rachel Gray it is both unknown and irrelevant.

In offering contrasted perspectives on the subject of success, *John Halifax* and *Rachel Gray* represent the finished form of the social novel in the decade. Their self-made man and anonymous seamstress reach back to the tradition of Stone's two novels *William Langshawe* and *The Young Milliner. John Halifax* derives from the study of Thornton in *North and South* as *Rachel Gray* descends from *Ruth* and the plain heroine of *Jane Rutherford.* Rachel Gray's distresses are not the fantastical ones suffered by the seamstress in *The Chimes,* nor is John Halifax the caricature that is Bounderby in *Hard Times.* In 1856, the female social novel reached a culmination, which was followed in the sixties by the achievements of two women, Elizabeth Gaskell with *Sylvia's Lovers* and George Eliot with *Felix Holt, the Radical.* George Eliot concluded that *Rachel Gray* failed as a novel, but it is doubtful if some influence of Kavanagh is not detectable in the rigorous honesty of her fiction.

5   The Achievement

The late fifties and the emerging succeeding decade were marked by social unrest that indicated the euphoria of the earlier years of the decade was becoming muted. Events like the Crimean War sullied the confidence of mid-Victorian Britain. Strikes, such as the London builders' action in 1859, indicated this malaise. Burn's description of the attitude of criminal legislators is indicative of the "more tolerant attitude towards centralization" (184) that marked the era. Intervention in the bleaching and dyeing industry in 1860 and in the lace industry in 1861, the repeal of the paper tax and the new Commission on Children's Employment the same year, the Taunton Commission on Education in 1861 (revealing the deplorable education of girls), the Adulteration of Food Act in 1860, and the Limited Liability Act of 1862 indicate the thorough movement of intervention. The Molestation of Workmen Act, which permitted peaceful picketing, and the Coal Mines Regulation Act of 1859, reveal the same government intervention in labor. The position of women had received attention with the debate over the Divorce and Matrimonial Causes Acts of 1857 relating to the status of income of formerly married women. The Nightingale School of Nursing in 1860 indicated a new alternative in professions for women. In the early 1860s with the American Civil War, distress became widespread from famine and the chaos in the cotton industry. Against this background the social novel entered a final phase, characterized by two texts, Elizabeth Gaskell's *Sylvia's Lovers* (1863) and George Eliot's *Felix Holt, the Radical* (1866).

Sylvia's Lovers and *Felix Holt* are important social novels for the very reason that they depart from the time of their composition to explore preceding generations. Both Gaskell and Eliot explain the origins of persisting social problems by returning to earlier eras, Gaskell to the last decade of the eighteenth century, Eliot to the months following the passage of the first Reform Bill in June 1832 and the subsequent December elections. Lansbury notes that Gaskell's dissenting background led her to focus on the Napoleonic Wars as the turning point in modern society, with "industry, commerce and social conscience" taking a new direction: "English society . . . would not have assumed the shape it did without the external pressure of war leading to the persecution of social and religious radicals and the widespread imposition of arbitrary regulations" (160).

A further reason for Gaskell's dramatic period in *Sylvia's Lovers* was noted by social reformers of the forties. Cooke Taylor cites the *Athenaeum* to the effect that "It was the misfortune of the factory system that it took its sudden start at the moment when the entire energies of the British legislature were preoccupied with the emergencies of the French revolution. . . . There thus crept into unnoticed existence a closely condensed population, under modifying influences the least understood, for whose education, religious wants, legislative and municipal protection, no care was taken" (3–4). Gaskell records seismographically the tremors that would shake later decades. Both novels deal with riots prompted by protest, Gaskell with a town riot against the press-gang, Eliot with an election riot, events that prefigure social disturbances in succeeding decades. Both women turn to the origin of social abuses — social, political, sexual — that the female protest novelist had used in her fictions. The political and social abuses recorded in *Felix Holt* and *Sylvia's Lovers* parallel the exposure of men's cruelty to women: the deception of Sylvia Robson by Philip Hepburn, and of Mrs. Transome by her son Harold and her lover Matthew Jermyn.

Because of their retrospective subject matter, *Sylvia's Lovers* and *Felix Holt* are culminations of the female social novel. This reversion to the past is not an evasion of contemporary questions but rather a deep probing of them. Both novels employ a typological method in studying history, that is, the use of previous history as a pattern of events occurring at their time of composition. It is not accidental that the exploration of the victimized status of women is examined in light of the legislation of the late fifties. If Sylvia Robson had been able to divorce, or had sufficient education to remain independent after separation, there might have been alternatives to her condition.

It is not accidental that Mrs. Transome is destroyed by a lawyer, since the law (until 1870 at least) regarded women as nonpersons, as do Jermyn and Harold Transome. In probing the working-class mind in both novels, each writer recognizes that by 1863 Manchester was losing the cotton trade to the United States. Both societies are in deep transition in the novels: in Gaskell from agricultural and marine to commercial; in Eliot from landed hegemony to gradual democratization by the franchise. Commerce over whaling in Gaskell and commerce over land in Eliot indicate the gradual change of the social system. There is a close connection between commercialism and the treatment of women.

Women are objects of commerce between men, an idea already suggested in Pimlico's *The Factory Girl.* Commercial competitiveness enables Philip Hepburn to deceive Sylvia and "win" her over Kinraid; Harold and Jermyn, truly father and son, treat Mrs. Transome as a manipulable cipher in their political and social struggle. It is because the patterns of behavior in the 1790s and the 1830s are conceived as prototypes of the circumstances of the sixties and as forerunners of the materials of the social novelists in the thirties, forties, and fifties, that *Sylvia's Lovers* and *Felix Holt* are summations of the female social novel. Brontë, Jewsbury, and Craik had already indicated the validity of analyzing one's own time through an earlier generation. In her review of Robert Mackay's *The Progress of the Intellect* in 1851, George Eliot observed: "It would be a very serious mistake to suppose that the study of the past and the labours of criticism have no important practical bearing on the present. Our civilization . . . [is] the offspring of a true process of development." This earlier period constituted "a pre-existence in the past" (Pinney 28–29). The use of the past as a pattern of the present is evident, for example, in the alternative titles of Gaskell's novel, *The Specksioneer* and *Philip's Idol,* which reveal the true status of women in the novel, as controlled by men, even as they were still in the sixties. The typological method is emphasized by Gaskell when she notes in the first volume of *Sylvia's Lovers*: "Yet, for all this, there were some who dared to speak of reform of Parliament, as a preliminary step to fair representation of the people, and to a reduction of the heavy war taxation that was imminent, if not already imposed. But these pioneers of 1830 were generally obnoxious" (178).

Many elements of *Sylvia's Lovers* anticipate subsequent subject matter of social novelists. This is evident in the early discussion about law by Philip Hepburn and Daniel Robson. Philip believes, "Let Government judge a bit for us. . . . I'm thankful to be governed by King George and a British Constitution," but Daniel counters, "I only ax 'em to govern me as I judge best, and that's what I call representation." To Philip "laws is made for the good of the nation, not for your good or mine," but Daniel believes, "Nation here! Nation theere! I'm a man and yo're another; but nation's nowheere" (42–43). Gaskell's discussion raises the question of government intervention and representation that was to characterize the following decades. Daniel later says: "They're for makking such a pack o' laws, they'll be for meddling wi' my fashion o' sleeping next. . . . They're a meddlesome set o' folks, law-makers is" (53). "Government did more to demoralise the popular sense of rectitude and uprightness than heaps of sermons could undo" (85). Gaskell mentions that the "corn laws" by the end of the century had "brought the price of corn up to a famine-rate" (508). When Bella, Sylvia and Philip's daughter, emigrates to America, Gaskell has established a matrix of typological significance: corn laws, interference, emigration, reform. Philip speculates: "Then he went on to wonder if the lives of one generation were but a repetition of the lives of those who had gone before, with no variation but from the internal cause that some had greater capacity for suffering than others" (254–55). Gaskell does see variation, does see alternatives, but she also realizes the tragedy in the recurrence of a typology.

The society of *Sylvia's Lovers* is undergoing a gradual transition. The conflict between the agricultural and the commercial is indicated by the opposition of Kester to Philip: "To Philip, Kester had an instinctive objection, a kind of natural antipathy such as has existed in all ages between the dwellers in a town and those in the country, between agriculture and trade" (192). To Sylvia Philip is "so full o' business and t' shop, and o' makin' money, and gettin' wealth" (208). Of the Foster brothers' shop, the narrator notes: "The separation of the business — the introduction of their shopmen to the distant manufacturers who furnished their goods . . . all these steps were in gradual progress" (137). The Foster brothers live in "the freshly-built rows of the new town of Monkshaven" (176). "The newer suburb was built in more orderly and less picturesque fashion on the opposite cliff" (20). The attorney Dawson resides "in one of the new streets on the other side of the river" (304). The demography indicates the typology of change.

Philip and Charley Kinraid represent two orders; their sexual combat for Sylvia indicates a societal fissure. Just as Philip deceives Kinraid and Sylvia, so "the Whitby whalers were to be outsailed by the New England clippers" (Lansbury 181). Philip's winning of Sylvia is the triumph of the commercial spirit over spontaneous marine enthusiasm. Sylvia's move to Philip's shop after her marriage is difficult: "Sitting in the dark parlour at the back of the shop . . . was much more wearying to her than running out into the fields," while "the idea of the house behind the shop was associated in her mind with two times of discomfort and misery" (361, 355). The opposition of farm and shop, of old and new town, reflects the transitional state of Whitby and the nation. Sylvia's departure from Haytersbank is the departure of the eighteenth century toward the mercantilism of the nineteenth. Philip's lack of sympathy and his calculation mark the commercial competitiveness that distinguishes the forthcoming era. Hepburn's concealing of Kinraid's impressment is the outgrowth of a competitive ethic that equates success with possession.

In this system, where women suffer severely, the typology is evident: "Men have plenty to say to men which in their estimation . . . women cannot understand; and farmers of a much later date than the one of which I am writing would have contemptuously considered it as a loss of time to talk to women" (93). When a partnership with the Fosters is negotiated, Jeremiah Foster notes about Hester Rose: "We have not thought it necessary to commend Hester Rose to you; if she had been a lad, she would have had a third o' the business along wi' yo. Being a woman, it's ill troubling her with a partnership; better give her a fixed salary till such time as she marries" (185). The typological point is evident in the exclusion of women from contracting and business that Gaskell saw in the sixties. When the men are taken by the press-gang, Philip says: "It's the law, and no one can do aught against it — least of all women and lasses" (30).

It is this oppression of women by law that encourages Philip to oppress Sylvia through his legally endowed rights after their marriage: "Kinraid's dead, I tell yo', Sylvie! And what kind of a woman are yo', to go dreaming of another man i' this way, and taking on so about him, when yo're a wedded wife, with a child as yo've borne to another man?" (374). The Fosters tell Sylvia about another dimension of the law: "Dost thee know that, by the law of the land, he may claim his child; and then thou wilt have to forsake it, or to be forsworn?" (436). The legally based discrimination in the public sector affects private action. Sylvia fantasizes that she will "lap thee round wi' my love, so as thou shall niver need a feyther's" (437). "I'm sick o' men and their cruel, deceitful ways. I wish I were dead" (435). Toward the end of the novel, she has realized bitterly: "Men takes a deal more nor women to spoil their lives" (502).

The social structure in the novel is full of conflict. "There is a sort of latent ill-will on the part of the squires to the tradesman, be he manufacturer, merchant, or shipowner, in whose hands is held a power of money-making, which no hereditary pride, or gentlemanly love of doing nothing, prevents him from using. . . . The squires . . . felt that the check upon the Monkshaven trade likely to be inflicted by the press-gang was wisely ordained by the higher powers . . . to prevent overhaste in getting rich" (9). Daniel's rebellion against intervention has a class basis. The law is no protection for Kinraid, who as a speck-sioneer ought to have been free from impressment. The discrepancy between passage of laws and enforcement, a central problem throughout the nineteenth century, is typologically indicated: "Of what use were laws, in those days of slow intercourse, with such as were powerful enough to protect?" (229). Appearing in the sixties, *Sylvia's Lovers* employs a typology of abuse in the military that intersected with the advocacy of Edward Cardwell to eliminate the purchase system in favor of a merit system. Although impressment had ceased in 1835, the debate about abuse of common men in the military was prominent in the sixties with its lingering post-Crimean disillusionment. Daniel Robson's revolt against law is not ignorant radicalism. It is the awareness of the legally sanctioned class distinctions that circumscribe him and his kind, like Kinraid. As Sylvia's name indicates, she is of the pastoral world, ignored by London and its legislators. When Daniel is executed, the law has been supported, but the precedent would make readers think of the Tolpuddle martyrs or others condemned for dissent. The widow Dobson speaks in a typological sense when she notes "t' famine comes down like stones on t' head o' us poor folk" (506). That a famine was occurring during 1862–1863 reveals Gaskell's typological intention in *Sylvia's Lovers*.

The most unusual element of the historical typology in *Sylvia's Lovers* is its confused chronology. By Gaskell's reckoning the story begins in 1796, but in the first volume she miscalculates and loses two years. Thus the "New Year" celebrated by Sylvia and Kinraid is not 1796, as the narrator claims, but 1798. The Siege of Acre (May 1799) by the chronology of Gaskell is May 1801. While thinking Kinraid returns in 1798, he actually does so in 1800. Gaskell had intended

Philip to return in 1800, but in fact it is 1802. This confusion of the internal chronology is significant, since she has made the change of century occur on Kinraid's return, not Philip's. The one event that would severely restrict the typology, the mutiny of the Nore in 1797, is not mentioned. Handley notes that "these errors do not militate against our appreciation of a fine novel" (303). This confusion masks a criticism of, or a cautionary statement about, the emerging century. If Philip returned at the turn of the century, it would indicate a spirit of forgiveness and the permanence of the competitive spirit.

The alteration of Philip Hepburn from merchant to soldier supports the argument of John Ruskin in *Unto This Last,* which had been serialized from August to November 1860 in the *Cornhill Magazine.* In February 1860 Gaskell had published "Curious if True" in the *Cornhill,* and other works, notably *Cousin Phillis* in 1863, were to appear in its pages. As a supporter of Ruskin, Gaskell almost certainly read these papers during the composition of *Sylvia's Lovers,* begun in 1859. Hepburn's involvement in the Siege of Acre, often regarded as a *deus ex machina,* may in fact have been a specific plan to parallel Ruskin's treatise. In the first paper, "The Roots of Honour," Ruskin contrasts the self-sacrifice of the soldier with the selfishness of the man of commerce. Philip Hepburn's transformation from merchant to soldier embodies the moral contrast studied by Ruskin with these two professions. Ruskin declares: "The reason [the world] honours the soldier is, because he holds his life at the service of the State. . . . The merchant is presumed to act always selfishly" (22–23). Changing from commercial selfishness to brotherly self-sacrifice, Philip exemplifies the necessity of ethics in economics advocated in *Unto This Last. Sylvia's Lovers* is a fictional and perhaps intentional version of Ruskin's harsh critique of political economy in his treatise. The typological use of the Siege of Acre, therefore, applies to contemporary literary history as well as to social history.

By having Kinraid return in 1800, Gaskell delivers an admonition to the emerging century. Gaskell's novel emphasizes the validity of some of the old values in face of the irresistible force of the new. The novel espouses a gradual transition that does not exclude previous values. The social, legal, and sexual issues are inextricable in these conflicts. There is a persistent system of abuse from squire to merchant, from government to citizen, from men to women, whether the issue is child custody, commercial partnership, the press-gang, unfair marriage laws, lack of women's education, or arbitrary legal power. The consequences of the commercial spirit on private lives were to be the matter of social novelists of the thirties, forties, and fifties. While Martineau in *The Rioters* supports harsh measures against the rebels, Gaskell sees the class basis of these revolts. Unlike Disraeli's desire in *Sybil* to revive previous orders, Gaskell sees in the past not a disjunction with the present but a disturbing continuity. The typological method reveals a basis of social unrest that eluded Tonna or Martineau. The fact that Gaskell had read *Adam Bede* prior to writing *Sylvia's Lovers* prompted her to return to the same decade. The returned lover, which she had treated in *The Manchester Marriage* in 1858, is not only a sign of Fate or a mark of Greek tragedy. It is a symbol of the distressing persistence of the typology of abuse and victimization. At the conclusion of the novel, Sylvia, Charley Kinraid, and Philip Hepburn have become a local legend in a very particular way: "A few old people can still tell you the tradition of the man who died in a cottage somewhere about this spot — died of starvation, while his wife lived in hard-hearted plenty not two good stone-throws away" (530). Sylvia's story has been interpreted typologically in light of the starvation prevalent in the sixties because of the disturbances in the cotton industry from the American Civil War. The fact that Sylvia's daughter emigrates to America, stated in the final paragraph of the text, emphasizes this typology. When George Eliot read Gaskell's novel she wrote: "I hope 'Sylvia's Lovers' is finding a just appreciation. It seems to me of a high quality both in feeling and execution" (Haight, *Letters* 4:79). Just as Gaskell had been influenced to return to the past by *Adam Bede,* so George Eliot may have followed Gaskell in chronicling early abuses in *Felix Holt, the Radical.*

When George Eliot (1819–1880) wrote *Felix Holt* she was aware of working in a tradition developed by women. She had observed in 1856 in her essay "Silly Novels by Lady Novelists" that the estimation of reviewers often was lofty according to the mediocrity of the female novelist's productions. She remarked that if a female writer "ever . . . reaches excellence, critical enthusiasm drops to the freezing point. Harriet Martineau, Currer Bell, and Mrs. Gaskell have been treated as cavalierly as if they had been men" (Pinney 322). Eliot cites three important predecessors in the social novel, of which *Felix Holt* forms a final expression. The novel contains rioting along the lines of *The Rioters* or *The Turn-out;* industrial debate as in *Shirley* or *The Hill and the Valley;* the working-class consciousness as in *Mary*

Barton or *North and South;* and an interest in women during periods of economic transition indicated by Stone, Jewsbury, Gaskell, and Brontë. Fred Thomson declares that *Felix Holt* is "not a political novel as the genre is ordinarily understood. . . . Equally remote from her purposes was the strain of social protest found in the fiction of Charles Kingsley or Mrs. Gaskell" ("Genesis" 576). This separation is arbitrary, however, for as Raymond Williams notes *Felix Holt* is concerned with issues like the "mob" (105). The novel shares many of the plot elements of works of social protest by both male and female predecessors. From Disraeli Eliot derives an inheritance affecting a lower-class woman, while Harold in his desire to marry Esther Lyon is a version of Egremont without the political ideology of Young England. The similarities to the protagonist of *Alton Locke* are clear: Felix is involved in a riot, sentenced as a leader. In Mary Barton's attempt to assist Jem Wilson at his trial Eliot found a precedent for Esther's speech at Felix's trial. The growth of Esther Lyon's social priorities parallels the growth of understanding of Margaret Hale in *North and South.*

Like that of several social novelists before her, Eliot's research was extensive: Samuel Bamford's *Passages from the Life of a Radical,* the *Committee Report on Agriculture* (1833), Mill and Comte, notes from the *Times,* the *Annual Register* of 1832 on election riots at Bolton, and the 1835 Parliamentary *Report* on bribery at elections. Eliot exposes the political situation on the eve of the Second Reform Bill by examining the conditions existing in the months after the passage of the First. Like *Sylvia's Lovers, Felix Holt* uses a typology, includes episodes of social unrest, and depicts a trial, but the main similarity between the two works lies in the careful interweaving of history with private lives: "These social changes in Treby parish are comparatively public matters, and this history is chiefly concerned with the private lot of a few men and women; but there is no private life which has not been determined by a wider public life" (45). Eliot's book also shares with Gaskell's novel an emphasis on women's hard treatment, noted by John Morley as "the evil usage which women receive at the hands of men . . . how hard or mean or cruel men are to women" (Haight, *Century* 34–35).

Events intervening between the publication of *Sylvia's Lovers* and *Felix Holt* show the nature of the typology in Eliot's novel. Following the 1862 Limited Liability Act, there was a growth of stock and bond speculation (noted by Dickens in *Our Mutual Friend*) and a rise in working men's associations, such as the National Association of Coal Miners and the Associated Iron Workers in 1863. The sudden financial collapse and panic of 1866, the Hyde Park disturbances in July, and the failure of Overend and Gurney made the year of the novel's appearance a tense one. Social disturbances appeared in many regions during 1866 and 1867: trade union unrest in Sheffield in 1866, the Trafalgar Square assembly of 10,000 in June 1866 after the defeat of the Reform Bill, the recurrence of disturbances in Sheffield in 1867, Fenian activity in Chester and Manchester, and street riots caused by the religious bigot Murphy in Wolverhampton and Birmingham. George Eliot's willingness to write the "Address to Working Men, by Felix Holt" for *Blackwood's* in 1868 is a fictional extension of the typology of the 1830s as a prototype of the 1860s.

This typology in *Felix Holt* parallels George Eliot's statements about "Historic Imagination" in "Leaves from a Note-Book," where she describes the purpose of the typological method: "The exercise of a veracious imagination in historical picturing seems to be capable of a development that might help the judgment greatly with regard to present and future events. By veracious imagination, I mean the working out in detail of the various steps by which a political or social change was reached, using all extant evidence and supplying deficiencies by careful analogical creation. . . . There has been abundant writing on such great turning-points, but not such as serves to instruct the imagination in true comparison. I want something different from the abstract treatment which belongs to grave history from a doctrinal point of view, and something different from the schemed picturesqueness of ordinary historical fiction. I want brief, severely conscientious reproductions, in their concrete incidents, of pregnant movements in the past" (Pinney 446–47). *Felix Holt* depicts such "movements," deliberately realized by the typological method that enables a "true comparison" to be elicited. The return of cholera in 1865–1866 would have recalled the vicious association of classes through disease. The first Trades Union Congress in 1868 revealed new working-class interests after the publication of the novel. In 1867 the Metropolitan Police Act and the Master and Servant Act were legislative results that showed the decade in as much flux as the thirties. The issue of women's political situation was accentuated by the Contagious Diseases Acts of 1864, 1866, and 1869 whereby a woman suspected of being a prostitute was compelled to undergo a pelvic examination. The outrage generated by these measures, the appearance of Mill's *The Subjection of Women* in 1869, and the Married Women's Property Act of 1870 indicate reformist attitudes about the situation of women that give point to the abuse by Harold and Jermyn of Mrs. Transome. The historical typology is Eliot's method of assessing and validating the theory of the gradual development of human cultures and beliefs, since it compares two such stages of development. Even if "the poor recede from the novels of the 1860s and early 1870s in the sense that the physical, urgent confrontation with them is lost" (Smith, *Nation* 266), *Felix Holt* and *Sylvia's Lovers* remain the summation of a tradition that extended over three decades.

The premise underlying *Felix Holt* is the concept of transition. The coach tour Eliot includes in her introduction portrays it sharply: "As the day wore on the scene would change: the land would begin to be blackened with coal-pits, the rattle of handlooms to be heard in hamlets and villages. Here were powerful men walking queerly with knees bent outward from squatting in the mine, going home to throw themselves down in their blackened flannel and sleep through the daylight . . . the pale eager faces of handloom-weavers, men and women, haggard from sitting up late at night to finish the week's work, hardly begun till the Wednesday. . . . The breath of the manufacturing town, which made a cloudy day and a red gloom by night on the horizon, diffused itself over all the surrounding country, filling the air with eager unrest. Here was a population not convinced that old England was as good as possible" (7–8). Treby Magna has undergone several phases of transition: "First came the canal; next, the working of the coal-mines at Sproxton, two miles off the town; and, thirdly, the discovery of a saline spring . . . together with the opportune opening of a stone-quarry." The town "took on the more complex life brought by mines and manufactures, which belong more directly to the great circulating system of the nation than to the local system to which they have been superadded. . . . The Independent chapel began to be filled with eager men and women" (41–43).

The consequence of this transition is a new relationship between private will and public necessity. The range of responses to this problem is extensive. There is Chubb, patron of the Sugar Loaf tavern: "The coming election was a great opportunity for applying his political 'idee,' which was, that society existed for the sake of the individual, and that the name of that individual was Chubb" (113). Felix declares, "I am a man of this generation; I will try to make life less bitter for a few within my reach" (225). This policy extends to the deflection of the Election Day riot: "He believed he had the power, and he was resolved to try, to carry the dangerous mass out of mischief till the military came" (268). Mrs. Transome and Esther Lyon are contrasted in terms of their public concern. For Mrs. Transome: "Here she moved to and fro amongst the rose-coloured satin of chairs and curtains—the great story of this world reduced for her to the little tale of her own existence" (280). Mrs. Transome is a distressing study of a woman "who had no other interests than her home" (P. Thomson 109), and Eliot shows the result of such insular selfishness. For Esther, Felix "was influence above her life, rather than a part of it . . . checking her self-satisfied pettiness with the suggestion of a wider life" (302).

Felix believes that the classes must act together for the social good: "Do you think there will ever be a great shout for the right—the shout of a nation as of one man . . . if every Christian of you peeps round to see what his neighbours in good coats are doing, or else puts his hat before his face that he may shout and never be heard?" (48). Mr. Lyon tells Felix that "true liberty can be nought but the transfer of obedience from the will of one or of a few men to that will which is the norm or rule for all men" (131). When Esther learns of her inheritance, her father advises her: "Your education and peculiar history would thus be seen to have coincided with a long train of events in making this family property a mean of honouring and illustrating a purer form of Christianity than that which hath unhappily obtained the pre-eminence in this land" (328–29). The extent of one's influence is moderate: "As to just the amount of result he may see from his particular work—that's a tremendous uncertainty: the universe has not been arranged for the gratification of his feelings. . . . There's some dignity and happiness for a man other than changing his station" (364). In his "Address to Working Men" Felix declares: "It is our interest to stand by each other, and . . . this being the common interest, no one of us will try to make a good bargain for himself without considering what will be good for his fellows" (415). This commitment to the social good is based on Eliot's doctrine of consequences, which binds the political to the private issues of the novel.

The conception of consequences is crucial to *Felix Holt* and its treatment of the interconnection of public and private moralities. In the introduction Eliot observes: "For there is seldom any wrong-doing which does not carry along with it some downfall of blindly-climbing hopes, some hard entail of suffering, some quickly-satiated desire that survives, with the life in death of old paralytic vice, to see itself cursed by its woeful progeny — some tragic mark of kinship in the one brief life to the far-stretching life that went before, and to the life that is to come after, such as has raised the pity and terror of men ever since they began to discern between will and destiny" (11). For Mrs. Transome this sequence assumes the shape of "the fatal threads about her, and the bitterness of this helpless bondage. . . . Nothing was as she had once expected it would be" (99). Matthew Jermyn, Mrs. Transome's lover and Harold's father, experiences an "inconvenience": "He had sinned for the sake of particular concrete things, and particular concrete consequences were likely to follow" (104). This lack of concern for consequences had been common to Jermyn and Mrs. Transome: "He and another bright-eyed person had seen no reason why they should not indulge their passion and their vanity, and determine for themselves how their lives should be made delightful in spite of unalterable external conditions" (190). Felix's killing of the constable entails a series of consequences. One is responsible even for the unforeseen consequences of one's actions. Felix's situation is but one illustration of what Eliot in 1851 had called "that inexorable law of consequences, whose evidence is confirmed instead of weakened as the ages advance" (Pinney 31).

The issue of consequences involves the problem of free agency. George Eliot had expressed in 1856, in "The Natural History of German Life," the nature of free will and its relationship to determinism in the social structure: "The external conditions which society has inherited from the past are but the manifestation of inherited internal conditions in the human beings who compose it; the internal conditions and the external are related to each other as the organism and its medium, and development can take place only by the gradual consentaneous development of both" (Pinney 287). It is with these external and internal determinants that the characters in *Felix Holt* struggle. From this struggle comes their occasionally painful growth in self-awareness. Harold Transome "was trusting in his own skill to shape the success of his own morrows, ignorant of what many yesterdays had determined for him beforehand" (161–62). When Felix is leading the rioters from further chaos, he has an insight: "But soon something occurred which brought with a terrible shock the sense that his plan might turn out to be as mad as all bold projects are seen to be when they have failed" (269–70).

For Eliot "It was that mixture of pushing forward and being pushed forward, which is a brief history of most human things" (268). The riot is a symbol of the oscillating forces of coercion, even as Mrs. Transome acknowledges that "I must put up with all things as they are determined for me" (294). Her son's moment of revelation is similar: "He felt the hard pressure of our common lot, the yoke of that mighty resistless destiny laid upon us by the acts of other men as well as our own" (386). "Converging indications and small links of incident" (331) form the filiation of human society. The Second Reform Bill, an indication of the convergence Eliot observed in *Middlemarch* and *Felix Holt,* is the typological consequence of the First. "The nature of things in this world has been determined for us beforehand" Felix Holt declares in the "Address to Working Men" in 1868 (417). Eliot was to write, in May 1865 during the composition of *Felix Holt,* that "railways, steamships, and electric telegraphs . . . are demonstrating the interdependence of all human interests" (Pinney 402).

For George Eliot, the interdependence of classes and the inevitability of consequences relate particularly to the role of women in *Felix Holt.* Most of the male characters, including Felix Holt, are marked by a disregard of women, whom they consider inconsequential. For Harold "his busy thoughts were imperiously determined by habits which had no reference to any woman's feeling" (19). He tells Mrs. Transome: "It doesn't signify what [women] think — they are not called upon to judge or to act . . . which properly belong to men" (36). "Harold Transome regarded women as slight things, but he was fond of slight things in the intervals of business" (153). When Harold learns that Esther has inherited Transome Court, he believes that "both the sex and the social condition were of the sort that lies open to many softening influences" (292). Felix regards women as a constraint on a man's self-realization: "I'll never marry, though I should have to live on raw turnips to subdue my flesh. I'll never look back and say, 'I had a fine purpose once — . . . but pray excuse me, I have a wife and children'" (66).

Felix later tells Esther: "I can't bear to see you going the way of the foolish women who spoil men's lives. Men can't help loving them, and so they make themselves slaves to the petty desires of petty creatures. That's the way those who might do better spend their lives for nought — get checked in every great effort — toil with brain and limb for things that have no more to do with a manly life than tarts and confectionary. That's what makes women a curse; all life is stunted to suit their littleness. That's why I'll never marry, if I can help it;

and if I love, I'll bear it, and never marry" (109). Eliot may have known John Galt's 1832 novel *The Radical* in which there are frequent outbursts against marriage as a constraint on a political individual. In *Felix Holt,* however, it is Mrs. Transome who suffers most at the hands of men. She tells Jermyn that Harold is as "good as men are disposed to be to women," but later she declares that "God was cruel when he made women" (101, 316). "I would not lose the misery of being a woman, now I see what can be the baseness of a man," she tells Jermyn in their last confrontation (337). "Men do not become penitent and learn to abhor themselves by having their backs cut open with the lash; rather, they learn to abhor the lash" (338). Despite this cruelty, Eliot regards women as not able to control their own lives: "After all, she [Esther] was a woman, and could not make her own lot. As she had once said to Felix, 'A woman must choose meaner things, because only meaner things are offered to her.' Her lot is made for her by the love she accepts" (342).

This situation aligns Esther with the protagonists of *Shirley, John Halifax,* and *Marian Withers.* When Esther and Felix acknowledge their love for one another, Eliot records: "She heard Felix say the word, with an entreating cry, and went towards him with the swift movement of a frightened child toward its protector" (365). Her choice of relinquishing her claim to Transome Court appears not an assertive but a submissive procedure, from one form of bondage (in fact from a situation where she might have control and influence) to a marriage where she will be the child: "I am weak — my husband must be greater and nobler than I am" (397). Although Basch describes Esther as "saved by marriage" (97), it is rather to control than to salvation that Esther yields. The disappointment of *Felix Holt* as a protest novel rests not so much in its political expression as in the failure of its attitude toward women to be as progressive as its attitude toward political progress. Eliot conceives Esther as "intensely of the feminine type, verging neither towards the saint nor the angel. She was 'a fair divided excellence, whose fulness of perfection' must be in marriage" (360). The "feminine type" is equated with "one who marries."

In *Felix Holt* George Eliot's politics are conservative, not radical; she espouses gradual change and condemns violence. She does not embrace the disappearance of social classes but rather, as she notes in Felix Holt's "Address," the "turning of Class Interests into Class Functions or duties" (416). George Eliot's theory of the organic society enforces a belief in unity that emphasizes interrelationship, but it is an interrelation of unequals. Harold's first wife, he tells Esther, was a slave, "bought, in fact" (353). Williams has recognized the "arbitrary" (106) nature of George Eliot's distinctions of political and social reform in *Felix Holt,* but this arbitrariness extends to her depiction of the situation of women. Neither Harold nor Felix shows deep awareness that legal remediation must exist before social attitudes are transformed. While one may object this would be anachronistic, Gaskell had already noted this inequity in *Sylvia's Lovers* regarding child custody. Jermyn's name indicates that unjust law is a germ in society, but Eliot does not suggest that politicians of any persuasion have realized the situation.

Felix Holt represents the culmination of the achievement of the social novel as written by women in England. In reverting to 1832 George Eliot brings the form back to the decade that saw its emergence as a serious narrative genre. Her focus on the corruption of the lawyer Jermyn indicates the central force, law, that would alter the condition of women in the sixties and cause a re-formation of protest literature at a later stage in the eighties and nineties, with novels like George Moore's *Esther Waters*, and into the Edwardian period with such texts as Netta Syrett's *Rose Cottingham.* It was only in the sixties, as Patricia Thomson observes, that "the Rights of Women movement did . . . assume the form of an organised campaign," when "the trial of the institution of marriage was really opened" (86, 89). While the importance of law had been a constant factor in social fiction for four decades, the sixties, making a shift from specific trade legislation to more universal application, produced changes that were only realized in later social fictions. The early stage of social fiction, commencing with Edgeworth, Martineau, and Tonna, through Trollope, Stone, Gaskell, Jewsbury, and Mayne, terminates with *Sylvia's Lovers* and *Felix Holt.* Lewes, writing in 1852, observed: "The appearance of Woman in the field of literature is a significant fact. It is the correlate of her position in society. . . . It is certain that the philosophic eye sees in this fact of literature cultivated by women, a significance not lightly to be passed over. It touches both society and literature" (129).

To determine the significance of this fact was not simple. Lewes went on to wonder: "What does the literature of women mean? . . . The advent of female literature promises woman's view of life, woman's experience: in other words a new element" (131). Four years later George Eliot less sympathetically but more perceptively noted it was unwise to classify women novelists by standards other than those used for evaluating men's achievements. In "Silly Novels by Lady Novelists" she writes, "Every critic who forms a high estimate of the share women may ultimately take in literature, will, on principle, abstain from any exceptional indulgence towards the productions of literary women" (Pinney 322). A reader of female social fiction, therefore, is obliged to reckon with both these attitudes: the critic must be sensitive to the appearance of women as a force in fiction and provide a just evaluation of their achievement. As a reviewer noted in the sixties, "A novelist is free to write a book with a purpose if he likes, but having done so, he must submit to be judged according to the nature of his purpose and the clearness with which he has developed it" ("Novels Purpose" 32).

Critics during the period noted the particular prominence of women in the social novel. After praising the fact that literature was exposing "the habitual thoughts and feelings of the great mass of the people," Charles Knight in 1861 noted the reformist impulse of social fiction: "Such are the duties which it is the especial honour of many of the present race of our writers of prose fiction to have successfully inculcated. . . . All honour to those beguilers of life's dull hours who have laboured to bring us all to a knowledge of each other by repeated efforts, such as those of Charles Dickens; to the illustrious females, such as Elizabeth Gaskell, who have seen in this work an especial vocation. . . . They have their reward, though not a complete one, in seeing the great change which marks the difference between 1831 and 1861" (Cazamian 293–94). For women writing during this period the genre of the novel was attractive because of its influence. It was the opinion of one contemporary essayist that "the novelist is now our most influential writer"; another commented that "there are peculiarities . . . in works of fiction which must always secure them a vast influence on all classes of societies and all sorts of minds. . . . Women . . . are the chief readers of novels; they are also, of late at least, the chief writers of them" ("Novels Purpose" 27; Greg, "False" 146–47). The novel was serious, and women writers of the stature of the social novelists realized the challenge and seized the opportunity. This was concomitant with a new attitude toward fiction itself: "It is only of recent days that critics have begun seriously to occupy themselves in the consideration of prose fiction" ("Novels Purpose" 25). Lewes speculated in his review of *Ruth* and *Villette:* "Should a work of Art have a moral? . . . A narrative can prove nothing . . . yet it is quite clear that the details of a narrative may be so grouped as to satisfy the mind like a sermon" (474–75). Women social novelists, while not necessarily desiring to "prove" a moral dogma, definitely sought to depict a moral dilemma and to suggest remediation of conditions. They were not philosophical moralists, but they were protesters.

The group of women considered in this study of the social novel until 1867 is a selected body of writers, those whose artistry was of some distinction and whose intentions were to some degree similar. While generalities are dangerous and suspect, one may isolate several traits that mark these women, most importantly their common use of fiction for social purposes, albeit those purposes might not be identical (as the problem of interventionism indicates). Most of these writers dealt with the economic, and therefore social, transition caused by the change from a cottage to a factory system, from an agriculturally based to an industrially based economic structure. The distinguishing mark of the social novel is not so much a focus on "the working classes" as its emphasis on the necessity of reform to eliminate exploitation in the transitional society existing because of industrialization. Many of these — Tonna, Gaskell, Brontë, and Eliot, for example — undertook serious research to authenticate their fictions. This may be coupled, as it was in the instance of Trollope and Mayne, with personal observations and exploration. The majority of the female social novelists incorporated specific historical events or allusions to substantiate the actuality of the conditions they were depicting: the Plug Plot Riots of *A Story of the Factories,* the first Chartist petition in *Mary Barton,* the last Chartist petition in *Rachel Gray,* the Reform Bill in *Felix Holt* and *John Halifax,* the assassination of Ashton in *William Langshawe.* The subjects of these novels bear some similarities: position in the industrial economic system (*The Young Milliner, Helen Fleetwood, A Story of the Factories*); the legal problems of women (*Jessie Phillips, Sylvia's Lovers*); the domestic consequences of industrialism (*The Wrongs of Woman, Jane Rutherford*); the question of assimilation of women (*William Langshawe, John Halifax*); the necessity of new roles for women (*Marian Withers, Shirley, Lucy Dean, North and South*). As a group these women writers discussed such questions in a context either explicitly industrial (Martineau, Tonna, Toulmin, Trollope) or in one that could not have existed apart from the period of transition to industrialism (Jewsbury, Meteyard, Craik, Gaskell). Social novelists regarded industrialism as a force exposing conditions not only peculiar to itself, such as hours of work, but auxiliary issues, such as husband/wife roles, that could be explored in industrial contexts. The assimilation that industrialism compelled, the transition that it provoked, were both public and private. Most of these writers espoused a reformist attitude but rarely did they advance a particular ideology like male practitioners of the form such as Kingsley and Disraeli. For most of the women writers belief in reform did not entail acceptance of a detailed political ideology. It is not legitimate to claim that all social fiction is perforce "propagandist." Advocates for reform proved capable of writing outside formulations that might limit their effectiveness.

G. M. Young has noted that "the fundamental issue of feminism was growing clearer all through the century" (*Victorian* 91), but the social novelists of this period dealt with feminist issues, such as marriage, child care, seduction, and prostitution, in the context of industrialism and its pressures. Feminist issues arose from industrial ones, for example the transformation of "overwork" in Stone and Tonna to "no work" in Jewsbury and Gaskell. Female novelists dealt with situations arising first from industrialism, then from feminism. As Young notes, it was only in late Victorian England that there appeared a concerted "Feminist movement" operating as a "calculable force" (*Victorian* 100). Feminism had existed during the period, although "it was not until the late eighties and nineties that the feminist movement began to gain any widespread support in England" (Branca 10). In the eyes of Tonna, Gaskell, Stone, Jewsbury, and Mayne, a woman's situation was never unaffiliated with economics. It was this affiliation that was the most striking of the insights in their depictions.

The extent of middle-class bias and the validity of these inquiries is an important question in evaluating the achievement of these writers. Too often Parliamentary investigators "found only what they were searching for. . . . Clearly enough, primary sources alone are insufficient. One needs the interpretation and drama of such writers as Mrs. Tonna and Mrs. Gaskell to make the mill girl and the dress-making apprentice flesh and blood figures. . . . A study of primary sources, together with literary data, has demonstrated the incompleteness of each. All this argues a plea for the historic method as applied to the study of literature" (Neff 245–46). These women, in using observation and sources, were writing the supporting material that prevented the distortion of the reports, not following them. Social fiction is a corrective to primary material, not its imitation. The justification of most of the female social novelists would be found in this statement from *Helen Fleetwood:* "You see, the facts are brought before Parliament, by having witnesses up to be examined on oath before the committee; these reports, as they are called, are printed, and sold too: but, Green, I don't think one lady in a thousand looks into them, to say nothing of other classes: and if they are not read, how can the statements be known?" (611).

Female social novelists sought to answer that question, to give their readers, especially women, a basis for reformist ideas even if they were not enfranchised. Writers as different as Tonna and Gaskell did not question the force of influence, even if they were unenfranchised. "Always, the novelist reached readers unaware of government publications" (Tillotson 81), and it was with this conviction that these women wrote. The Victorian period was "the age of inquiry and of experiments in the method of inquiry" (Young, "Victorian" 159), and the social protest novel fulfilled Carlyle's behest for such inquiry in *Chartism.* George Eliot noted, "How little the real characteristics of the working-classes are known to those who are outside them. . . . Our social novels profess to represent the people as they are, and the unreality of their representations is a grave evil" (Pinney 268, 270). She called for "the natural history of our social classes" (272). It needs to be kept in mind, as Marcus notes, that "these two 'nations' are really parts of one" (*Engels* 233). Female social novelists would not have written had they not recognized the interconnection of social classes, even if some did embrace their separation. Through their use of documents and personal observation they confronted Eliot's indictment of "unreality"; Tonna includes documents specifically to avoid the charge of being "unreal." It is important when assessing the use of data to realize that the "extreme" style of a Tonna or a Trollope may heighten the treatment but not invalidate the social information of the text. Several writers, such as Martineau, Stone, and Gaskell, deliberately avoid the distorting artificiality of story that mars a work like *The Factory Girl* or *Hard Times.* Many of these women were ahead of their time as practitioners of the novel by this very deemphasis on dramatic incident, most conspicuously a writer like Julia Kavanagh. These women were creators of the social novel, initiating and advancing its use of statistics in combination with personal evidence, promoting social reform through the practice of literary form.

The "inquiry" for which Carlyle called in *Chartism* had been undertaken before his 1839 essay and was pursued following it. The writings of female social novelists supplemented rather than imitated Blue Books, providing a form of inquiry that differed from that of the male-dominated Parliamentary committees. In this respect, female social fiction appropriated to itself a territory occupied by male legislators, redefining in the process the subject and influence of the productions of female writers. They did successfully expose conditions, and the selectivity of their data was an asset in achieving accessibility. The historical value of their work lies in its role as a complement to primary evidence. The need for such appraisals was obvious to contemporaries like Cooke Taylor, who quotes a document stating: "This distress, heightened as it now is by the severity of the weather, has arrived at a pitch of which it is impossible to convey any adequate idea by mere statistical information" (219–20). The appeal of Tonna to her female readers assumes their conscientious interest in improving women's condition. It is important that the abuses were recorded at all as a first stage of social progress. Beyond the historical value of this material is the final legacy of female social fiction: a new authority for the female writer, a new seriousness in the reception of her work, and a place for her in the transition that industrialism compelled in the nineteenth century. While the artistry of female social fiction was of variable quality, this variation reflects transition, not stasis; dynamism rather than conformity; progress rather than perfection; distinguishing signs of the era itself. After the work of female social novelists, the seriousness of women's narratives could not be refuted. The social narrative provided women a means of influence in the legislative process despite their disenfranchisement. It also requires that their importance be reflected in a revision of the literary canon that includes the practitioners of this form. If, as Mill noted, the key mark of his era was that "human beings are no longer born to their place in life, and chained down" (143), female social novelists had their place in such an age, both in society and in the canon of literary history.

Bibliography
Index

Bibliography

This Bibliography is divided into two sections: Books, and Essays and Reviews. The Books section is further subdivided into Documents, Literary Works, and Historical and Literary Studies. Throughout the text, documentation is by parenthetical page reference to author or, if necessary, author and short title, followed by page number or, if necessary, volume and page number.

Books

Documents

Bauer, Carol, and Lawrence Ritt, eds. *Free and Ennobled.* New York: Pergamon, 1979.

Black, Eugene C., ed. *British Politics in the Nineteenth Century.* New York: Harper, 1969.

Black, Eugene C., ed. *Victorian Culture and Society.* New York: Harper, 1973.

Bowditch, John, and Clement Ramsland, eds., *Voices of the Industrial Revolution.* Ann Arbor: University of Michigan Press, 1961.

British Parliamentary Papers. Shannon: Irish University Press, 1968.

Chadwick, Edwin. *Report on the Sanitary Condition of the Labouring Population of Great Britain,* ed. M. W. Flinn. Edinburgh: University Press, 1965.

Checkland, S. G., ed. *The New Poor Law Report of 1834.* London: Penguin, 1974.

Cole, G. H., and A. W. Filson, eds. *British Working Class Movements: Select Documents.* New York: St. Martin's, 1967.

Cole, G. H., and Margaret Cole, eds. *The Opinions of William Cobbett.* London: The Cobbett Publishing Company, 1944.

Gash, Norman, ed. *The Age of Peel.* New York: St. Martin's, 1968.

Hellerstein, Erna, Leslie Hume, and Karen Offen, eds. *Victorian Women.* Stanford: Stanford University Press, 1981.

Hollingsworth, Brian, ed. *Songs of the People: Lancashire Dialect Poetry of the Industrial Revolution.* Manchester: Manchester University Press, 1977.

Hollis, Patricia, ed. *Class and Conflict in Nineteenth-Century England, 1815–1850.* London: Routledge and Kegan Paul, 1973.

Hollis, Patricia, ed. *Women in Public, 1850–1900.* London: Allen and Unwin, 1979.

McCulloch, J. R. *A Statistical Account of the British Empire.* 2 vols. London: Knight, 1837.

Mitchell, B. R., and Phyllis Deane, eds. *Abstract of British Historical Statistics.* Cambridge: Cambridge University Press, 1962.

Mitchell, B. R., and Phyllis Deane, eds. *European Historical Statistics, 1750–1970.* New York: Columbia University Press, 1975.

Mitchell, B. R., and H. G. Jones, eds. *Second Abstract of British Historical Statistics.* Cambridge: Cambridge University Press, 1971.

Mulhall, Michael G. *The Dictionary of Statistics.* London: Routledge, 1899.

Murray, Janet Horowitz, ed. *Strong-Minded Women and Other Lost Voices from Nineteenth-Century England.* New York: Pantheon, 1982.

Pike, E. Royston, ed. *Human Documents of the Industrial Revolution in Britain.* London: Allen and Unwin, 1966.

Pike, E. Royston, ed. *Human Documents of the Victorian Golden Age.* London: Allen and Unwin, 1967.

Young, G. M., and W. D. Handcock, eds. *English Historical Documents: 1833–1874.* New York: Oxford University Press, 1970.

Literary Works

Brontë, Charlotte. *The Professor.* London: Dent, 1965.

Brontë, Charlotte. *Shirley.* Oxford: Clarendon, 1979.

Brown, John. *A Memoir of Robert Blincoe.* Firle, Sussex: Caliban Books, 1977.

Carlyle, Thomas. *Characteristics.* In *The Works of Thomas Carlyle,* vol. 28. London: Chapman and Hall, 1896–1899.

Carlyle, Thomas. *Chartism.* In *The Works of Thomas Carlyle,* vol. 29. London: Chapman and Hall, 1896–1899.

Carlyle, Thomas. *Diderot.* In *The Works of Thomas Carlyle,* vol. 28. London: Chapman and Hall, 1896–1899.

Carlyle, Thomas. *Past and Present.* In *The Works of Thomas Carlyle,* vol. 10. London: Chapman and Hall, 1896–1899.

Carlyle, Thomas. *Signs of the Times.* In *The Works of Thomas Carlyle,* vol. 27. London: Chapman and Hall, 1896–1899.

Craik, Dinah Mulock. *John Halifax, Gentleman.* London: Dent, 1961.

Dickens, Charles. *The Chimes.* London: Chapman and Hall, 1845.

Dickens, Charles. *Hard Times.* London: Bradbury and Evans, 1854.

Dickens, Charles. *Nicholas Nickleby.* London: Chapman and Hall, 1838–1839.

Dickens, Charles. *Oliver Twist.* London: Bentley, 1838.

Dickens, Charles. *Sketches by Boz.* London: Oxford University Press, 1957.

Disraeli, Benjamin. *Coningsby.* Oxford: Oxford University Press, 1982.

Disraeli, Benjamin. *Sybil.* Oxford: Oxford University Press, 1981.

Edgeworth, Maria. *The Absentee.* In *Tales and Novels,* vol. 6. London: Routledge, 1893.

Edgeworth, Maria. *Castle Rackrent.* London: Oxford University Press, 1964.

Eliot, George. *Felix Holt, the Radical.* Oxford: Clarendon, 1980.

Ellen Linn, the Needlewoman. Tait's Edinburgh Magazine 17 (August 1850), 465–70.

Galt, John. "The Seamstress." In *Selected Short Stories,* ed. Ian Gordon. Edinburgh: Scottish Academic Press, 1978.

Gaskell, Elizabeth. *Libbie Marsh's Three Eras.* In *The Works of Mrs. Gaskell,* vol. 1. London: Smith, Elder, 1906.

Gaskell, Elizabeth. *Lizzie Leigh.* In *The Works of Mrs. Gaskell,* vol. 2. London: Smith, Elder, 1906.

Gaskell, Elizabeth. *Mary Barton.* In *The Works of Mrs. Gaskell,* vol. 1. London: Smith, Elder, 1906.

Gaskell, Elizabeth. *North and South.* In *The Works of Mrs. Gaskell,* vol. 4. London: Smith, Elder, 1906.

Gaskell, Elizabeth. *Ruth.* In *The Works of Mrs. Gaskell,* vol. 3. London: Smith, Elder, 1906.

Gaskell, Elizabeth. *The Sexton's Hero.* In *The Works of Mrs. Gaskell,* vol. 1. London: Smith, Elder, 1906.

Gaskell, Elizabeth. *Sylvia's Lovers.* In *The Works of Mrs. Gaskell,* vol. 6. London: Smith, Elder, 1906.

Jewsbury, Geraldine. *The Half-Sisters.* London: Chapman and Hall, 1854.

Jewsbury, Geraldine. *Marian Withers.* 3 vols. London: Colburn, 1851.

Kavanagh, Julia. *Rachel Gray.* London: Hurst and Blackett, 1856.

Kingsley, Charles. *Alton Locke,* with *Cheap Clothes and Nasty.* London: Macmillan, 1895.

Kingsley, Charles. *Yeast.* London: Dent, 1928.

A London Dressmaker's Diary. Tait's Edinburgh Magazine 9 (November 1842), 709–18.

Martineau, Harriet. *The Hill and the Valley.* In *Illustrations of Political Economy,* vol. 1. London: Fox, 1834.

Martineau, Harriet. *A Manchester Strike.* In Ivanka Kovacevic, *Fact into Fiction.* Leicester: Leicester University Press, 1975.

Martineau, Harriet. *The Rioters.* Wellington, Salop: Houlston, 1827.

Martineau, Harriet. *The Turn-out.* Wellington, Salop: Houlston, 1829.

Mayne, Fanny. *Jane Rutherford; or the Miners' Strike.* In *The True Briton,* NS, 1–2 (9 June to 20 October, 1853).

Meteyard, Eliza. *Lucy Dean; The Noble Needlewoman.* In *Eliza Cook's Journal* 2 (16 March to 20 April 1850).

More, Hannah. *The Lancashire Collier Girl* and *Village Politics.* In Ivanka Kovacevic, *Fact into Fiction.* Leicester: Leicester University Press, 1975.

Paley, William. *Equality, as consistent with the British Constitution.* In Ivanka Kovacevic, *Fact into Fiction.* Leicester: Leicester University Press, 1975.

Pimlico, Paul. *The Factory Girl.* In *Reynolds's Miscellany* 3 (20 October 1849), 201 – (24 November 1849), 283.

"A Rambler." *The Lancashire Collier-Girl.* In *The Gentleman's Magazine* 65 (March 1795), 197–99.

"A Rambler." *Letter.* In *The Gentleman's Magazine* 65 (December 1795), 993.

"A Rambler." *Promotion to the Lancashire Collier Girl.* In *The Gentleman's Magazine* 68 (December 1798), 1030–31.

Reynolds, G. M. W. *The Seamstress.* In *Reynolds's Miscellany* 4 (23 March 1850), 129–5 (10 August 1850), 46.

Stone, Elizabeth. "The Widow's Son." In *Chambers's Miscellany.* Edinburgh: Chambers, 1844.

Stone, Elizabeth. *William Langshawe, the Cotton Lord.* 2 vols. London: Bentley, 1842.

Stone, Elizabeth. *The Young Milliner.* London: Cunningham and Mortimer, 1843.

[Tonna], Charlotte Elizabeth. *Combination.* New York: Dodd, 1844.

[Tonna], Charlotte Elizabeth. *Helen Fleetwood.* In *The Works of Charlotte Elizabeth,* vol. 1. New York: Dodd, 1849.

[Tonna], Charlotte Elizabeth. *The System.* London: Westley and Davis, 1827.

[Tonna], Charlotte Elizabeth. *The Wrongs of Woman.* In *The Works of Charlotte Elizabeth,* vol. 2. New York: Dodd, 1849.

Toulmin, Camilla. *The Orphan Milliners. A Story of the West End.* In *Illuminated Magazine* 2 (April 1844), 279–85.

Toulmin, Camilla. *A Story of the Factories.* In *Chambers's Miscellany.* Edinburgh: Chambers, 1846.

Trollope, Frances. *Jessie Phillips.* London: Colburn, 1844.

Trollope, Frances. *Michael Armstrong, the Factory Boy.* London: Colburn, 1840.

Historical and Literary Studies

Abel, Elizabeth, ed. *Writing and Sexual Difference.* Chicago: University of Chicago Press, 1982.

Altick, Richard D. *The English Common Reader.* Chicago: University of Chicago Press, 1957.

Ashton, T. S. *The Industrial Revolution: 1760–1830.* New York: Oxford University Press, 1948.

Aspin, Christopher. *Lancashire: The First Industrial Society.* Helmshore, Lancashire: Helmshore Local History Society, 1969.

Auerbach, Nina. *Communities of Women.* Cambridge: Harvard University Press, 1978.

Banks, J. A., and Olive Banks. *Feminism and Family Planning in Victorian England.* New York: Schocken, 1974.

Basch, Françoise. *Relative Creatures: Victorian Women in Society and the Novel.* New York: Schocken, 1974.

Baym, Nina. *Woman's Fiction.* Ithaca: Cornell University Press, 1978.

Best, Geoffrey. *Mid-Victorian Britain: 1851–1875.* New York: Schocken, 1971.

Branca, Patricia. *Silent Sisterhood: Middle-Class Women in the Victorian Home.* London: Croom Helm, 1975.

Brantlinger, Patrick. *The Spirit of Reform.* Cambridge: Harvard University Press, 1977.

Briggs, Asa. *The Age of Improvement.* New York: Harper, 1959.

Briggs, Asa, ed. *Chartist Studies.* London: Macmillan, 1959.

Briggs, Asa. *Victorian Cities.* New York: Harper, 1963.

Briggs, Asa. *Victorian People.* New York: Harper, 1959.

Brinton, Crane. *English Political Thought in the Nineteenth Century.* New York: Harper, 1962.

Brougham, Henry. *Practical Observations upon the Education of the People.* London: Taylor, 1825.

Buckley, Jerome Hamilton. *The Victorian Temper.* Cambridge: Harvard University Press, 1951.

Buckley, Jerome Hamilton, ed. *The Worlds of Victorian Fiction.* Cambridge: Harvard University Press, 1975.

Burn, W. L. *The Age of Equipoise.* New York: Norton, 1965.

Butler, Marilyn. *Maria Edgeworth.* Oxford: Clarendon, 1972.

Cazamian, Louis. *The Social Novel in England 1830–1850,* trans. Martin Fido. London: Routledge and Kegan Paul, 1973.

Chapple, J. A. V., and Arthur Pollard, eds. *The Letters of Mrs Gaskell.* Cambridge: Harvard University Press, 1967.

Checkland, S. G. *The Rise of Industrial Society: 1815–1885.* London: Longman, 1964.

Clark, G. Kitson. *The Making of Victorian England.* New York: Athenaeum, 1967.

Colby, Robert. *Fiction with a Purpose.* Bloomington: Indiana University Press, 1951.

Colby, Vineta. *Yesterday's Woman.* Princeton: Princeton University Press, 1974.

Colvin, Christina, ed. *Maria Edgeworth: Letters from England, 1813–1844.* Oxford, Clarendon, 1971.

Craig, David. *The Real Foundations: Literature and Social Change.* New York: Oxford, 1974.

Craik, Dinah Mulock. *A Woman's Thoughts about Women.* Philadelphia: Peterson, 1858.

Craik, W. A. *Elizabeth Gaskell and the English Provincial Novel.* London: Methuen, 1975.

Creeger, George R., ed. *George Eliot: A Collection of Critical Essays.* Englewood Cliffs, New Jersey: Prentice-Hall, 1970.

Crouzet, François. *The Victorian Economy,* trans. A. S. Foster. London: Methuen, 1982.

Cruikshank, Marjorie. *Children and Industry.* Manchester: Manchester University Press, 1981.

Dalziel, Margaret. *Popular Fiction 100 Years Ago.* London: Cohen and West, 1957.

Deane, Phyllis. *The First Industrial Revolution.* Cambridge: Cambridge University Press, 1967.

Delamont, Sara, and Lorna Duffin. *The Nineteenth-Century Woman.* London: Croom Helm, 1978.

Digby, Anne, and Peter Searby. *Children, School and Society in Nineteenth-Century England.* London: Macmillan, 1931.

Dodd, William. *The Factory System Illustrated in a Series of Letters to the Right Hon. Lord Ashley.* London: Murray, 1842.

Dodd, William. *A Narrative of the Experience and Sufferings [of] William Dodd, A Factory Cripple.* London: Seeley, 1841.

Dyos, H. J., and M. Wolff, eds. *The Victorian City.* 2 vols. London: Routledge and Kegan Paul, 1979.

Easson, Angus. *Elizabeth Gaskell.* London: Routledge and Kegan Paul, 1979.

Engels, Friedrich. *The Condition of the Working Class in England,* trans. W. O. Henderson and W. H. Chaloner. Stanford: Stanford University Press, 1968.

Ensor, Robert. *England, 1870–1914.* Oxford: Clarendon, 1936.

Faber, Richard. *Proper Stations.* London: Faber, 1971.

Fielden, John. *The Curse of the Factory System.* London: Cobbett, 1836.

Finlayson, Geoffrey. *Decade of Reform.* New York: Norton, 1970.

Finlayson, Geoffrey. *The Seventh Earl of Shaftesbury.* London: Methuen, 1981.

Flinn, Michael. *British Population Growth, 1700–1850.* London: Macmillan, 1970.

Forster, John. *The Life of Charles Dickens.* New York: Doubleday, Doran, 1928.

Fraser, Derek. *The Evolution of the British Welfare State.* London: Macmillan, 1976.

Fraser, Derek, ed. *The New Poor Law in the Ninetenth Century.* London: Macmillan, 1976.

Gash, Norman. *Reaction and Reconstruction in English Politics, 1832–1852.* New York: Oxford University Press, 1965.

Gaskell, Peter. *Artisans and Machinery.* London: Parker, 1836.

Gaskell, Peter. *The Manufacturing Population of England.* London: Baldwin and Craddock, 1833.

Gérin, Winifred. *Charlotte Brontë*. New York: Oxford University Press, 1967.

Gérin, Winifred. *Elizabeth Gaskell*. New York: Oxford University Press, 1980.

Gilbert, Sandra M., and Susan Gubar. *The Madwoman in the Attic*. New Haven: Yale University Press, 1979.

[Greg, William Rathbone]. *An Enquiry into the State of the Manufacturing Population*. London: Ridgway, 1831.

Griest, Guinevere L. *Mudie's Circulating Library and the Victorian Novel*. Bloomington: Indiana University Press, 1970.

Haight, Gordon S., ed. *A Century of George Eliot Criticism*. Boston: Houghton Mifflin, 1965.

Haight, Gordon S., *George Eliot: A Biography*. New York: Oxford University Press, 1968.

Haight, Gordon S., ed. *The George Eliot Letters*. 9 vols. New Haven: Yale University Press, 1954–1978.

Haller, John, and Robin M. Haller. *The Physician and Sexuality in Victorian America*. New York: Norton, 1974.

Hammerton, A. James. *Emigrant Gentlewomen: Genteel Poverty and Female Emigration 1830–1914*. London: Croom Helm, 1979.

Hammond, J. L., and Barbara Hammond. *The Town Labourer*. New York: Doubleday, 1968.

Harrison, Fraser. *The Dark Angel*. London: Fontana, 1977.

Harrison, J. F. C. *Early Victorian Britain, 1832–1851*. London: Fontana, 1971.

Hartley, Allan J. *The Novels of Charles Kingsley*. Folkestone, Kent: Hour-Glass Press, 1977.

Hewitt, Margaret. *Wives & Mothers in Victorian Industry*. London: Rockcliff, 1958.

Himmelfarb, Gertrude. *The Idea of Poverty: England in the Early Industrial Age*. New York: Knopf, 1984.

Hobsbawm, E. J. *Labouring Men*. London: Weidenfeld and Nicholson, 1964.

Holloway, John. *The Victorian Sage*. New York: Norton, 1965.

Houghton, Walter E. *The Victorian Frame of Mind*. New Haven: Yale University Press, 1957.

Houghton, Walter E., ed. *The Wellesley Index to Victorian Periodicals 1824–1900*. Toronto: University of Toronto Press, 1966–1979.

House, Humphry. *The Dickens World*. New York: Oxford, 1960.

House, Madeline, and Graham Storey, eds. *The Letters of Charles Dickens*, vol. 1. Oxford: Clarendon, 1965.

Howe, Susanne. *Geraldine Jewsbury*. London: Allen and Unwin, 1935.

Hutchins, B. L., and A. Harrison. *A History of Factory Legislation*. New York: Kelley, 1966.

James, Louis. *Fiction for the Working Man, 1830–1850*. London: Oxford University Press, 1963.

Jay, Elisabeth. *The Religion of the Heart.* Oxford: Clarendon, 1979.

Kay, James Phillips. *The Moral and Physical Condition of the Working Classes Employed in the Cotton Manufacture in Manchester.* London: Ridgway, 1832.

Kay, James Phillips. *The Training of Pauper Children.* London: Clowes, 1839.

Keating, P. J., ed. *Working Class Stories of the 1890s.* London: Routledge and Kegan Paul, 1975.

Keating, P. J. *The Working Classes in Victorian Fiction.* London: Routledge and Kegan Paul, 1975.

Knoepflmacher, Uli C. *Religious Humanism and the Victorian Novel.* Princeton: Princeton University Press, 1965.

Kovacevic, Ivanka. *Fact into Fiction.* Leicester: Leicester University Press, 1975.

Lansbury, Coral. *Elizabeth Gaskell.* London: Elek, 1975.

Laslett, Peter. *The World We Have Lost.* New York: Scribner's, 1965.

Leavis, F. R. *The Great Tradition.* New York: New York University Press, 1964.

Llewellyn, Alexander. *The Decade of Reform: The 1830s.* New York: St. Martin's Press, 1972.

Lucas, John. *The Literature of Change.* Sussex: Harvester, 1977.

Malthus, Thomas Robert. *An Essay on the Principle of Population.* New York: Norton, 1976.

Manchester As It Is. Manchester: Love and Barton, 1839.

Marcus, Steven. *Dickens: From Pickwick to Dombey.* New York: Basic Books, 1965.

Marcus, Steven. *Engels, Manchester, and the Working Class.* New York: Random House, 1974.

Marcus, Steven. *The Other Victorians.* New York: New American Library, 1966.

Martin, Robert. *Charlotte Brontë's Novels.* New York: Norton, 1966.

Martin, Robert. *The Dust of Combat.* London: Faber, 1959.

Martineau, Harriet. *Autobiography.* 2 vols. Boston: Osgood, 1877.

Martineau, Harriet. *The Factory Controversy.* Manchester: Ireland, 1855.

Martineau, Harriet. *History of the Peace, 1816–1854.* 4 vols. Boston: Walker, Wise, 1865.

Mayhew, Henry. *London Labour and the London Poor.* 4 vols. New York: Dover, 1968.

Mayhew, Henry. *The Unknown Mayhew,* ed. Eileen Yeo. New York: Schocken, 1971.

Melada, Ivan. *The Captain of Industry in English Fiction, 1821–1871.* Albuquerque: University of New Mexico Press, 1970.

Mill, John Stuart, and Harriet Taylor. *Essays on Sex Equality,* ed. Alice Rossi. Chicago: University of Chicago Press, 1970.

Mitchell, Sally. *The Fallen Angel: Chastity, Class, and Women's Reading 1835–1880.* Bowling Green: Bowling Green University Popular Press, 1981.

Moers, Ellen. *Literary Women.* New York: Doubleday, 1977.

Morris, R. J. *Cholera 1832.* London: Croom Helm, 1976.

Neff, Wanda. *Victorian Working Women.* New York: Columbia University Press, 1929.

Nightingale, Florence. *Cassandra.* Old Westbury, New York: Feminist Press, 1979.

Norton, Caroline. *English Laws for Women in the Nineteenth Century.* London: Wertheimer, 1854.

O'Neill, William. *The Woman Movement.* London: Allen and Unwin, 1969.

Pichanick, Valerie. *Harriet Martineau.* Ann Arbor: University of Michigan Press, 1980.

Pinchbeck, Ivy. *Women Workers and the Industrial Revolution, 1750–1850.* London: Routledge, 1930.

Pinney, Thomas, ed. *Essays of George Eliot.* New York: Columbia University Press, 1963.

Pratt, Annis. *Archetypal Patterns in Women's Fiction.* Bloomington: Indiana University Press, 1981.

Reach, Angus. *Manchester and the Textile Districts in 1849.* Helmshore, Lancashire: Helmshore Local History Society, 1972.

Reach, Angus. *The Yorkshire Textile Districts.* Helmshore, Lancashire: Helmshore Local History Society, 1974.

Ricardo, David. *The Principles of Political Economy and Taxation.* London: Dent, 1973.

Roberts, David. *Paternalism in Early Victorian England.* London: Croom Helm, 1979.

Roberts, David. *Victorian Origins of the British Welfare State.* New York: Archon, 1969.

Rostow, W. W. *British Economy of the Nineteenth Century.* Oxford: Clarendon, 1948.

Rubenius, Aina. *The Woman Question in Mrs. Gaskell's Life and Works.* Cambridge: Harvard University Press, 1950.

Ruskin, John. *Unto This Last.* Lincoln: University of Nebraska Press, 1967.

Showalter, Elaine. *A Literature of Their Own.* Princeton: Princeton University Press, 1977.

Slaney, R. A. *The State of Education of the Poorer Classes in Large Towns.* London: Hatchard and Son, 1837.

Smith, Sheila. *The Other Nation.* Oxford: Clarendon, 1980.

Spacks, Patricia. *The Female Imagination.* New York: Knopf, 1975.

Strong, Roy. *Recreating the Past.* New York: Thames and Hudson, 1978.

Sussman, Herbert. *Victorians and the Machine.* Cambridge: Harvard University Press, 1968.

Sutherland, James. *Victorian Novelists and Publishers.* Chicago: University of Chicago Press, 1976.

Taylor, William Cooke. *Notes of a Tour in the Manufacturing Districts of Lancashire.* London: Duncan and Malcolm, 1842.

Thomas, Maurice. *The Early Factory Legislation.* Westport, Connecticut: Greenwood, 1970.

Thompson. E. P. *The Making of the English Working Class.* New York: Vintage, 1966.

Thomson, Patricia. *The Victorian Heroine.* London: Oxford University Press, 1956.

Tillotson, Kathleen. *Novels of the Eighteen-Forties.* New York: Oxford University Press, 1961.

[Tonna, Charlotte Elizabeth]. *The Perils of the Nation.* London: Seeley, 1843.

[Tonna], Charlotte Elizabeth. *Personal Recollections.* New York: Scribner's, 1850.

Toynbee, Arnold. *The Industrial Revolution.* Boston: Beacon, 1956.

Tufnell, E. C. *Character, Object, and Effects of Trades' Unions.* London: Ridgway, 1834.

Ure, Andrew. *The Philosophy of Manufactures.* London: Knight, 1835.

Vicinus, Martha. *The Industrial Muse.* London: Croom Helm, 1974.

Vicinus, Martha, ed. *Suffer and Be Still.* Bloomington: Indiana University Press, 1972.

Vicinus, Martha, ed. *A Widening Sphere.* Bloomington: Indiana University Press, 1977.

Walkley, Christina. *The Ghost in the Looking Glass: The Victorian Seamstress.* London: Peter Owen, 1981.

Ward, John Trevor. *The Factory Movement, 1830–1855.* New York: St. Martin's, 1962.

Watt, Ian, ed. *The Victorian Novel.* New York: Oxford, 1971.

Webb, Igor. *From Custom to Capital: The English Novel and the Industrial Revolution.* Ithaca: Cornell University Press, 1981.

Webb, R. K. *Harriet Martineau: A Radical Victorian.* New York: Columbia University Press, 1960.

Wheeler, James. *Manchester: Its Political, Social and Commercial History, Ancient and Modern.* London: Whittaker, 1836.

Wheeler, James, ed. *Manchester Poetry.* London: Charles Tilt, 1838.

Wiesenfarth, Joseph, ed. *George Eliot: A Writer's Notebook, 1854–1879.* Charlottesville: University of Virginia Press, 1981.

Wiesenfarth, Joseph. *George Eliot's Mythmaking.* Heidelberg: Carl Winter, 1977.

Williams, Raymond. *Culture and Society, 1780–1950.* New York: Harper, 1958.

Woodward, Llewellyn. *The Age of Reform, 1815–1870.* Oxford: Clarendon, 1962.

Woolf, Virginia. *A Room of One's Own.* Harmondsworth: Penguin, 1945.

Woolf, Virginia. *The Second Common Reader.* New York: Harcourt, Brace and World, 1960.

Young, G. M. *Victorian England: Portrait of an Age.* London: Oxford, 1953.

Essays and Reviews

"Alton Locke," *Blackwood's Magazine* 68 (November 1850), 592–610.

Ashton, T. S. "Some Statistics of the Industrial Revolution in Britain," *Transactions of the Manchester Statistical Society* (1947–48), 1–21.

Ashton, T. S. "The Standard of Life of the Workers in England," In *Capitalism and the Historians,* ed. F. A. Hayek. London: University of Chicago Press, 1954.

"The Author of John Halifax," *British Quarterly Review* 44 (1866), 32–58.

Aydelotte, William. "The Conservative and Radical Interpretation of Early Victorian Social Legislation," *Victorian Studies* 11 (December 1967), 225–36.

Aydelotte, William. "The England of Marx and Mill as Reflected in Fiction," *Journal of Economic History,* Supplement 8 (1948), 42–58.

Banks, J. A. "Population Change and the Victorian City," *Victorian Studies* 11 (March 1968), 277–89.

Best, Geoffrey. "The Scottish Victorian City," *Victorian Studies* 11 (March 1968), 329–58.

Bland, D. S. "*Mary Barton* and Historical Accuracy," *R.E.S.* 1 (January 1950), 58–60.

Brantlinger, Patrick. "Bluebooks, the Social Organism, and the Victorian Novel," *Criticism* 14 (Fall 1972), 328–44.

Brantlinger, Patrick. "The Case against Trades Unions in Early Victorian Fiction," *Victorian Studies* 13 (September 1969), 37–52.

Brebner, J. B. "Laissez Faire and State Intervention in Nineteenth-Century Britain," *Journal of Economic History,* Supplement 8 (1948), 59–73.

Briggs, Asa. "The Language of 'Class' in Early Nineteenth-Century England," *Essays in Labour History.* London: Macmillan, 1960.

Briggs, Asa. "Private and Social Themes in *Shirley,*" *Brontë Society Transactions* 13 (1958), 203–19.

Briggs, Asa. "The Victorian City: Quantity and Quality," *Victorian Studies* 11 (Summer 1968), 711–30.

Carnall, Geoffrey. "Dickens, Mrs. Gaskell, and the Preston Strike," *Victorian Studies* 8 (September 1964), 31–48.

Chaloner, W. H. "Mrs. Trollope and the Early Factory System," *Victorian Studies* 4 (December 1960), 159–66.

Clark, G. Kitson. "Hunger and Politics in 1842," *Journal of Modern History* 25 (December 1953), 355–74.

"Coningsby," *Athenaeum* (18 May 1844), 446–47.

Craik, Dinah M. "Concerning Men," *Cornhill Magazine* n.s. 9 (1887), 368–77.

Craik, Dinah M. "To Novelists — and a Novelist," *Macmillan's* 3 (1861), 441–48.

Cyples, William. "Morality of the Doctrine of Averages," *Cornhill Magazine* 10 (1864), 218–24.

Deutsch, Felix. "Artistic Expression and Neurotic Illness: *Alton Locke*," *American Imago* 4 (December 1947), 64–102.

Dunn, Richard. "Dickens and Mayhew Once More," *Nineteenth-Century Fiction* 25 (December 1970), 348–53.

Dyos, H. J. "The Slums of Victorian London," *Victorian Studies* 11 (September 1967), 5–40.

Eagleton, Terry. "Class, Power and Charlotte Brontë," *Critical Quarterly* 14 (Autumn 1972), 225–35.

Eastlake, Elizabeth. "Vanity Fair, Jane Eyre, and the Governesses' Benevolent Institution – Report for 1847" *Quarterly Review* 84 (December 1848), 153–85.

Edelstein, T. J. "They Sang 'The Song of the Shirt': The Visual Iconology of the Seamstress," *Victorian Studies* 23 (Winter 1980), 183–210.

[Eliot, George]. "Rachel Gray," *Leader* 7 (5 January 1856), 19.

Fahnestock, Jeanne. "Geraldine Jewsbury: The Power of the Publisher's Reader," *Nineteenth-Century Fiction* 28 (December 1973), 253–72.

Fido, Martin. "Sources of Working Class Passages in Disraeli's *Sybil*," *Modern Language Review* 72 (April 1977), 268–84.

Fido, Martin. "The Treatment of Rural Distress in Disraeli's *Sybil*," *Yearbook of English Studies* 5 (1975), 153–63.

Fielding, K. J., and Anne Smith. "*Hard Times* and the Factory Controversy," *Nineteenth-Century Fiction* 24 (March 1970), 404–27.

Fryckstedt, Monica. "Charlotte Elizabeth Tonna: A Forgotten Evangelical Writer," *Studia Neophilologica* 52 (1980), 79–102.

Fryckstedt, Monica. "Charlotte Elizabeth Tonna and *The Christian Lady's Magazine*," *Victorian Periodicals Review* 14 (1981), 43–51.

Fryckstedt, Monica. "The Early Industrial Novel: *Mary Barton* and Its Predecessors," *Bulletin of the John Rylands University Library* 63 (Autumn 1980), 11–30.

Fryckstedt, Monica. "New Sources on Geraldine Jewsbury and the Woman Question," *Research Studies* 51 (June 1983), 51–63.

Gorsky, Susan. "The Gentle Doubters: Images of Women in Englishwomen's Novels, 1840–1920." In *Images of Women in Fiction: Feminist Perspectives,* ed. Susan Cornillon. Bowling Green: Bowling Green University Popular Press, 1972.

Gorsky, Susan. "Old Maids and New Women: Alternatives to Marriage in Englishwomen's Novels, 1847–1915," *Journal of Popular Culture* 7 (Summer 1973), 68–85.

[Greg, William Rathbone]. "False Morality of Lady Novelists," *National Review* 7 (1859), 144–67.

[Greg, William Rathbone]. "Mary Barton," *Edinburgh Review* 89 (1849), 402–35.

[Greg, William Rathbone]. "Prostitution," *Westminster Review* 53 (1850), 238–68.

Greg, William Rathbone. "Why Are Women Redundant?" In *Literary and Social Judgments.* Boston: Osgood, 1873.

Hamilton, Robert. "Disraeli and the Two Nations," *Quarterly Review* 288 (January 1950), 102–15.

Handley, Graham. "The Chronology of *Sylvia's Lovers,"* *Notes and Queries* 210 (August 1965), 302–03.

Heineman, Helen. "Frances Trollope's *Jessie Phillips:* Sexual Politics and the New Poor Law," *International Journal of Women's Studies* 1 (1978), 96–106.

Henriques, U. R. Q. "Bastardy and the New Poor Law," *Past and Present* 37 (July 1967), 103–29.

Hobsbawm, E. J. "Custom, Wages, and Work-Load in Nineteenth-Century Industry," in *Essays in Labour History.* London: Macmillan, 1960.

"Jessie Phillips," *Athenaeum* (28 October 1844), 956–57.

[Jewsbury, Geraldine]. "Alton Locke," *Athenaeum* (7 September 1850), 944–46.

[Jewsbury, Geraldine]. "A Woman's Thoughts about Women," *Athenaeum* (6 February 1858), 177.

"John Halifax, Gentleman," *Athenaeum* (26 April 1856), 520–21.

Kestner, Joseph. "Interview with Germaine Greer." In *Women Writers Talking,* ed. Janet Todd. London: Holmes and Meier, 1983.

Kettle, Arnold. "The Early Victorian Social-Problem Novel." In *Pelican Guide to English Literature,* vol. 6. Baltimore: Penguin, 1958.

Korg, Jacob. "The Problem of Unity in *Shirley,"* *Nineteenth-Century Fiction* 12 (September 1957), 125–36.

Kovacevic, Ivanka, and S. Barbara Kanner. "Blue Book into Novel: The Forgotten Industrial Fiction of Charlotte Elizabeth Tonna," *Nineteenth-Century Fiction* 25 (September 1970), 152–73.

Kowaleski, Elizabeth. "'The Heroine of Some Strange Romance': The *Personal Recollections* of Charlotte Elizabeth Tonna," *Tulsa Studies in Women's Literature* 1 (Fall 1982), 141–53.

Lalumia, Matthew. "Realism and Anti-Aristocratic Sentiment in Victorian Depictions of the Crimean War," *Victorian Studies* 27 (Autumn 1983), 25–51.

[Lewes, G. H.]. "Currer Bell's *Shirley,"* *Edinburgh Review* 91 (January 1850), 153–73.

[Lewes, G. H.], Vivian. "A Gentle Hint to Writing-Women," *Leader* 1 (18 January 1850), 189.

[Lewes, G. H]. "The Lady Novelists," *Westminster Review* 58 (1852), 129–41.

[Lewes, G. H.]. "Marian Withers, *Leader* (30 August 1851), 825–26.

[Lewes, G. H.]. "Ruth and Villette," *Westminster Review* 59 (1853), 474–91.

[Ludlow, J. M.]. "Ruth," *North British Review* 19 (1853), 151–74.

"Marian Withers," *Athenaeum* (30 August 1851), 920–21.

Martin, Robert. "Charlotte Brontë and Harriet Martineau," *Nineteenth-Century Fiction* 7 (December 1952), 198–201.

Martineau, Harriet. "Some Autobiographical Particulars of Miss Harriet Martineau," *Monthly Repository* 7 (1833), 612–15.

"Mary Barton," *Athenaeum* (21 October 1848), 1050–51.

"Mary Barton," *Fraser's Magazine* (April 1849), 429–32.

"Mary Barton," *Westminster Review* 50 (1849), 26–34.

[Mayne, Fanny]. "What I Saw and Heard in the Manufacturing Districts," *The True Briton* 2 (January 1854), 383–85.

"Michael Armstrong," *Athenaeum* (10 August 1839), 587–90.

Mitchell, Jack. "Aesthetic Problems of the Development of the Proletarian-Revolutionary Novel in Nineteenth-Century Britain." In *Marxists on Literature: An Anthology,* ed. David Craig. Baltimore: Penguin, 1975.

Mitchell, Sally. "Lost Women: Implications of the Fallen in Works by Forgotten Women Writers of the 1840's," *Papers in Women's Studies* 1 (June 1974), 110–24.

Neale, R. S. "Class and Class-Consciousness in Early Nineteenth-Century England: Three Classes or Five?," *Victorian Studies* 12 (September 1968), 5–32.

"The Needlewomen's Farewell," *Punch* 18 (12 January 1850), 14.

"North and South," *Athenaeum* (7 April 1855), 403.

"Novels with a Purpose," *Westminster Review* 82 (1864), 24–49.

"The Point of the Needle," *All the Year Round* (5 September 1863), 36–41.

"Rachel Gray," *Athenaeum* (12 January 1856), 40–41.

"The Rioters," *Athenaeum* (29 October 1842), 930.

"Ruth," *Athenaeum* (15 January 1853), 76–78.

Scrope, George Poulett. "Miss Martineau's *Monthly Novels,"* *Quarterly Review* 49 (April 1833), 137–52.

Shanley, Mary Lyndon. "'One Must Ride Behind': Married Women's Rights and The Divorce Act of 1857," *Victorian Studies* 25 (Spring 1982), 355–76.

"Shirley," *Athenaeum* (3 November 1849), 1107–9.

Showalter, Elaine. "Dinah Mulock Craik and the Tactics of Sentiment," *Feminist Studies* 2 (1975), 5–23.

Showalter, Elaine. "Feminist Criticism in the Wilderness." In *Writing and Sexual Difference,* ed. Elizabeth Abel. Chicago: University of Chicago Press, 1982.

"The Slaves of the Needle," *The True Briton* 2 (March 1854), 533.

Smith, Sheila M. "Blue Books and Victorian Novelists," *Review of English Studies* 21 (1970), 23–40.

Smith, Sheila M. "Willenhall and Wodgate: Disraeli's Use of Blue Book Evidence," *Review of English Studies* 13 (1962), 368–84.

[Stephen, Fitzjames]. "The License of Modern Novelists," *Edinburgh Review* 106 (July 1857), 64–81.

Sucksmith, Harvey. "Dickens and Mayhew: A Further Note," *Nineteenth-Century Fiction* 24 (December 1969), 345–49.

"Sybil," *Athenaeum* (17 May 1845), 477–79.

Thomson, Fred C. "*Felix Holt* as Classic Tragedy," *Nineteenth-Century Fiction* 16 (June 1961), 47–58.

Thomson, Fred C. "The Genesis of *Felix Holt,*" *PMLA* 74 (December 1959), 576–84.

Tonna, Charlotte Elizabeth, ed. *The Christian Lady's Magazine* 1 (January 1834) – 25 (June 1846).

Webb, R. K. "The Victorian Reading Public." In *Dickens to Hardy,* ed. Boris Ford. Baltimore: Penguin, 1960.

"William Langshawe, the Cotton Lord," *Athenaeum* (1 October 1842), 846.

"William Langshawe, the Cotton Lord," *Examiner* (5 November 1842), 709.

"Women's Heroines," *Saturday Review* 23 (1867), 259–61.

Young, G. M. "Victorian Centenary." In *Today and Yesterday.* London: Rupert Hart-Davis, 1948.

"The Young Milliner," *Athenaeum* (6 May 1843), 437.

Index

233